GEIR ØVENSEN

RESPONDING TO CHANGE
TRENDS IN PALESTINIAN HOUSEHOLD ECONOMY

Special consultant: Jon Pedersen

Sponsored by
The Norwegian Ministry of Foreign Affairs
with additional support provided by
The John D. and Catherine T. MacArthur Foundation
in the framework of
The Common Security Forum

FAFO International
Jerusalem, P.O.Box 21751
Tel. 822358, Fax. 822856

FAFO report 166

© FAFO 1994
ISBN 82-7244-121-4

Also by the author:
Marianne Heiberg and Geir Øvensen
Palestinian Society
in Gaza, West bank and Arab Jerusalem
A survey of Living Condition
(FAFO 1993)

Printed in Norway by
Cover and design by Jon S. Lahlum

Contents

Preface 5

Chapter 1 A society facing economic shocks 9
Model for household adaptation 12

Chapter 2 Labour-force participation, under-utilization of labour and employment patterns 17
Introduction 17
Labour-force participation 18
    Concepts of labour-force, employment and work 18
    Crude labour-force participation rates 21
    Determinants of labour-force participation 25
    Composition of the labour force 27
Under-utilization of labour 28
    Unemployment 30
    "Discouraged workers" 34
    Visible and invisible under-employment 39
    Three types of labour under-utilization 44
Employment patterns 50
    Introduction5 50
    Changes in employment from 1992 to 1993 51
    Male employment by main area of work 58
    Employment by gender and area of residence 61
    Individual engagement
    in income-generating household activities 61
Future labour-force scenarios 66
    Labour-force scenarios for Gaza 66
    Concluding remarks 73

Chapter 3 Household economy 77
Introduction 77
Household income-generating activities as adaptation strategy 78
Household income types and employment 88
    The index for household possession of consumer durables 88
    Distribution of the index for household possession of
    consumer durables by region and socio-economic group 90
    Types of household income 91

Prevalence and importance of household income types 92
Changes in income since 1992 94
Income types and the index for
household possession of consumer durables 96
The "family employment network" hypothesis 99
Dependence on public support,
employment and household wealth 103
Summing up household income types and employment 111
The role of net liquid wealth as household coping strategy 112
Indicators for net liquid household wealth 113
Indicators for net liquid household wealth
by socio-economic group 114
Interpreting indicators for net liquid household wealth 115
Net liquid household wealth and employment
problems among household members 119
Reducing net liquid wealth as coping strategy:
Household prototypes 120

Chapter 4 Report conclusion 127

Appendix1 The sample of the FALUP study
By Jon Pedersen 133
The Gaza sample 134
The West Bank sample 135
Response rates and errors in the data files 136
Conclusion 136

Appendix 2 The field work
By Neil Hawkins 140
Recruitment 140
Training 141
Sampling 142
Organisation and field work 143

Appendix 3 Tables to chapter 2 145

Appendix 4 Tables to chapter 3 183

References 223

PREFACE

Responding to Change comes at a time when the march of events in the Middle East is accelerating. The breakthrough in the Peace Process and the establishment of Palestinian self-rule in Gaza and the Jericho area are reshaping the region before our very eyes, politically, economically and psychologically. Possibilities that could hardly be dreamed of not long ago, now appear within reach.

FAFO has been privileged to follow developments at close hand. The present study builds on and extends the FAFO study on living conditions in the Occupied Territories, FALCOT 92, the results of which were outlined and discussed in *Palestinian Society*. This report was presented to the Refugee Working Group (Multilateral Peace Process) in Oslo in May 1993. As it happened, that meeting took place at a propitious time in the Peace Process. At the Oslo meeting, we were encouraged to undertake an update which would capture changes since the border closure. With the backing of the Norwegian Ministry of Foreign Affairs, therefore, we immediately proceeded to plan a follow-up study, named FALUP. Although the focus and substantive content of the new study were altered somewhat, we could make full use of experiences, findings and models from FALCOT. We decided to focus on the economic conditions of refugees and displaced persons in West Bank camps and in the whole of Gaza.

The results of FALUP are now available in *Responding to Change*. Our ambition is that they should enter the general policy dialogue about the future of Gaza and the West Bank. Above all, it is our hope that the new report will give Palestinian authorities valuable input and help in the formulation of national policies for economic development. If the economic situation of the people in Gaza and the West Bank continues to deteriorate, not only will the daily lives of ordinary people be adversely affected, but the whole Peace Process may be placed in jeopardy. On the positive side, it must be noted that the international community is gradually becoming conscious of the gravity of the situation. We sincerely hope that the new report will help focus efforts, so that international programmes take into consideration, and address, crucial changes in the socio-economic realities in Gaza and on the West Bank.

The project would not have been possible without the commitment and support of a number of Palestinian individuals and institutions. As indicated, the survey and the report should be seen in the context of efforts to enhance Palestinian capacities for data collection and analysis, with a view to laying the foundations for informed policy planning. The cooperation between FAFO and the Palestinian Bureau of Statistics (PBS) is a cornerstone in ongoing work towards these ends. We are indebted to the Director of PBS, Dr. Hasan Abu Libdeh, for his support and advice.

Neil Hawkins, FAFO's Middle East Coordinator, worked unceasingly to ensure that survey operations would be conducted smoothly and efficiently. FAFO's local staff must be thanked for their dedication and hard work. Our gratitude is due to Rena Zaqqout and Akram Atallah, who worked tirelessly to ensure the quality of the survey, and who efficiently supervised and directed every stage of the field work from recruitment to data entry. The FAFO supervisory staff in both Gaza and the West Bank must be commended for their contributions to the design of the questionnaire, the field work organisation and the management of the field work. They made this survey theirs by their tremendous enthusiasm as well as their extensive experience. It gives me great pleasure to mention them by name: Ghassan Hamed-Sana'assi, Abeer Mansour, Sobheya Hilew, Reem Moughraby, Badia Tahboub, Mohammed Al Ashqar, Najwa El Jikhlip, Rudayna Al Smari, and Maher Dahlan.

Our thanks are also extended to Hani Dada and Arwa Da'na, who were essential in organising the data entry, and Khalid El Sirr, who once again proved his competence in the sampling process. The twenty-five data collectors, most of whom had worked on FALCOT, have a major share in the success of the FALUP survey. Their commitment and energy were impressive. They adopted a professional attitude from the start. Our thanks also go to all those anonymous volunteers who devoted time and effort to assisting our field staff in their work.

We have been fortunate in having a close working relationship with the Gaza Trade Unions. Rassem el Bayyary was generous in allowing us to use the Unions' facilities and office in Khan Younis in Gaza.

I wish to salute the ten FAFO staff members who are being transferred to the newly established Palestinian Bureau of Statistics (PBS), which is being funded by the Norwegian Ministry of Foreign Affairs. We feel sad about finishing our acquaintance with them, but also proud that they will be able to play a vital role in this key Palestinian institution. They, and the PBS, will benefit from all those years of training and experience. We wish them every success in their new jobs.

On the Israeli side, Freddy Zach once again provided valuable help. We are also grateful to Professor Moshe Sicron, Dr. Zvi Eisenbach and Elisha Palgi of the Israel Central Bureau of Statistics for their informed comments on FALCOT. Ambassador Joseph Hadass' kind advice and encouragement have been greatly appreciated.

Support from the UN system was very much in evidence. Roger Guarda, Resident Representative of the UNDP in Jerusalem, played an important role by securing financial support for the training of FAFO staff prior to the survey. Consequently, our staff was fully prepared to tackle the many challenges related to the survey.

At UNRWA, Lee O'Brien and Dr. Alex Pollock must be thanked for their very useful advice on the construction of the questionnaire, as well as their input at the analytical stage. Their scrupulous and knowledgeable counsel really made a difference.

We are grateful that the Norwegian Ministry of Foreign Affairs took quick action to support the project. FALUP has been financed by the Ministry. Warm thanks go to Deputy Minister Jan Egeland and Deputy Minister Asbjørn Mathisen. Deputy Director Hans Fredrik Lehne was also most obliging. Funds from The John D. and Catherine T. MacArthur Foundation, based in Chicago, helped us carry out project plans, for which we are highly appreciative.

Clearly, *Responding to Change* is the result of assistance from a multitude of sources, and of an impressive pooling of talents and efforts. But if anyone deserves special mention, it must be Geir Øvensen, main author of the report. Geir Øvensen, who received important support and advice from Research Director Jon Pedersen throughout the process, worked with vigour, thoroughness and an ever inquisitive mind. Professor Knud Knudsen offered comprehensive and highly valuable comments on early drafts of the manuscript.

I am pleased to record the contributions of FAFO's Norwegian staff. Liv Jorunn Stokke provided indispensable help in the training of supervisors and data collectors, while Steinar Tamsfoss assisted in sampling work with characteristic professionalism. Research Director Jon Hanssen-Bauer aided ably in the coordination and planning of the project, particularly in the early stages. Special Adviser Jan Dietz should be commended for his organising skills and imaginative contributions to report work. Gudrun Thoner read the manuscript critically and constructively, in addition to helping assemble the many informative figures in the report. Further, Dag Tuastad offered useful comments.

Jon S. Lahlum did an excellent job on the technical side, steering the production of the report with a steady, imperturbable hand. I also want to thank Susan Høivik for her proofreading of the manuscript and her valuable suggestions.

Work to broaden and deepen our knowledge of living conditions in the Middle East must not only simply go on. It must advance - in terms of both quantity and quality. The Peace Process may be contingent on such progress. The Refugee Working Group in the Multilateral Peace Process will be an important catalyst in future endeavours to promote economic development, bridge political differences, narrow social gaps and create regional cooperation in the Middle East. FAFO wishes to play its part, being ready to cooperate with all institutions that have an interest in applied science and in translating theoretical insights into political action. The publication of *Responding to Change* will, I hope, be interpreted as a sign of FAFO's continuing commitment.

Geir O. Pedersen
Director
Centre for International Studies, FAFO
Oslo, May 1994

CHAPTER 1
A SOCIETY FACING ECONOMIC SHOCKS

The survey presented in this report aims to depict the situation for households in Gaza and the West Bank refugee camps as of autumn 1993. Like all small, open economies, the Occupied Territories are highly vulnerable to shocks from the outside world. Israeli military occupation has made the dependency on external events even stronger than in otherwise comparable economies.

The 1967 war brought with it profound changes in regional economic relations in the Middle East and had a penetrating impact on the economy of the Occupied Territories. Contacts with neighbouring Arab states were disrupted, and the economy of the Occupied Territories became oriented completely towards the much stronger Israeli economy. These changes have provided the backdrop for all subsequent changes in the economic environment in the area.

Mainly through export of manual labour to the Israeli economy, the Occupied Territories experienced rapid economic growth in the 1970s and early 1980s. After the outbreak of the Intifada in 1987, economic performance in the Occupied Territories has stalled, and developments have been even more heavily influenced by outside forces, due to a sequence of external political and economic shocks.

In its September 1993 report on the economy of the Occupied Territories, the World Bank lists four unusual features of the policy environment after 1967 (World Bank 1993:25):

- Asymmetric market relations with Israel and other countries that caused a bias towards export of labour
- Regulatory restrictions that held back the expansion of the private productive sector
- Fiscal compression that led to under-provision of public goods
- A declining natural resource base

The structural distortions described above have rendered the economy of the Occupied Territories highly vulnerable to economic fluctuations in Israel, but also to developments in the Gulf States, Jordan, and other countries in the Middle East importing Palestinian products and labour. The absence of Palestinian-controlled instruments for macro-economic policy has magnified the impact of the shocks, which have affected the Occupied Territories almost unmitigated by attempts at alleviation.

In recent years, three major shocks have shaken the economy of the Occupied Territories. These are the Intifada continuing from 1987, the Gulf War in January 1991, and the Israeli border closure in March 1993.

The outbreak of the *Intifada* has had a pervasive influence on the economy of the Occupied Territories. Normal economic activity has been disrupted through strikes, curfews and periodic border closures. Workers' earnings have been affected, both as a consequence of the above-mentioned factors, and through reduced demand for labour in Israel. The Intifada has led to a situation of general instability and unpredictability in the Occupied Territories. Together with increased and firm Israeli enforcement of taxation, it has created strong incentives against private investment and economic activity.

The *Gulf War* had dramatic short-run effects in early 1991 due to a 24-hour curfew, which for six weeks virtually paralysed the economy of the Occupied Territories. Stricter restrictions on employment in Israel after the initial complete border closure were to have more lasting effects, in particular in Gaza, where new permits were required for entry to Israel. Some of these restrictions were, however, later softened somewhat.

Public and private transfers also dropped sharply as a consequence of the Gulf War. Many households lost remittances, due to expulsions of Palestinians from several Gulf States. Furthermore, the loss of Arab grants distributed through the PLO deprived many households and institutions in the Occupied Territories of substantial financial means. Adding to the severe economic problems stemming from the Gulf War, the extremely harsh winter of 1991-92 caused extensive damage to West Bank agriculture.

Perhaps even more critical to the economy of the Occupied Territories was the March 1993 *border closure*, following incidents involving Palestinian workers in Israel. After an initial complete closure, some workers were re-admitted to their workplaces, but in far smaller numbers than before. New, meticulous and time-consuming security checks were introduced at the border checkpoints. Because many of the economic incentives for Palestinian employment in Israel still exist both among employers and workers, it is hard to predict how permanent the border closure will be.

All these shocks add up to a large adverse change in external sources of income growth. Loss of income from remittances and employment in Israel have only partly been counter-balanced by other factors. There has been some increase in demand for Palestinian workers in construction due to immigration to Israel from the former Soviet Union, as well as increased local construction in the Occupied Territories due to families returning from the Gulf after the war, but this demand has failed to compensate for the negative effects of the dramatic shocks described.

Today the economy of the Occupied Territories is in the process of adapting to a new situation of reduced household income. If employment in Israel is cut off permanently, there will be a far more urgent need to reorient the labour force and the economy towards domestic production.

Figure 1.1 places the negative shocks to the economy of the Occupied Territories in recent years along a time axis, highlighting the Gulf War and the border closure. The present survey must also be seen against the background of the Intifada, which is in effect low-intensity warfare with more or less active phases.

The same figure indicates the fieldwork periods of FAFO's two living condition surveys in the area. FALCOT 92 took place in the summer of 1992, after the Gulf War but before the border closure. FALUP 93 was carried out in October/ November 1993 and should thus be able to record effects from both these events as well as the Intifada.

The general aim of FALUP 93 has been to get a better understanding of the mechanisms at work among individuals and households with regard to adaptation to economic shocks. In pursuing this goal we have also updated economic data from FALCOT 92 and hence monitored developments in the area.

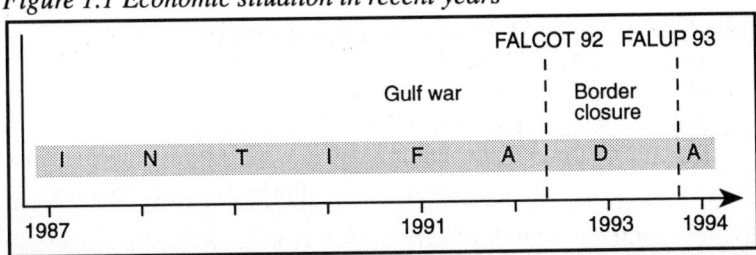

Figure 1.1 Economic situation in recent years

For reasons of time and cost, the scope of FALUP 93 has been limited in two ways compared to FALCOT 92. First, FALUP's geographical coverage is confined to Gaza and the West Bank/Arab Jerusalem refugee camps. Second, FALUP 93 investigates only conditions of employment and aspects of the household economy.

As to geographical coverage, we wished to select those areas which had scored lowest on the household wealth index in FALCOT 92. Emphasis was further put on employment and household economy because these living condition components were assumed to be most affected by the border closure. Moreover, there is little reason to believe that other aspects of living conditions, such as health or education, would be measurably affected during this short time-span.

Because of the diversity and magnitude of the shocks described above, it is important to specify what is really measured. We are plainly measuring the *long-term effects of occupation and Intifada*, the *medium-term effects of Gulf War* factors, and the *short-term effects of the border closure*, in one and the same survey.

The problem of interpretation is amplified because the survey has been conducted in two distinct geographical areas. Did for example the shocks have the same timing and impact in the two areas?

The answers to such questions will be left for the conclusion of the report. In the subsequent discussions we shall to some degree use FALCOT 92 as a point of reference for comparison with the new data. In Gaza, this approach should be straightforward, as FALUP 93 was conducted in the same localities as FALCOT 92, although other households were interviewed. In the West Bank refugee camps, however, the FALCOT 92 sample was generally too small to enable comparisons of results, and so none have been attempted.

We will now proceed by outlining a simplified model for possible household adaptation strategies in a situation of reduced labour income.

MODEL FOR HOUSEHOLD ADAPTATION

In what ways have households and individuals in the Occupied Territories responded to the economic shocks described above? To give an overview of household adaptation strategies and coping mechanisms, figure 1.2 presents a simplified model of the household economy.

The input side of the model comprises three main components: income from (formal) labour activity, income from household activities, and public and private transfers. Income from formal labour activity increased substantially after 1967, constituting the main share of disposable household income. The recent cuts in Palestinian employment, particularly among those employed in Israel, have led to a sharp drop in labour income.

The importance of household income-generating activities declined steadily after 1967. The Intifada brought some revival of these activities, as self-reliance and reduced dependence on Israel could be highly desirable for ideological reasons.

Transfers comprise both public and private transfers. UNRWA support to refugees who fled in 1948 and to their descendants is the most important type of public transfers. Some UNRWA support is means-tested and distributed only to particularly needy households, the "special hardship cases". Other kinds of means-tested "public" transfers are social benefits from the Israeli Civil Administration, funds distributed through religious institutions (*Zaqat*), and from political organizations (e.g. "Martyr money" for families of Intifada victims, prisoners).

Private transfers are mainly remittances from family members working in the Gulf or in Western countries. Support among members of the extended family in the same localities is also common.

UNRWA support and social benefits per capita have remained relatively unchanged in recent years, but remittances have dropped dramatically after the Gulf War, as has support from the PLO.

The output side of the household economy model comprises various household consumption expenditures and investments. Average household consumption expenditures in the Occupied Territories increased sharply after 1967, mainly because of increased income, but also due to

Figure 1.2 The household model

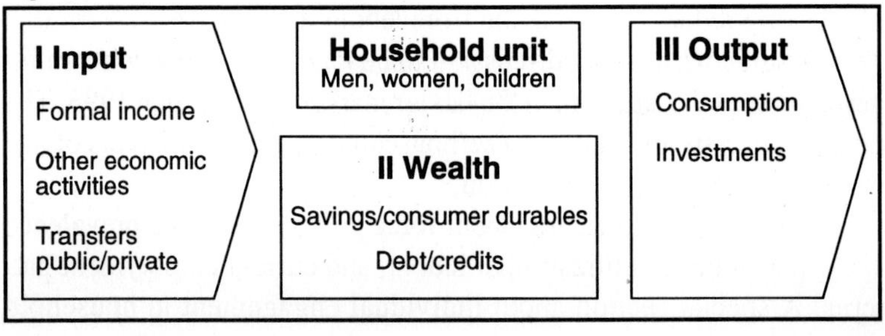

I Input	Household unit Men, women, children	III Output
Formal income		Consumption
Other economic activities	II Wealth	Investments
Transfers public/private	Savings/consumer durables Debt/credits	

the decline in the self-subsistence economy. The Intifada brought a halt to this rising trend. "Investments" comprise traditional material investments, but also non-material investments like education of household members or sending them abroad to work or study.

The level of household wealth reflects cumulative differences between household income and consumption expenditures over time. The primary indicators for changes in net household wealth are developments in the household's stock of consumer durables, gold and other savings, and utilization of debt and credits. Household wealth increased from 1967 to 1987, but has most likely declined since the outbreak of the Intifada.

How have households in Gaza and the West Bank refugee camps responded to the sharp drop in labour income after the border closure in March 1993? On the basis of the simplified model about household economy, we may identify three principal coping strategies.

First, compensation may take place on the input side, through greater involvement in household income-generating activities, or through increased public or private transfers.

Second, the output side may be adjusted to the new low level of input through reductions in household consumption and investment expenditures.

Third, households can, at least in the short run, avoid having to adjust output by drawing on reducing their net wealth. Net wealth may decrease through sales of savings, by taking up loans or credits, or through a combination of these measures. For most households, this strategy can only be used as a temporary remedy.

It seems reasonable to assume that households will tend to choose some mixture of these three adaptation strategies. Since it is still not clear whether the cut-off of Palestinian employment in Israel will be permanent or temporary, an important question is how the composition of adaptation strategies will vary over time, depending on expectations of a lasting reduction in income from labour activity.

We will continue this discussion in chapter two below, with an investigation of the situation in the labour market as of autumn 1993. The units of analysis are all *individual* household members, 15 years of age or older, in the survey population.

Of principal concern are labour force participation, the prevalence and types of under-utilization of labour, and current employment patterns. A special section about individual engagement in household income-generating activities has also been included. Finally, we present some scenarios for future labour-force participation.

Chapter three focuses on how households as economic units adapt to the effects of the border closure. The first part of the chapter investigates income-generating activities on the *household* level, and whether household production have been increased to compensate for the loss of formal labour income.

The second part discusses the relationship between household income types, the household wealth index, and employment. Here we focus on household systems for re-distributing economic resources among members, and to which extent households seem dependent on transfers from non-private sources like UNRWA.

The third part discusses net household wealth, measured through sales of savings, or through taking up loans or credits. We look into the prevalence of savings, as well as the use of and sources of credits and debt. Finally, we turn to the role of net wealth as a household coping strategy for various types of households.

CHAPTER 2
LABOUR-FORCE PARTICIPATION, UNDER-UTILIZATION OF LABOUR AND EMPLOYMENT PATTERNS

INTRODUCTION

This chapter focuses on the employment situation of Palestinians living in Gaza and the West Bank refugee camps after the March 1993 Israeli border closure. It is our hypothesis that there has been a dramatic reduction in employment since the closure. Thus we seek to develop indicators which can measure this reduction, and help us to understand how it has manifested itself in various socio-economic groups.

The chapter is divided into four parts. The first part will discuss various aspects of labour-force participation – crude labour-force participation rates, determinants of labour-force participation and the composition of the labour force.

The second part will document the effects of the border closure on the employment situation for various socio-economic groups, with a focus on the under-utilization of labour.

The third part deals with changes in individuals' employment situation and workplace from 1992 to 1993. We will also discuss the situation of employed persons, their workplace, type of work and the economic sectors in which they are found. A special section concerning individual involvement in household income-generating activities, has also been included.

The concluding part of the chapter will discuss scenarios for future labour supply in Gaza on the basis of results from the present data set. We also present alternative projections from the Work Force and Labour Modules of the World Bank's macro-economic model for the Occupied Territories.

In family-based Palestinian society, decisions on income-generating activities are usually seen as household rather than individual matters. A person's labour activities may thus be viewed as a result of *household* optimization strategies, rather than individual strategies unconstrained by the household. Why then, have we chosen to focus on the labour activities of *individuals*? There are two reasons for this: 1) it is the individual who is actually employed, and 2) the household may be treated as a set of contextual variables.

The economic importance of labour for the household, and its role in household coping strategies, are left for the subsequent chapter. Each adult individual in the sample will consequently be treated as a separate case, even though the labour activities of individual household members may be expected to be highly inter-related.

LABOUR-FORCE PARTICIPATION

The size of the labour force is the most common indicator for the amount of labour available to the economy.[1] Here we shall discuss labour-force participation in terms of three questions: First, what are the crude labour-force participation rates in Gaza and the West Bank refugee camps? Second, what determines labour-force participation in these areas? And finally, what is the current composition of the labour force by gender, age and educational background?

CONCEPTS OF LABOUR-FORCE, EMPLOYMENT AND WORK

Let us begin with a brief introduction of the adapted version of ILO's labour-force framework used in our analysis. Figure 2.1 gives an overview of the main categories used in the survey. (Heiberg & Øvensen 1993:182) The same categories were used in the previous FAFO survey.[2]

On the basis of a person's activities in the so-called "reference week" the labour force framework divides the survey population, 15 years or older, into three exhaustive and mutually exclusive categories: the employed, the unemployed, and persons outside the labour force.

In the FALUP 93 survey the "reference week" varied over geographical areas in the time period from September to October 1993. Work

---

[1] The present survey, based on a randomly selected sample of the population in Gaza and the West Bank refugee camps, can give only relative results as percentage distributions. Estimation of absolute results – e.g. the size of the labour force in the survey areas is crucially dependent on the accuracy of estimates of the *total* population in the survey areas.

[2] Heiberg, Marianne and Geir Øvensen (1993), *Palestinian Society in Gaza, West Bank and Arab Jerusalem*: A Survey of Living Conditions, Oslo: FAFO report 151. p. 182. The survey upon which this book is based, will subsequently be referred to as FALCOT 92).

activities conducted by prisoners, children under the age of 15, or by Israeli settlers are not included in the survey. No upper age limit for respondents was introduced because of the relatively small proportion of old persons in the population.

The "employed" (box Ia, Ib and Ic) comprise all persons who worked at least one hour in the reference week, or persons who were temporarily absent. Persons working 34 hours or less during the reference week were defined as part-time workers; those working 35 hours or more as full-time workers.

The "unemployed" (box II) are persons who did not work even one hour in the designated week, but who were actively seeking work. Employed and unemployed persons taken together make up the "currently economic active population" or "labour-force". Persons 15 years or older who are not "currently economic active" and children together make up the "not in the labour force" category (box III and IV).

The ILO labour-force classification system is based on *time* worked rather than income. Working for many hours by no means guarantees correspondingly high income levels. On the contrary, many low-productivity jobs are implicitly based on long working hours that compensate for low hourly wages.

All the same there are two main reasons for adhering to time- rather than income-based definitions for labour activities. First, income, unlike time worked, may be transferred among reference periods, and thus may be difficult to integrate into a labour-force framework with a short reference period. This problem is manifest in agricultural work where

Figure 2.1 Labour survey definitions used by FAFO

Total population					
Working age population persons 15 year or older					Persons under 15 years
Persons included in labour force				Not in labour force	
Employed persons			Unemployed persons	i.e. not "employed" or "unemployed" and did not seek work in the determinant week	
Full time 35 hours or more in the determinant week	Part time 34 hours or less in the determinant week	Temporarily absent	not "employed" but sought work in the determinant week		
Ia	Ib	Ic	II	III	IV

income appears when the produce is sold, even though work has been carried out throughout the whole agricultural season.

Second, fear of taxation and scepticism towards strangers asking about money matters, make it extremely challenging to obtain reliable informationon income from employment. Under-reporting and concealment of money inflows would be the most likely result.

Contrary to the intentions of the ILO definitions, many respondents in household surveys tend to understand "work" as regular employment only. This misunderstanding leads to frequent under-reporting of much labour activities typical of developing countries, like casual work, unpaid family work and work remunerated in kind. In particular, under-reporting of female labour activities may be expected.

To cope with this problem a particular section focusing on income-generating household activities rather than individual persons, was included in the survey questionnaire. Even though most income-generating household activities take place in a domestic setting, some, like trade and services, are normally carried outside the home.

In spite of several problematic borderline cases, "income-generating household activities" was thus applied to activities that brought *supplementary* income to households. Activities carried out in the home and resembling ordinary employment, like for example sub-contracting and piecework arrangements, were covered by the standard labour-force framework questions. Results from the section about income-generat-

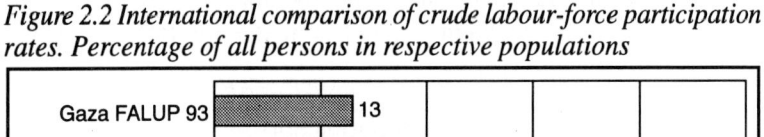

Figure 2.2 International comparison of crude labour-force participation rates. Percentage of all persons in respective populations

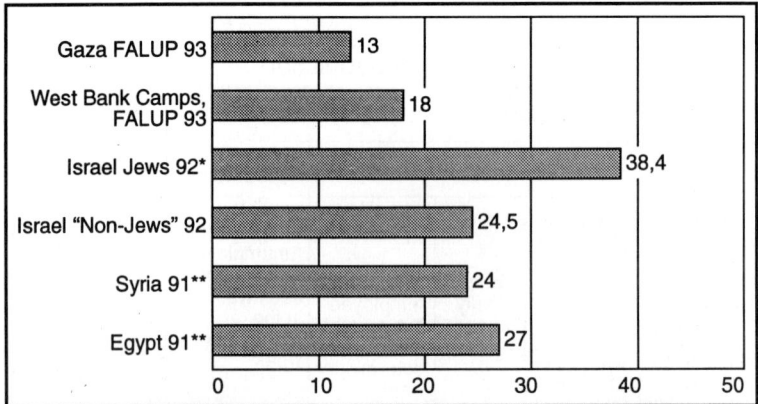

Gaza FALUP 93	13
West Bank Camps, FALUP 93	18
Israel Jews 92*	38,4
Israel "Non-Jews" 92	24,5
Syria 91**	24
Egypt 91**	27

* Source: "Statistical Abstract of Israel 1993, tables 12.1, 12,8, Main Series A.
** Source: World Bank "An Investment in Peace"; volume 6 page 12.

ing household activities will be discussed further at the end of the section about employment patterns, page 63.

CRUDE LABOUR-FORCE PARTICIPATION RATES

See tables 2.1 to 2.7 in appendix 3 as references to the discussion in this section.

The proportion of the population involved in the labour force is called the crude labour-force participation rate. This rate may be seen as directly reflecting two factors: the age distribution of the population, and the propensity of various population categories to work.

Figure 2.2 presents a comparison between crude labour-force participation rates in Gaza and the West Bank refugee camps with those in Syria and Egypt, and for Jews and "Non-Jews" in Israel.

The 1993 crude labour-force participation rates in Gaza and the West Bank refugee camps are not only far below that for Jews in Israel, but even lower than for other countries in the region. What can explain the extremely low participation rates in Gaza and the West Bank refugee camps? Table 2.1 gives some useful insights.

Table 2.1 Labour-force participation rates, by gender and source

	Gaza FAFO 93	WBC FAFO 93	Gaza FAFO 92	WBC FAFO 92
Percentage of total population in LF	13	18	20	25
n	3535	1865	958	87
Percentage of total population, 15 years or more	49	55	50	56
n	3535	1865	958	87
Percentage of adults in labour force	26	32	39	45
n	3535	1865	958	87
Percentage of males in sample	49	48	50	50
n	3549	1865	*	*
Percentage of adult males in LF	47	57	72	76
n	1744	903	477	42
Percentage of adult females in LF	6	9	7	14
n	1792	962	481	45

* The sex rate in the FALCOT 92 report was fixed to 50% male/female. (The gender of the Randomly Selected Individual had to be pre-selected due to a number of questions which required female interviewers to interview female respondents.)

As in most Middle Eastern populations, except for Israeli Jews, much of the population in Gaza and the West Bank refugee camps are young people below working age. This very young population implies unfavourable dependency ratios – i.e. the ratio of persons under and above working age to that of persons of working age – and hence low crude labour-force participation rates.

Children's work was omitted when the crude labour-force participation rates were estimated. Even though children's work does exist in the

Figure 2.3 Gaza labour-force participation, by gender and sub-region. Percentage of all adults in respective groups in Gaza

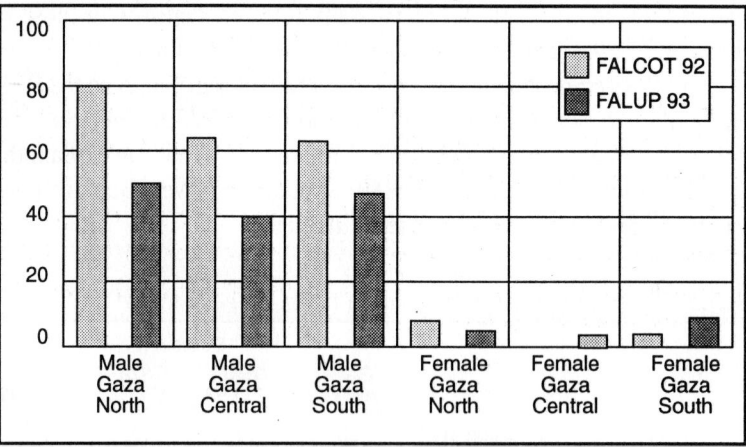

Figure 2.4 Gaza labour-force participation, by gender and refugee status. Percentage of all adults in respective groups in Gaza

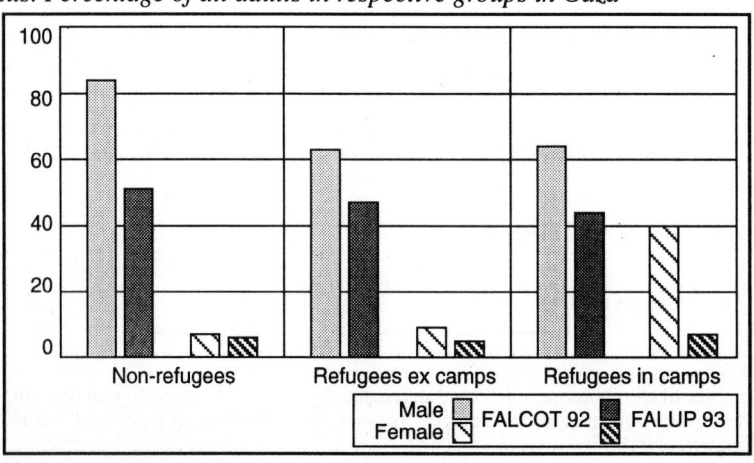

area, the nature of this work is such that reliable measurement would require a specially designed survey.

Another important explanation for the extremely low crude labour-force participation rates in Gaza and the West Bank refugee camps is the very low participation rates for females – which again is the pattern found in most Middle Eastern populations except for Israeli Jews.

For adult males the FALCOT 92 report found relatively high labour-force participation rates in both Gaza and the West Bank refugee camps. The 1993 adult male rates, however, seem to have dropped dramatically – in Gaza this decrease amounts to half of the males in the labour force in 1992.

Which population groups have in particular seen a decrease in labour-force participation from 1992 to 1993? Figures 2.3, 2.4 and 2.5 compare Gaza labour-force participation by sub-region, refugee status and number of adult males in household, as measured by the FALUP 93 and the FALCOT 92 surveys. (The FALCOT 92 sample for the West Bank refugee camps was too small to permit comparison).

The greatest relative drop in male labour-force participation has been among non-refugees, who are over-represented in Greater Gaza City. Gaza males living in households with many other adult males have the largest reduction in labour-force participation.

Figure 2.5 Gaza labour-force participation by, gender and number of adult males in household. Percentage of all adults in respective groups in Gaza

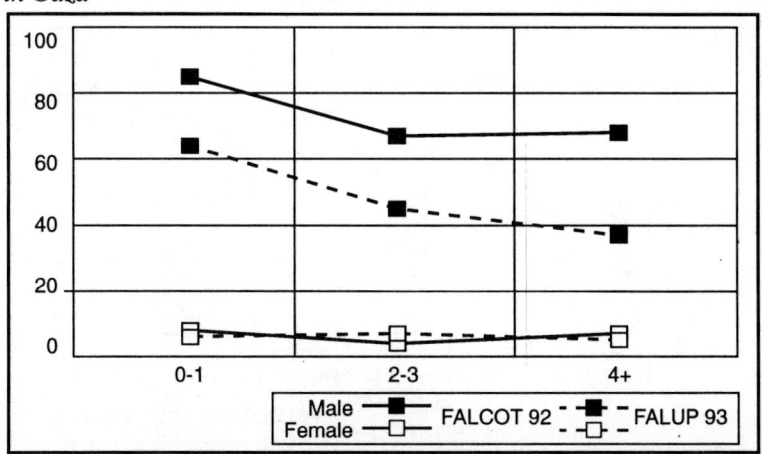

Figures 2.6, 2.7 and 2.8 compare Gaza labour-force participation in the FALUP 93 survey and the FALCOT 92 survey by individual characteristics such as gender, age, education and marital status. For males, the participation rate seems to have dropped for all groups, but most for those who are young, unmarried and less educated.

The substantial drop in adult male participation indicates the occurrence of a dramatic loss of employment after the March 1993 border closure. The employment situation among various socio-economic

Figure 2.6 Gaza labour-force participation, by gender and age. Percentage of all persons in respective groups in Gaza

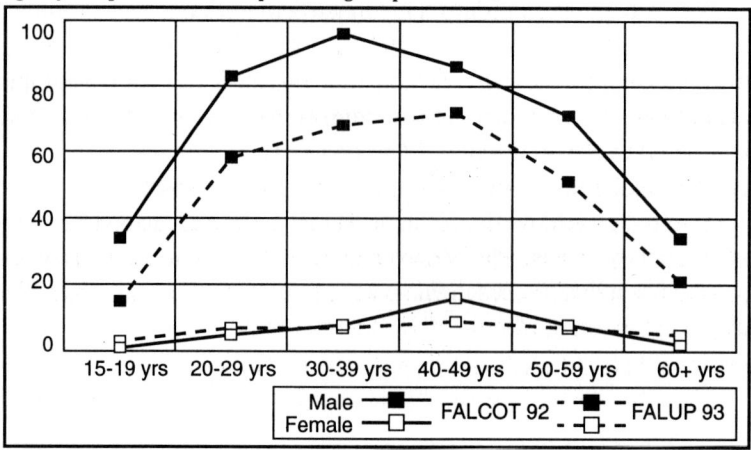

Figure 2.7 Gaza labour-force participation, by gender and education. Percentage of all adults in respective groups in Gaza

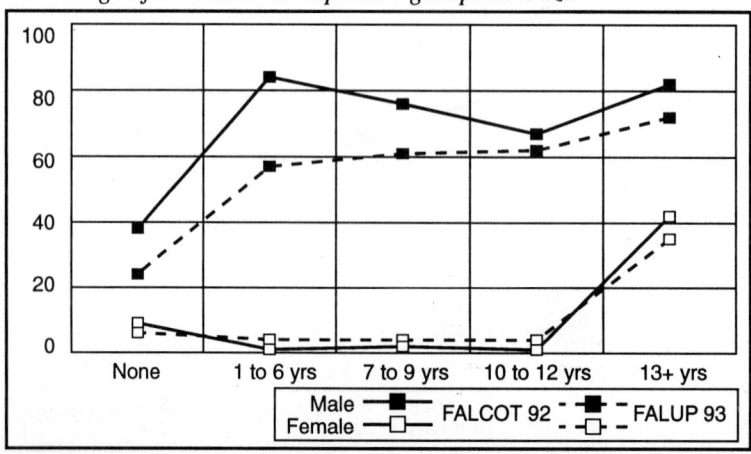

groups after the border closure will be discussed in greater detail in the section about under-utilization of labour.

What determined labour-force participation in Gaza and the West Bank refugee camps in the autumn of 1993? As labour-force participation is influenced by numerous economic, political and cultural factors, working together in a complex interplay, a multi-variate analysis is required.

DETERMINANTS OF LABOUR-FORCE PARTICIPATION

See appendix 3 as reference to the discussion in this section.
An individual's position in the labour market may be seen as the outcome of a chain of decisions. Most important is the decision to be economically active or not – i.e. whether the person will seek work. Among those who are economically active, additional decisions will have to be taken regarding the number of working hours, employment status, type, sector and workplace.

Who make these decisions? Many economic models for Western countries are based on the assumption that decisions on labour activities are primarily the result of one adult individual maximizing his or her utility. This maximization process implies weighing up payment for work against alternative use of time, whether for other obligations or for leisure. The process is constrained by such factors as the person's physical ability to work, his or her skills, and the preferences of other household members.

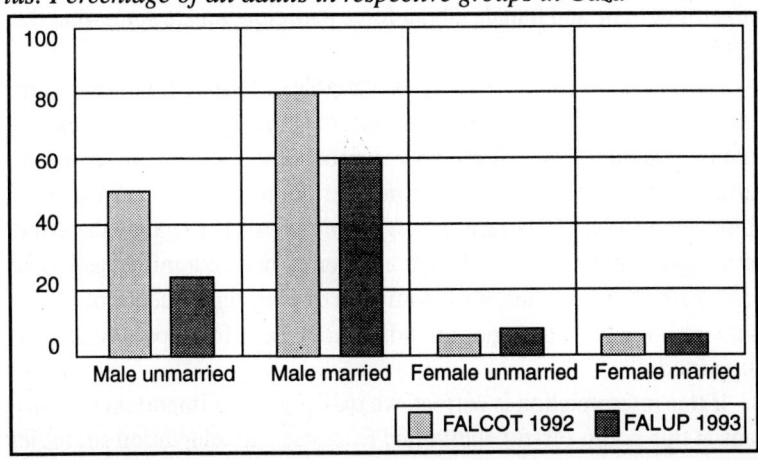

Figure 2.8 Gaza labour-force participation, by gender and marital status. Percentage of all adults in respective groups in Gaza

Palestinian society is family-based, so a model that sees decisions on income-generating activities basically as a household matter, seems more applicable. In this model, individual labour activities is considered primarily as the outcome of *household* rather than individual optimization strategies.

In this sub-section we seek to highlight factors influencing the decision of individuals to become economically active, and possibly confirm the appropriateness of the household decision model. Our tool of analysis is logistic regression analysis estimating the propensity of individuals to join the labour force.

Logistic regression is a statistical method where a dependent variable which describes an outcome or event is explained by one or more independent (explanatory) variables. A logistic regression model furnishes estimates of how the probability of the outcome is affected by the explanatory variables. Because the model focuses on outcomes, it is well suited for analyses of how decisions are influenced by the characteristics of individuals or groups.

In our case, the outcome is whether or not an individual is a member of the labour force, i.e. if the decision to join the labour force has been taken. The explanatory variables may be seen as falling in two groups. The first group consists of variables relating to the position of individuals as ascribed by birth or inherent in their life cycle: gender, age, position in the household and marital status. The second group consists of variables that reflect the process of social differentiation more directly such as refugee status, education or place of residence. The analysis was carried out separately for men and women, since the determinants of male and female labour force participation are somewhat different.

It appears that it is the group of variables ascribed by birth and inherent in the life cycle that has the most explanatory power. The exception is education, which is the only variable of the second group that we have found to influence labour force participation. As the West Bank sample comprises 97% refugees, it is only possible to gauge the effect of refugee status in Gaza, where it apparently does not influence labour force participation. Thus, the assumption of a strong influence of household optimization strategies on individual labour force participation is supported.

If this interpretation is correct, we may draw two important conclusions at this point. Firstly, individual response and adaptation strategies to meet the economic shocks affecting the Occupied Territories are closely linked with household coping strategies. Secondly, public policy for influencing labour-force participation must not only aspire to change an individual's choice patterns, such as years of education, but also try to influence behavioural and attitudinal norms, such as what is seen as appropriate work for women.

In the next section we present the composition of the labour force. This composition is, of course, a product of the factors identified as significant in the regression equations above.

COMPOSITION OF THE LABOUR FORCE

See tables 2.8 to 2.11 in appendix 3 as references to the discussion in this section.

Labour resources available to the economy are dependent not only on the size, but also on the "quality" of the labour force. In particular, the workers' formal education and occupational training are important for labour productivity.

Does the labour force in fact comprise the most productive segments of the adult population? Figure 2.9 presents a regional comparison of average age by gender and labour-force status.

As could be expected, those in the labour force in both main areas are better educated than are those outside the labour force. Regardless

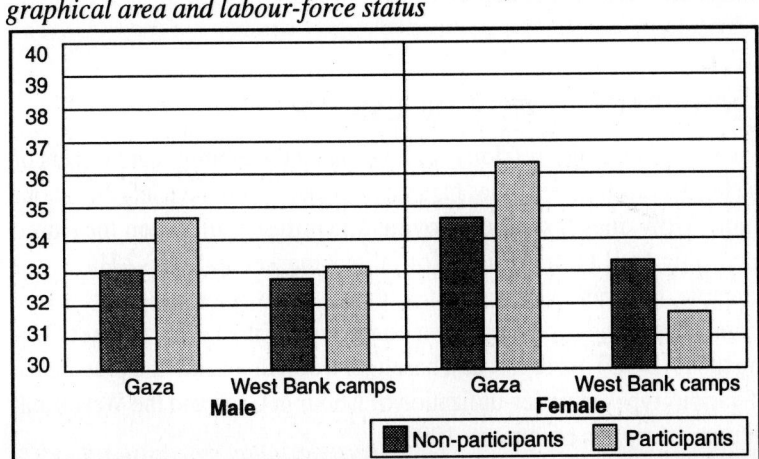

Figure 2.9 Average age of adults, 15 years or older, by gender, main geographical area and labour-force status

of sex, those in the labour force have on average 2-3 more years of education than non-participants.

With regard to average age, differences by labour force status are small, due to two effects which tend to counteract each other. On the one hand, labour-force participation is lower among young adults because many are still students; on the other, it is also low among the elderly, who are often unwell.

For male labour-force participants, regional differences in average age and years of education are relatively small. For (the small sample of) women, regional differences are larger, in particular with regard to average age. Interestingly, the difference between male and female labour-force participants takes opposite directions in Gaza and in the West Bank refugee camps. Gaza women are older and have less formal schooling than their male counterparts, whereas in the West Bank refugee camps the pattern is the inverse.

Female participation in both areas is highest, *relative* to male participation, at the extremities of the educational ladder – in particular at the top. This pattern was also observed in the FALCOT 92 report, which noted that "work" among women primarily tends to be understood as employment outside the home. Because of the greater acceptance of females working in professional rather than manual jobs, relatively many employed women hold mid-level professional jobs in public services (nursing, teaching, etc.).

Table 2.1 clearly confirms the hypothesis of a dramatic reduction in male labour-force participation in Gaza and the West Bank refugee camps after the Israeli border closure in March 1993.

UNDER-UTILIZATION OF LABOUR

The main aim of this section is to investigate the employment effects of the border closure. What has happened to those who have left the labour force? How does loss of employment manifest itself when measured according to ILO definitions for labour market statistics? Have, for example, the unemployment rates surged, or do other indicators give a more valid expression of present conditions in the labour market? Using the FALCOT 92 report as a baseline, we shall discuss the prevalence of various types of under-utilization of labour in Gaza and the West Bank refugee camps as of autumn 1993.

If the present extraordinary low labour-force participation is a result of structural factors outside the control of the individual, it indicates a deterioration in welfare and living conditions. We will argue that the change in adult male labour-force participation is most probably rooted in the difficult labour market situation currently prevailing in the Occupied Territories. The apparently involuntary character of the situation would seem to validate claims of an under-utilized labour potential.

Before proceeding with the discussion, some definitions and concepts must be clarified. Figure 2.10 gives a schematic overview of different types of under-utilization of labour. Note that the figure is based on the ILO classification system presented in figure 2.1.[3] In the FALCOT 92 report it was argued that unemployment rates were misleading as measures of the prevalence of under-utilization of labour in the Occupied Territories, for two main reasons. First, many "employed" persons in the labour force are in reality under-employed. Second, many persons outside the labour force can be labelled "discouraged workers" because they have simply given up trying to find work. In the survey, "discouraged workers" were identified as persons currently neither working nor seeking work, but who would like to work *if* an "acceptable" job for an "acceptable" wage could be found.

In addition to the persons completely out of work – the regular "unemployed" – many employed persons also desire additional employment. These persons may be labelled *visibly* under-employed. Further, many workers are full-time employed in jobs with very low-productivity

Figure 2.10 Types of labour under-utilization

II	III	I a, b, c	
Unemployed (ILO def.)	Not in labour force (ILO def.)	Employed (ILO def.)	
Unemployment		Underemployment	
Visible	Invisible	Visible	Invisible
ILO definition of unemployment	Discouraged workers	Seeking additional work	Low prouctivity Difficult to measure
1	2	3	4

3 Heiberg, Marianne and Geir Øvensen (1993), p. 189.

and wages. These workers can be characterized as *invisibly* under-employed. Finally, many persons outside the labour force are in reality so-called discouraged workers because they have simply given up trying to find work at all.

UNEMPLOYMENT

See tables 2.12 to 2.17 in appendix 3 as references to the discussion in this section.

"Unemployed" persons (box II) are defined by the ILO as those who did not work as much as one hour during the week prior to the interview, but who at the same time were actively seeking work. The state of unemployment may be considered as one extreme on a continuous scale from high labour activity to complete inactivity in the labour market.

Figure 2.11 presents visible unemployment by gender and main area as share of the labour-force participants in each group. The 1992 unemployment rate as measured by the FALCOT 92 report has been used as a reference for Gaza males.

From figure 2.11 we see that 1993 male unemployment rates in Gaza are higher than in the West Bank refugee camps. In both main areas, unemployment is higher for women than for men, which may indicate particularly strict requirements as to "acceptable" workplace and type of work for women.

Figure 2.11 Unemployment rates, by gender and main geographical area (ILO definitions). Percentage of labour-force participants in respective groups

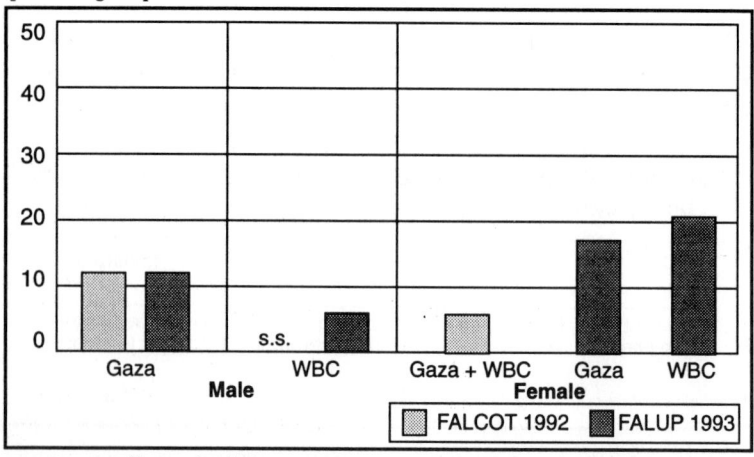

s.s. = too small sample size

The critical question concerning unemployment is why the general 1993 visible unemployment rates in Gaza and the West Bank refugee camps are in fact so much lower than many might have expected.

The March 1993 border closure could have been expected to generate a steep increase in unemployment rates in the short term. First, there is a direct effect of workers losing employment in Israel. Second, workers' loss of income induces negative domestic multiplier effects on aggregate demand. From figure 2.11, we see that unemployment in Gaza as of late 1993 is, however, the *same* as measured by the FALCOT 92 report. (The sample size for the West Bank refugee camps in the FALCOT 92 report is too small to permit comparison.)

Several hypotheses may be suggested to explain the lack of change in the Gaza unemployment rate:

First, the *"no change"* hypothesis stipulates that access for Gaza workers to the Israeli labour market had already been restricted ever since the Gulf War in January 1991. The March 1993 border closure thus made little difference.

Second, the *"smooth adaptation"* hypothesis assumes that Gaza workers were willing to accept lower wages to obtain employment. That is, most workers who lost employment in Israel quickly acquired and accepted lower paid employment locally in Gaza. Third, the *"measurement problem"* hypothesis claims that open unemployment rates have little validity as indicators of under-utilization of labour in the Occupied Territories. They consequently must be supplemented with other measures.

Returning to the "no change" hypothesis, let us compare the share of workers who mainly worked in Israel in the autumn of 1993 with the corresponding share for the same period in 1992. Both shares are calculated as a percentage of the total number of persons employed at least one week in the two respective four-week periods. Figure 2.12 presents the results by gender and main geographical area.

Figure 2.12 rejects the "no change" hypothesis. Both in Gaza and in the West Bank refugee camps, the *net* reduction of (male) employment in Israel exceeds 1/3. The regional breakdown in figure 2.13, however, shows a tendency towards less reduction in employment in Israel in Northern Gaza and the Southern/Central West Bank refugee camps.

The Southern and Central West Bank refugee camps are the only region where the "no change" hypothesis may have some relevance. 20% of the population live in Arab Jerusalem (Shufat and Kalandia refugee camps), and consequently do not need permits to enter Israel.

In the Jerusalem area, many Israeli checkpoints can also be by-passed on foot by not using the roads. Still, even in this group, the net reduction of employment in Israel is as high as 23%.

The "smooth adaptation" hypothesis assumes that Gaza workers were willing to accept lower wages locally to obtain employment. To test this hypothesis, we investigated the present labour-force status of males who mainly worked in Israel in the autumn of 1992, but *not* in the autumn of 1993. These workers (the *gross* reduction of employment in Israel), comprised approximately 1/2 of the workers who had worked mainly in Israel in the autumn of 1992. Figure 2.14 presents the results for this group of workers by main geographical area.

We can see that only 2 out of 5 persons who lost work in Israel from 1992 to 1993 found new employment in the Occupied Territories. As many as 70-80% of those who *found* employment stated that they want to work more.

Very few workers who lost jobs in Israel from 1992 to 1993 show up in the statistics as "unemployed" as defined by the ILO. The largest group among these workers in both Gaza and the West Bank refugee camps is that of "discouraged workers". Among Gaza workers who lost their jobs in Israel from 1992 to 1993, the group of "discouraged work-

Figure 2.12 1993 and 1992 employment in Israel, by gender and main geographical area of residence. Percentage of adults in respective groups employed one week or more during a four-week period prior to the survey (October/November 1993), and the corresponding period in 1992

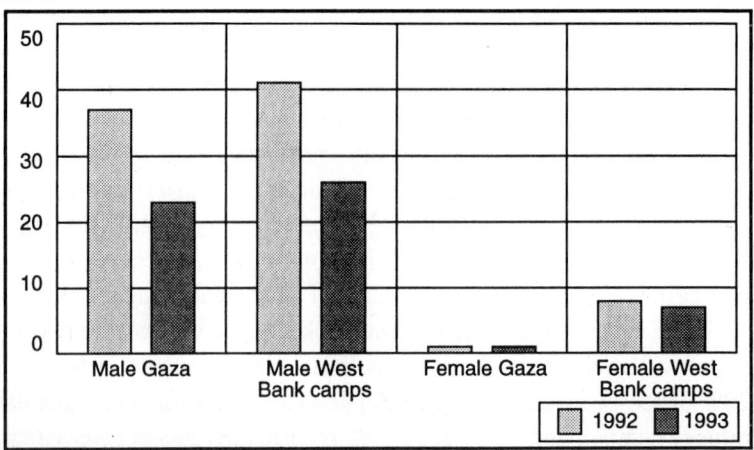

ers" is 4 times as large as the number of "unemployed" persons. In the West Bank refugee camps it is 9 times as large.

These results have two important implications. First, the (open) unemployment rate alone is not able to capture developments in under-utilization of labour for this group of workers.

Figure 2.13 1993 and 1992 male employment in Israel by sub-area. Percentage of adults in respective groups employed one week or more during a four-week period prior to the survey, (October/November 1993), and the corresponding period in 1992

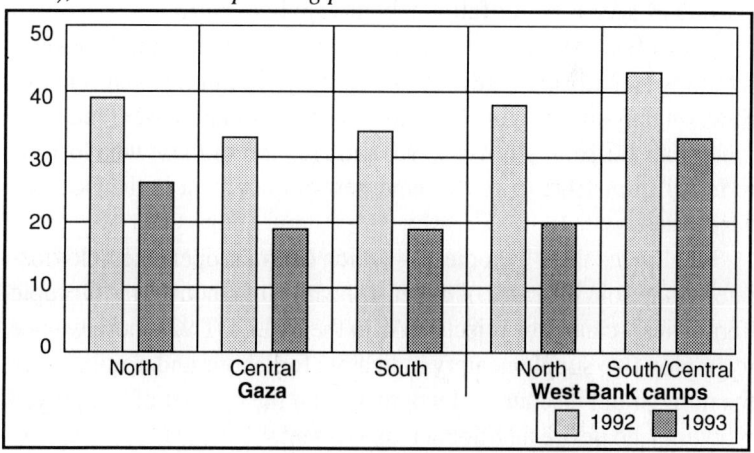

Figure 2.14 1993 employment situation of men who worked in Israel in 1992 but not in 1993, by main geographical area of residence. Percentage of men in respective groups employed one week or more during a four-week period in october/november 1992, but not in the corresponding period in 1993

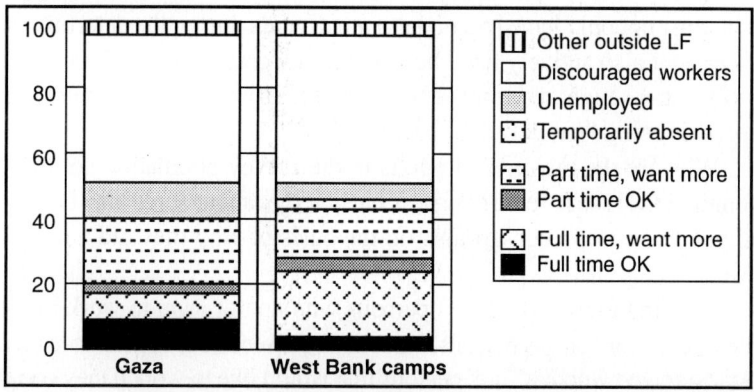

Second, it is misleading to take the low and comparatively stable unemployment rates to indicate that the labour market in the Occupied Territories quickly adjusted to a reduced labour demand through lower wages. We have shown that the decrease in employment after the border closure is far greater than indicated by the unemployment rate.

Also the downward trend in workers' reservation wages (i.e. the lowest wage for which they will offer employment), seems much lower when we take into consideration the unemployment rates *as well as* the high number of "discouraged workers". This topic will be further dealt with in the fourth and final part of the employment chapter, in the discussion of scenarios for future labour supply in Gaza.

The dramatic reduction in adult male labour-force participation after the border closure hardly shows up in the unemployment statistics. Still, net employment for Palestinian workers in Israel was reduced by more than 1/3 from 1992 to 1993, and only 2/5 of these who lost jobs in Israel from 1992 to 1993 found new employment in the Occupied Territories.

Finally, the third hypothesis – which distrusts open unemployment rates as the sole indicator of under-utilization of labour in the Occupied Territories – cannot be rejected. As in the FALCOT 92 report, we need to employ two supplementary indicators for labour under-utilization – the number of "discouraged workers", and the number of "employed" workers who desire additional employment.

"Discouraged workers"

See tables 2.18 to 2.22 in appendix 3 as references to the discussion in this section.

To be classified as "unemployed" in the labour force framework, a person must not only have had no labour activities during the determinant week, but also actively have been seeking work. Persons who neither worked nor sought work are either classified as not belonging the labour force or being "temporarily absent".

Why are the majority of adults in the survey population not to be found in the labour force? Persons outside the labour force may be subdivided into two main groups, on the basis of why they did not seek work.

The first group comprises persons who do not *want* to work in the short term, for various reasons. Persons in the second group are so-called "discouraged workers", i.e. persons that would like to work *if* they could find an "acceptable" job at an "acceptable" wage. Figure 2.15 shows the distribution of the two main groups among persons outside the labour force, by gender and main geographical area. (The comparison with the FALCOT 92 report is only illustrative, due to the small sample size, variations in question formulation and differences with regard to geographical coverage).

Those who do not want any work in the short term were mostly housewives, students and old or unwell persons. Figure 2.16 shows the distribution of reasons for neither working nor seeking work among persons in this group, by gender and main geographical area.

Figure 2.16 shows considerable gender-specific differences, but for both sexes, small variations by area. While most of the large group of women who do not want to work are housewives, most men in this group are either students or old/unwell.

In a possible accelerated process of development in the Occupied Territories even more persons may become students. Constantly higher requirements for labour productivity may further squeeze more workers into the group of (too) "old/ sick" persons. The number of housewives, on the contrary, is likely to decrease if fertility starts declining, if attitudes towards what is "appropriate" work for women change, and if female educational levels continue to rise.

If these assumptions hold true, female labour-force participation rates may increase in the future. Male participation, on the contrary, is likely to stay stable or even fall in the youngest and oldest age groups.

Figure 2.15 "Discouraged workers", by gender and main geographical area. Percentage of adults outside the labour force in respective groups

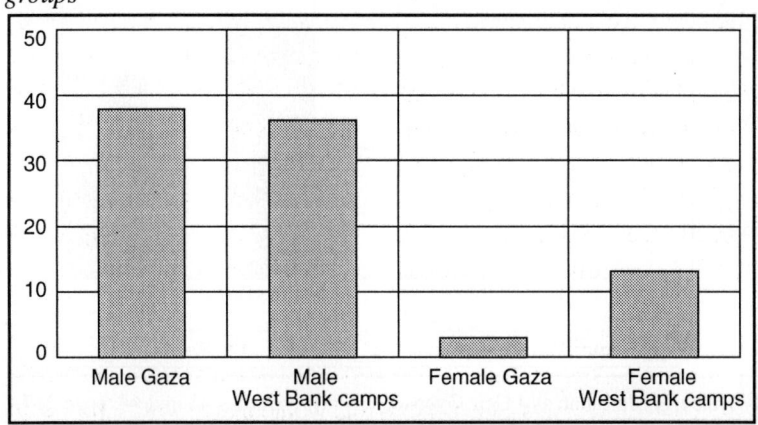

The gender distribution of reasons for neither working nor desiring to work illustrates that a substantial female labour reserve may be available in the long term.

The other main group among persons outside the labour force is the group of so-called "discouraged workers", i.e. persons who state that they would like to work if "acceptable" jobs for "acceptable" wages could be found. Figure 2.17 shows the reasons for neither working nor seeking work among persons in this group by gender and main geographical area.

Figure 2.17 indicates large differences by gender, and for women, also by area of residence. For men, the main reasons stated by respondents in both areas are security-related. These include "administrative measures" like "green card", lack of permit, town arrest, etc. Note that persons imprisoned for "security" reasons have already been excluded from the survey population).[4] Most of these measures relate to restrictions on employment in Israel or in Israeli institutions and settlements in the Occupied Territories.

The high number of males defined as "discouraged workers" because they do not seek work due to security-related measures, can be interpreted in several ways: First, "discouraged Palestinian workers" seem

Figure 2.16 Persons outside the labour force who do not want to start working, by gender and main geographical area. Percentage of adults in respective groups who are outside the labour force and not "discouraged workers"

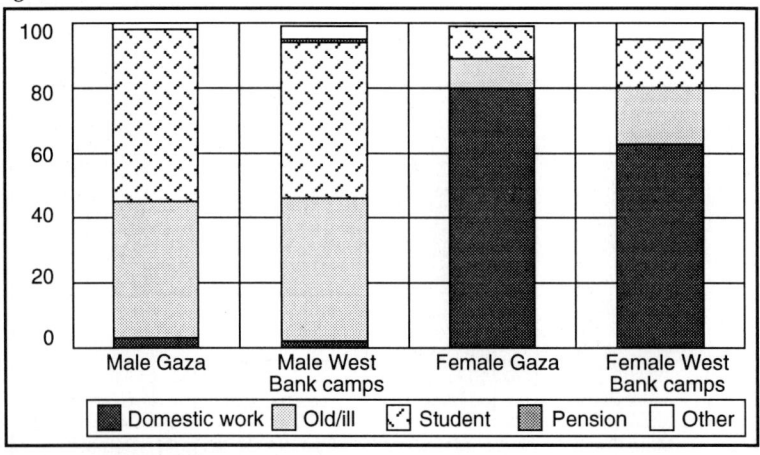

4 Heiberg, Marianne and Geir Øvensen (1993), endnotes 43 and 44, page 217.

to blame Israeli policy for lack of effort in even looking for work. Israel is consequently the target for frustrations due to lack of employment among these persons.

Second, there seems to be a widespread Palestinian desire for employment in Israel, or in Israeli institutions and settlements in the Occupied Territories, despite the inconvenience, and degradation often associated with border control procedures. This indicates that wage levels for workers from the Occupied Territories employed by Israelis are relatively high compared to other employment available to Palestinians, even if they are less well paid than their Jewish colleagues.

Third, the reservation wage of the "discouraged workers" (i.e. the lowest wage for which they will offer employment), still seems above the wage level currently obtainable in the Occupied Territories. The real search for (*any kind of*) local employment has thus not yet been launched.

Finally, the large proportion of male "discouraged workers" giving security-related reasons for not seeking work, may possibly indicate that the border closure is regarded as a temporary situation. Expectations of improvement in the future are based upon the experience of numerous fluctuations between tighter and more relaxed border restrictions in recent years. Among women living in West Bank refugee camps, security-related measures are cited as important reasons for not working,

Figure 2.17 Reasons for not working or seeking jobs among "discouraged" workers, by gender and main geographical area. Percentage of adult "discouraged" workers in respective groups

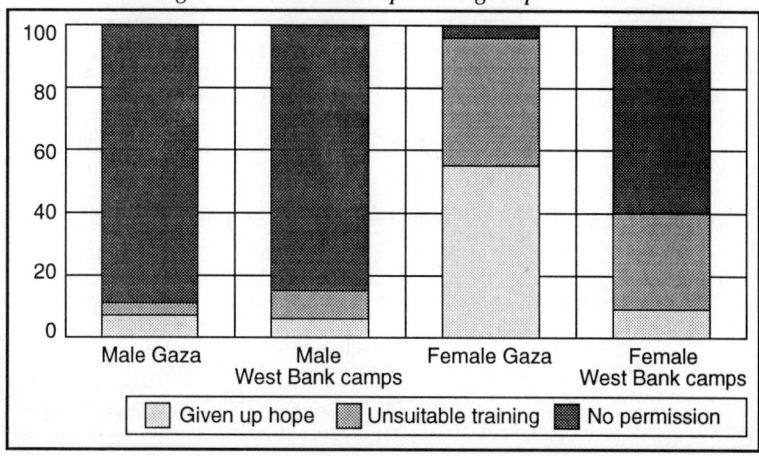

whereas they are of little importance to Gaza women. A possible explanation for this regional difference is that scepticism to female employment in Israel is particularly strong in Gaza.

A relatively high number of women report that they have given up looking for work or finding work that accords with their vocational training. As for unemployed women, this may indicate particularly strict

Figure 2.18 Discouraged workers, by main geographical area, gender and age. Percentage of persons in respective groups who are outside the labour force

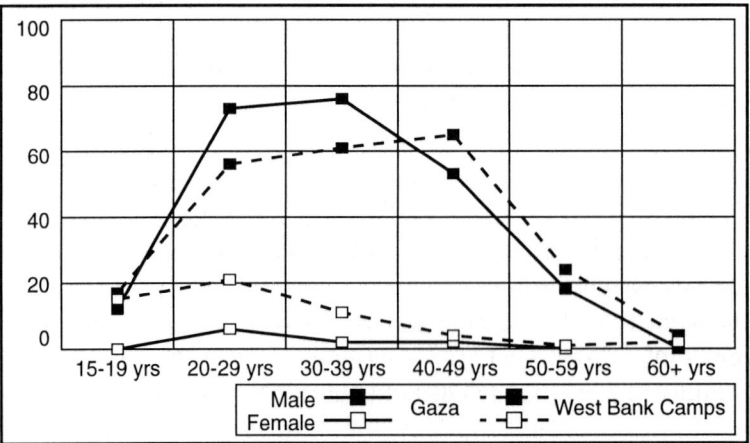

Figure 2.19 Discouraged workers, by main geographical area, gender and education. Percentage of adults in respective groups who are outside the labour force

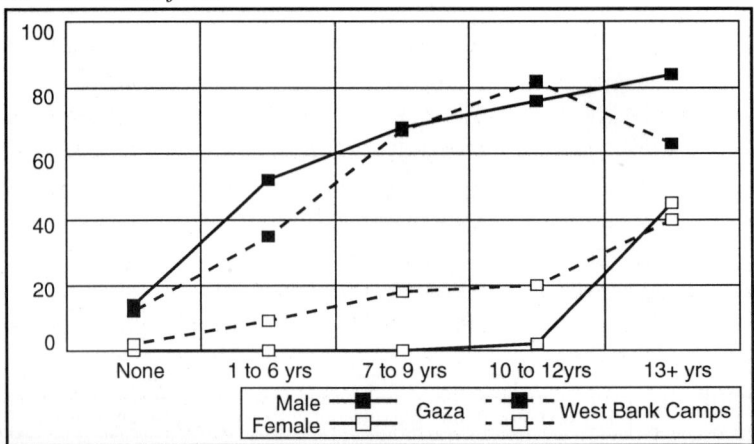

requirements as to "acceptable" female workplaces and types of occupation.

Figures 2.18 and 2.19 show regional distributions of "discouraged workers" by gender, age and education. In both main geographical areas, "discouraged workers" are predominantly young males with above average education. No difference in the prevalence of "discouraged workers" could be found across refugee status in Gaza.

From these findings, "discouraged workers" would appear to score better than average in attractiveness in the labour market. It seems reasonable to assume that this "attractiveness" is reflected in self-perceived status, and consequently causes lighter expectations and a more discriminating attitude with respect to place and type of job. These factors, rather than inability to find *any* kind of work at all, may explain why these persons have not set about searching in earnest for local employment in Gaza and the West Bank.

VISIBLE AND INVISIBLE UNDER-EMPLOYMENT

See tables 2.23 to 2.27 in appendix 3 as references to the discussion in this section.

In the introductory statement concerning under-employment, *visible* under-employment was described as insufficiency in the volume of employment. *Invisible* under-employment, on the other hand, was described as mis-allocation of labour resources, e.g. in the form of low-productivity and under-utilization of a worker's skills.

Many employed persons, both full-time and part-time workers, desire additional employment. Could these persons be labelled as visibly under-employed? According to ILO definitions, a visibly under-employed person must both be working less than normal duration of time, and seeking and being available for additional work. Statistical measurements of visible under-employment following these definitions strictly would, however, be highly problematic, as one would have to estimate the normal weekly working hours in a person's usual type of activities, as well as the time actually worked during the week.

Using low income as a criterion for invisible under-employment is problematic because low income may reflect the institutional set-up rather than low labour productivity. This is perhaps most clearly exemplified by unpaid family labour among women and children. In family enterprises it may be particularly difficult to trace the individual income components required to measure invisible under-employment.

Rather than follow the ILO definitions rigidly we have chosen to use the number of employed persons who express desire for more work as an empirical indicator of *visible* under-employment. Among part-time workers, it may be assumed that the desire for more work indicates the involuntary character of such labour activities.

Full-time workers who desire additional employment, on the contrary, can hardly be classified as visibly under-employed, since they already hold jobs of normal duration. It is, however, reasonable to assume that many of these workers hold full-time jobs with insufficient productivity and payment, and that their desire for even more work should be interpreted as an indication of *invisible* under-employment.

Figure 2.20 shows the share of full-time and part-time employed labour-force participants by main geographical area and gender. Comparisons between the FALUP 93 and the FALCOT 92 surveys must be made with care, due to different definitions applied by the two surveys. In the FALUP 93 survey, persons who worked more than 35 hours the last week prior to the interviewing were classified as full-time workers, and those who worked from 1 to 34 hours as part-time workers. The FALCOT 92 report defined part-time workers as those working 6 weeks

Figure 2.20 Full-time, part-time and unemployment rates, by gender and main geographical area. Percentage of adults who worked 35 hours or more the week before the 1993 survey, and 6 weeks or more during the two months before the 1992 survey (july/august 1992)

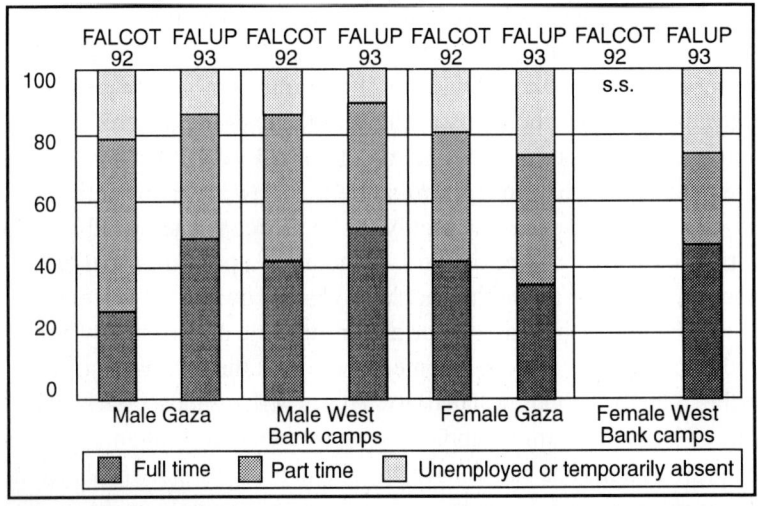

s.s. = too small sample size

or less during the last two months prior to the survey; full-time workers were persons working 7 weeks or more during the same period.

All the same, it still seems that *relatively* more Gaza males were working full-time in 1993 than in 1992. Due to frequent strikes, curfews and border-crossing restrictions in 1992, employment in Israel was much less stable than in the Occupied Territories. Consequently 88% of Gaza workers who worked in Israel were classified by the FALCOT 92 report as part-time workers.

In contrast, part-time workers constituted 58% of those employed locally in Gaza. Many workers employed full-time were employed by institutions like UNRWA or the (Israeli) Civil Administration. Unlike those employed in Israel or in marginal employment in the Occupied Territories, these workers were hardly (directly) affected by the border closure.

A possible explanation for the *relative* increase in full-time employment among Gaza males is that the dramatic drop in labour-force participation from 1992 to 1993 was caused by a reduction in "part-time" employment. In the West Bank refugee camps similar mechanisms may have been at work, in particular, with regard to employment in Israel. The sample of merely 32 persons in this group in the FALCOT 92 report is, however, too small to permit meaningful comparisons with FALUP 93 data.

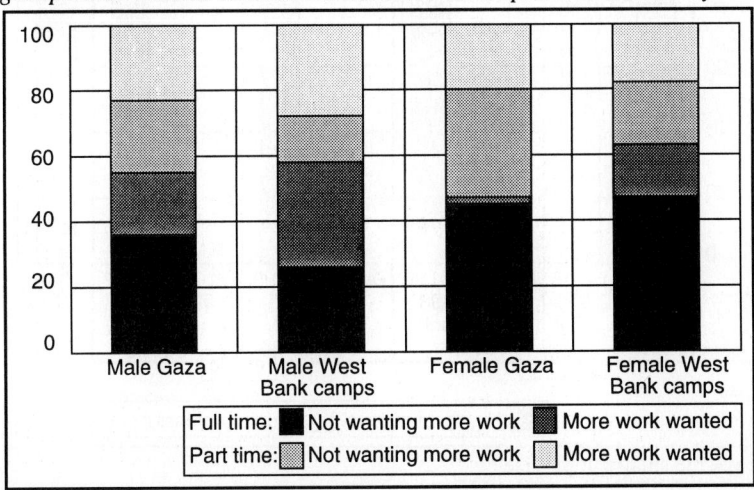

Figure 2.21 Employed persons wanting/ not wanting more work, by gender and main geographical area. Percentage of adults in respective groups who worked at least one hour the week prior to the survey

Figure 2.21 shows the 1993 distribution of part-time and full-time workers by gender and main geographical area. Both part-time and full-time groups have been sub-divided according to whether the respondent desired additional employment or not.

In both areas, and for both part-time and full-time workers, the proportion of employed men who desire more work is larger than that for employed women. Since most Palestinian women are also responsible for household domestic tasks like child care and housekeeping, this result is not surprising. Ensuring that work does not get in the way of family obligations is an absolute requirement for women who accept conventional employment. As could be expected, desire for more work among employed women is lowest in the more traditional Gaza Strip.

Because of very low female labour-force participation, the number of employed women was too small to be broken down by age and educational groups. Table 2.24 in the Appendix shows that the proportion of part-time and full-time employed men desiring additional employment is highest in the two age groups 20-29 years and 30-39 years. Probably due to a mix of health problems and cultural norms regarding obligations and privileges for men of mature age, a vast majority of

Figure 2.22 Employed persons with 10 or more years of education by, gender, main geographical area and type of job. Percentage of employed adults in respective groups with at least 10 years of education

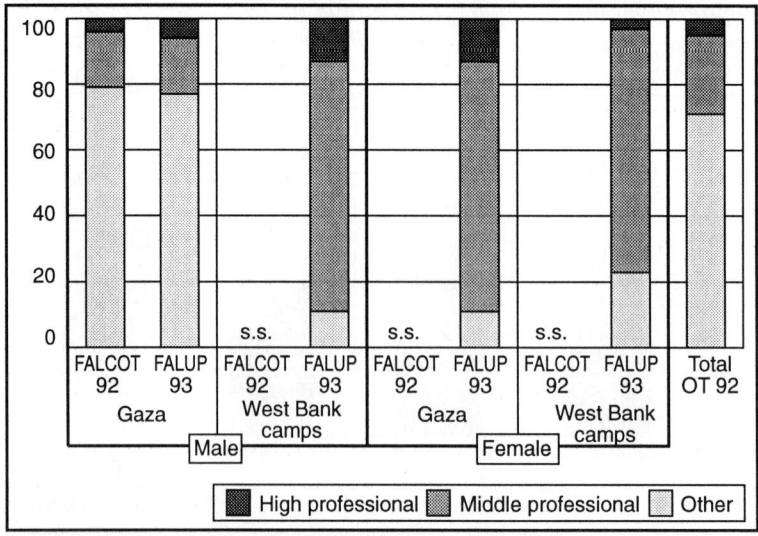

s.s. = too small sample size

employed men over 50 years of age express no desire to increase their present labour market activities.

A greater share of highly educated males seems to desire more work than among those with little education. In the West Bank refugee camps, a majority of men with more than 7 years of formal schooling, both among part-time and full-time workers, state that they want additional work. However, the strong negative correlation between age and education may underline much of these results.

Measuring invisible under-employment was described by the FALCOT 92 report as even more challenging than measuring visible under-employment. One would have to establish thresholds below which income is considered abnormally low, as well as under-utilization of skills, or insufficient productivity. Information on the economic productivity of individual economic units would have to be augmented by information on the characteristics of individual workers.

As an *indicator* of under-utilization of *skills*, the job types of persons correlated with level of schooling is shown in figures 2.22 and 2.23. Results from the FALUP 93 survey are very similar to observations made by the FALCOT 92 report.

Figure 2.23 Employed persons with 13 or more years of education by, gender, main geographical area and type of job. Percentage of employed adults in respective groups with at least 13 years of education

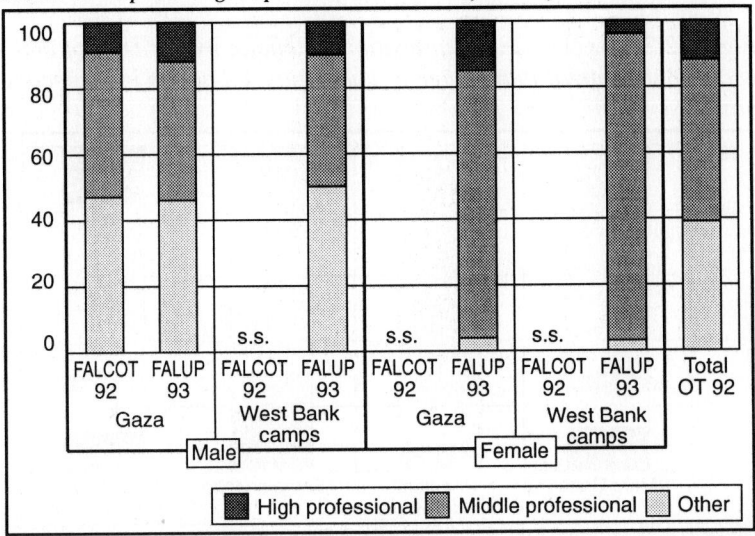

s.s. = too small sample size

We note the strong effect of gender with regard to correspondence between education and employment. Among employed men with 10 or more years of education 80% hold non-professional jobs. In the group of men with 13 or more years of education this rate drops to 50%.

For the small sample of employed women, only a low proportion in both educational groups hold non-professional jobs. This emphasizes how important jobs of high social status are for acceptance of female labour activities outside the home.

THREE TYPES OF LABOUR UNDER-UTILIZATION

See tables 2.28 to 2.33 in appendix 3 as references to the discussion in this section.

Under-utilization of labour manifests itself in various ways. Can one single measure capture the situation of labour under-utilization in Gaza and the West Bank refugee camps?

Here we have described three different indicators of labour under-utilization: the (open) unemployment rate, the number of "discouraged workers" and the number of employed workers who want more work. Despite challenging problems of measurement and interpretation, these criteria can be summed up in an aggregate classification system.

The first group comprises workers employed part-time or full-time who do not want more work. The second group consists of persons

Figure 2.24 Types of under-utilization of labour, by gender and main geographical area. Percentage of under-utilized adults in respective groups

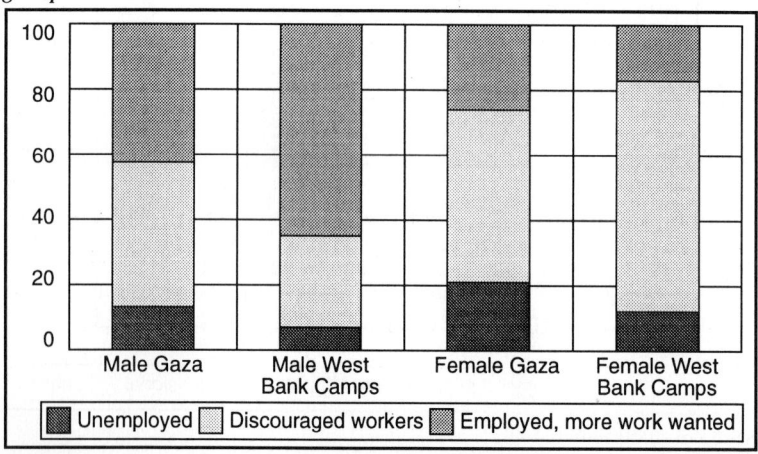

presently outside the labour force with no (immediate) desire to start working. People in both these groups generally seem to be satisfied with their current labour-force status.

The third and final group however, is constituted by persons who express desire for more work, or if presently inactive, the desire to start working. It seems reasonable to assume that most of these persons in one way or the other are frustrated with their present labour-force status. Here we combine employed persons who want to work more, "discouraged workers", and (regularly) unemployed workers into a group which we have labelled "under-utilized persons".

Figure 2.24 shows the distribution of this group by gender and main geographical area.

On average just slightly more than one-tenth of this group are the regularly unemployed. In both regions the majority are employed persons who desire more work, or "discouraged workers". The variations in the content of the group of under-utilized persons will be further discussed in the next section concerning future labour-force scenarios for Gaza.

A caveat is called for concerning both these two last sub-groups. The desire for (more) work among these persons obviously has implicit references to "acceptable" jobs and "acceptable" wage levels. It is thus not clear under exactly what conditions they would be willing to take on (more) work, and what specific efforts they might consider or initiate to obtain (more) employment.

ILO's standard "labour-force framework" is based on actual (objective) behaviour rather than perceptions and opinions. The reference to "acceptable" jobs and "acceptable" wage levels introduces a fairly subjective and hypothetical element into the ideally "objective" description of the labour-market situation.

Still, this classification system may be useful for at least three reasons. Firstly, because most of the under-utilized persons can be assumed to be frustrated with their current labour-force status, it represents an important indicator of social frustration and discouragement. In particular the group of "discouraged workers" expresses a mixture of a sense of resignation (expressed by lack of belief in the point of even *trying* to look for a suitable job), and targeted dissatisfaction (Israel is the scapegoat, by failing to issue various permits indispensable in many types of jobs).

Second, the less than full utilization of under-utilized persons represents a severe loss in well-being at the societal, the household and the individual levels. Unemployed persons and "discouraged workers" represent a productivity loss for society, as their whole potential output is lost as long as their involuntary inactivity persists. Permanent reduction in the productive potential of both unemployed persons and "discouraged workers" may be one of the lasting effects of such undesired inactivity.

Third, the group of under-utilized persons in many ways proves the existence of a reserve army of workers which, under certain conditions, could increase their individual labour activities within relatively *short* periods of time. This labour reserve should be seen in contrast to the labour reserve among "non-discouraged workers" outside the labour force (housewives, etc), which is likely to become available only over a longer period of time.

It is reasonable to assume that an increase in wages stemming from a positive shift in demand for labour will generally also lead to an increase in supply of labour. The size of the group of under-utilized persons is an important factor to be considered in employment planning. It has particular relevance when evaluating short-term effects of shifts in demand for labour, but also when making labour-force projections for the long term. These points will be further discussed at the end of this chapter.

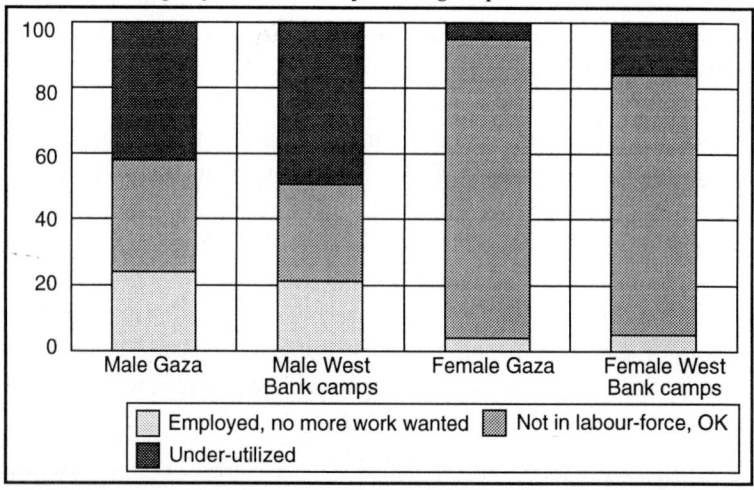

Figure 2.25 Employment situation, by gender and main geographical area. Percentage of adults in respective groups

We may now turn to the section of the prevalence of under-utilization of labour in Gaza and the West Bank refugee camps. Here we divide the working age population into the three main groups described above: Employed, no more work wanted; non-active, no more work wanted; and under-utilized persons.

As can be seen from figure 2.25, almost half the of adult males in both areas are under-utilized. In particular for Gaza, where all types of localities are represented in the survey population, these results paint a worrisome picture of profound social frustration.

The vast majority of women, on the contrary, do not express dissatisfaction with their current labour-force status. Most women in both areas are inactive in the labour market, and do not express desire for work because they are either housewives, students or old/ill.

Breaking the results down by sub-regions, we note a somewhat surprising but nontheless explainable lack of variation in the distribution of the three groups by sub-region and refugee status in Gaza. The FALCOT 92 report showed that Greater Gaza City, where non-refugees are over-represented, at that time had the least difficult employment situation. In the preceding section, however, we saw that these localities had the greatest decrease in male labour-force participation from 1992 to 1993. The border closure thus paradoxically seems to have equalized regional differences in Gaza, bringing all localities up to the same high level of under-utilization of adult male labour.

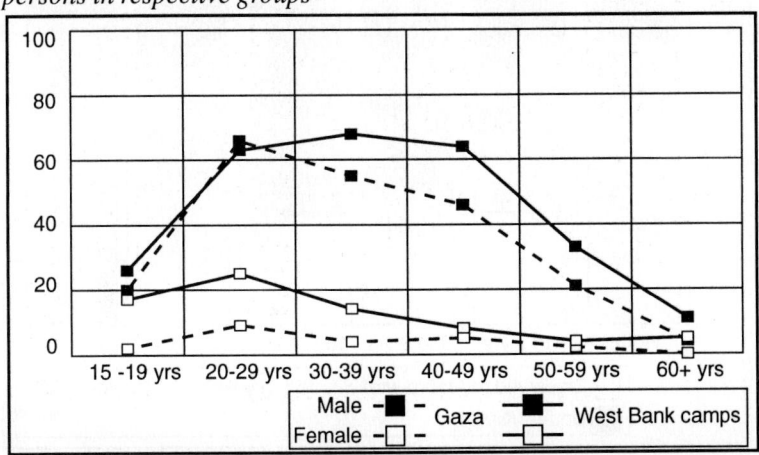

Figure 2.26 Labour under-utilization, by gender and age. Percentage of persons in respective groups

For the West Bank refugee camps (97% UNRWA refugees), regional differences in the distribution of the three groups were even smaller. The only exception was a relatively large number of under-utilized women in the Central/ Southern camps.

More important than variations by locality are variations according to individual characteristics. Figures 2.26, 2.27, 2.28 and 2.29 present the distribution of the three groups by gender, age and education.

Figure 2.27 Labour under-utilization, by gender and education. Percentage of adults in respective groups

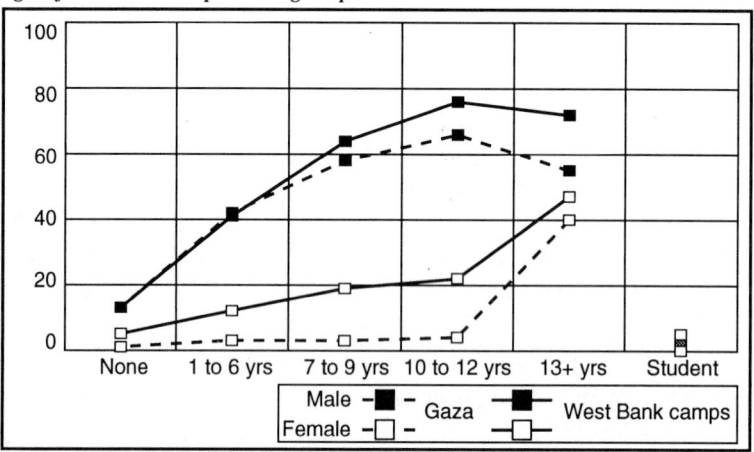

Figure 2.28 Male employment situation, by gender and education in Gaza. Percentage of adult men in respective groups

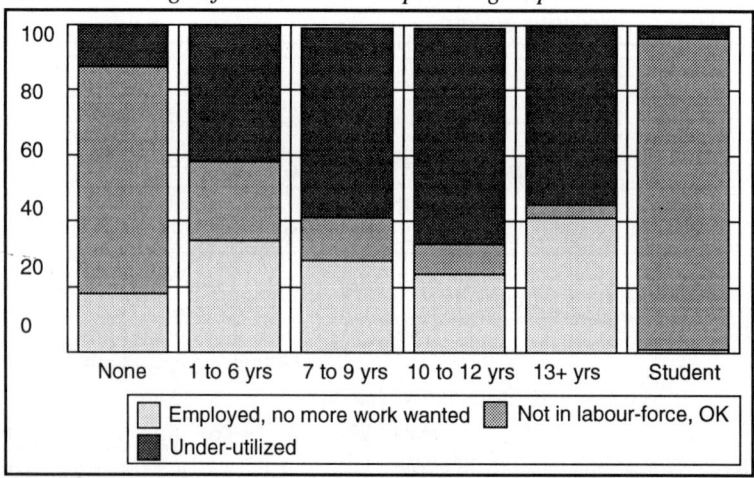

A breakdown of the results for women by age and education indicates that the future may see major changes in the pattern of "inactive" women with no desire to join the labour force. The aggregate results seem to cover strong effects along a dimension of exposure to modern society and thinking. On the one hand, there is a majority of voluntarily inactive old or less educated women, particularly in Gaza. On the other, we find a minority of young, highly educated women who want more work, or who wish to start to work, particularly in the West Bank refugee camps.

In both main geographical areas a high number of young and middle-aged, well-educated men want to change their current labour-force status. Two-thirds of Gaza men aged 20-29 years can be classified as under-utilized. Almost as high levels are reached for men of the same age in the West Bank refugee camps. This high under-utilization of youth and middle-aged, well-educated men represents a tremendous waste of some of the most productive groups in the Occupied Territories. The problem is aggravated by the risk of a permanent reduction in the productive potential of those completely inactive, the unemployed and "discouraged workers".

The high number of under-utilized youth and middle-aged men, culturally expected to provide for their families, proves the existence of a reserve army of male workers. An outward shift in demand for labour is likely to lead to a steep increase in labour supply within relatively

Figure 2.29 Female employment situation, by gender and education in Gaza. Percentage of adult women in respective groups

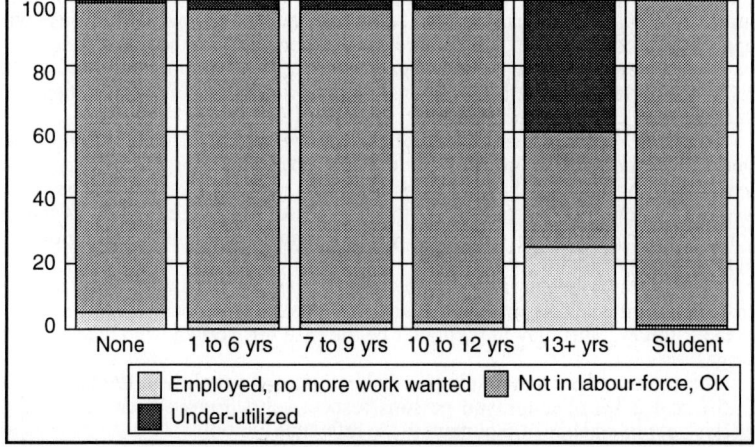

short periods of time. The size of the group of under-utilized persons is thus an important factor to be considered in labour market planning.

The most serious problem stemming from the large numbers of young, well-educated and under-utilized men is the vast potential they represent for social unrest and violence. These males – with ample resources, and most probably frustrated with their current employment situation – seem to direct much of their dissatisfaction towards Israel.

Failure to defuse this "social bomb" in the very near future may jeopardize the creation of conditions necessary for economic growth. Reducing under-utilization of labour in the Occupied Territories will thus be a crucial challenge for the Palestinian self-governing authority. If it does not succeed, it may end up replacing Israel as the scapegoat for social frustration and dissatisfaction.

EMPLOYMENT PATTERNS

INTRODUCTION[5]

We begin this section by following changes in the employment situation of individuals in the sample from 1992 to 1993. Here we are particularly interested in the direct and indirect employment effects of the border closure.

Did the workers who lost their jobs in Israel from 1992 to 1993 come from any particular type of locality? Were persons with any particular

---

5 ILO's labour force classification is based on a person's activities the last *week* prior to the survey. In the discussion below the concept «employed persons» will apply to all persons in the (adult) survey population who worked at least one week in a one *month* reference period, regardless of age or labour force status. The reference period either refers to the last month prior to the survey (October/ November 1993), or the same month in 1992.

The use of one month as a reference period for employment characteristics was made to reduce vulnerability to sudden political events or possible seasonal variations. In general the two groups «labour force» and «employed persons» overlap. Ninety-four per cent of «employed persons» were classified as labour force members, and 85% of labour force members belonged to the group of «employed persons».

Work types and sectors where many workers have very sporadic labour activity may, however, be under-represented among «employed persons» compared to the «labour force». This may in particular be the case for workers who receive daily wages.

The number of persons holding secondary jobs was very low in 1992 and 1993, (1.5% and 2.5% of employed persons respectively). Employment thus refers exclusively to «main» employment in the reference period.

individual characteristics more affected than others? The earlier section about under-utilization of labour showed that only about a half of those who lost employment in Israel between 1992 and 1993 found new employment in the Occupied Territories. Did these workers "squeeze out" other workers? Are they content with their 1993 employment situation?

The second aim of this section will be to look into the employment characteristics of workers who held jobs in 1993. By "employment characteristics" we here mean the distribution of workers according to types and sectors of work, as well as intensity of work, types of payment and status at the workplace.

Many workers in our sample are still employed in Israel. Do those employed in Israel mainly perform unskilled, service and vocational work, as before? Are they predominantly employed in the construction, service and agricultural sectors?

Do the 1993 employment characteristics vary by gender? Do employed women primarily hold low status jobs, and do they tend to work fewer hours than employed men?

Finally, we will discuss individual engagement in household income-generating activities. Who works in household production? Is household production an alternative to "formal" labour activities?

CHANGES IN EMPLOYMENT FROM 1992 TO 1993

See tables 2.34 to 2.43 in appendix 3 as references to the discussion in this section.

Initially the border closure was very comprehensive, preventing almost all Palestinian workers in Israel access to their jobs. Restrictions were then gradually relaxed. The Israelis still refused, however, to admit individuals considered to be "security threats".

The loss of employment in Israel may be termed the "direct" employment effect of the border closure in March 1993. The loss of income from wages also led to adverse multiplicator effects on local demand and hence employment in the Occupied Territories. This effect may be termed the "indirect" employment effect of the border closure.

Three main groups can be identified for further investigation as to the direct and indirect effects of the border closure, on the basis of the survey population's pre-closure employment status. The first group comprises persons who worked in Israel in 1992. The second group persons who worked in the Occupied Territories in 1992, and the third group persons not active in the labour market in 1992.

Figures 2.12 and 2.13 present a comparison between the percentages of workers who worked mainly in Israel in October/November 1993, and the corresponding percentages for the same months in 1992. It seems reasonable to interpret the difference in employment percentages as the *direct* effect of the border closure. In both main survey areas there was a *net* reduction of employment in Israel of more than 1/3 since 1992.

Our principal indicator for measuring the direct effects of the border closure is to take the group of workers who in 1992 were employed in Israel, and investigate their employment status and workplace, if any, in 1993. As can be seen from figure 2.30, this *gross* reduction of employment in Israel from autumn 1992 to autumn 1993 amounted to 50%. Only 1 out of 4 persons employed in Israel in 1992 started working in the Occupied Territories in 1993. Almost 2 out of 3 of those who had been working in Israel in 1992 expressed a desire for more work in 1993.

Figure 2.31 presents results for the sub-group which *lost* employment in Israel. In Gaza only 1 out of 3 persons who lost their jobs in Israel between 1992 and 1993 found new employment in the Occupied Territories. In both areas more than 80% wanted to work more in 1993, the highest level found for any group.

Have workers who lost employment in Israel "squeezed out" other workers in local employment? The results do not support such a hypo-

Figure 2.30 Main area of work in 1993 of those working in Israel in 1992, by main geographical region of residence. Percentage of adults in respective groups

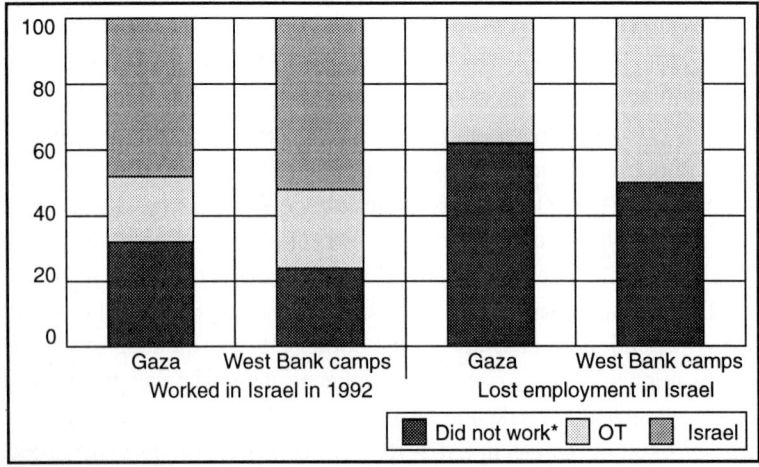

* i.e worked less than one week in the designated month

thesis. First, less than half of the workers previously employed in Israel found employment locally. Second, employment characteristics of these workers indicate a group of marginal workers, employed in low-status jobs with high instability and insecurity.

Figure 2.31 Employment situation of those working in Israel in 1992, by main geographical region of residence. Percentage of adults in respective groups

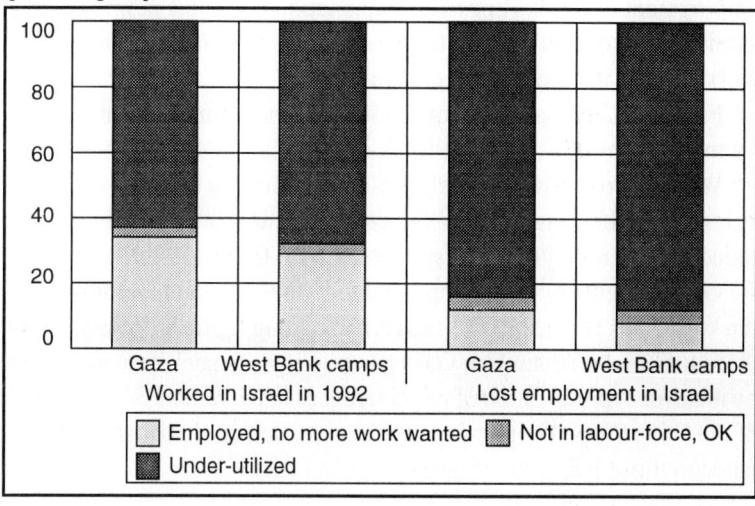

Figure 2.32 1993/1992 male employment in Israel, by refugee status. Percentage of adults in respective groups employed one week or more during a four-week period prior to the survey, (October/November 1993), and the corresponding period in 1992

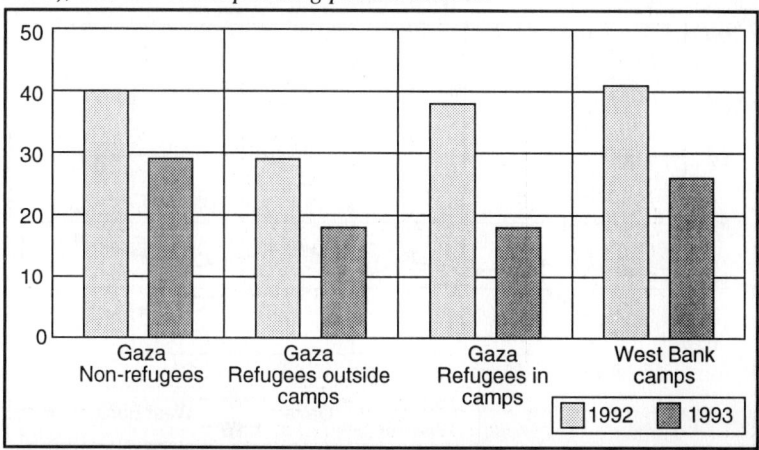

We have noted that there was a net reduction of 1/3 among Palestinian workers in Israel from 1992 to 1993. Which socio-economic groups have been affected in particular six months after the border closure? To answer this question, we need a more detailed discussion of the *net direct effects* of the closure on various regions and socio-economic groups.

Table 2.16 in the Labour table appendix showed that the areas most remote from Israeli population centres have the largest net reduction in employment in Israel. A possible explanation is that the new time-consuming security checks at the border crossings are most burdensome for workers with the longest travel distances.

Figure 2.32 compares reduction in Gaza male employment in Israel by refugee status, using West Bank refugee camps as reference.

Workers from the Gaza refugee camps seem to be the group most severely hit. In terms of the *1992* employment share in Israel, the net reduction of employment in Israel is 28% for Gaza non-refugees, 38% for Gaza refugees outside camps, and 53% for Gaza camp refugees. For the West Bank refugee camps the corresponding figure is 36%. Some of the substantial reduction for Gaza camp refugees may be accounted for by the over-representation of camp refugees in the remote Southern part of the Gaza Strip. Another possible explanation could be Israeli reluctance to those living in refugee camps in Gaza.

Figure 2.33 Employed males who worked mainly in Israel, by main geographical area and age. Percentage of males employed one week or more during a four-week period prior to the survey, (October/ November 1993), and for the corresponding period in 1992

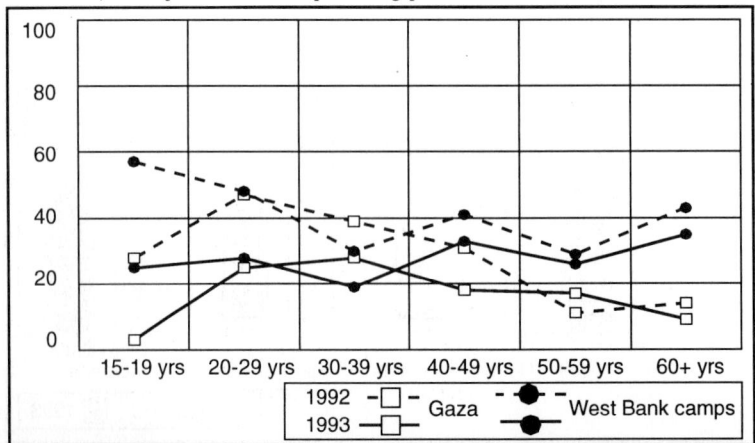

The March 1993 employment restrictions were particularly targeted at young, unmarried men. As expected, figures 2.33, 2.34 and 2.35 show that the net reduction in employment in Israel is particularly marked for young, unmarried males with above average education.

Figure 2.34 Employed males who worked mainly in Israel, by main geographical area and education. Percentage of adult males in respective groups employed one week or more during a four-week period prior to the survey, (October/November 1993), and the corresponding period in 1992

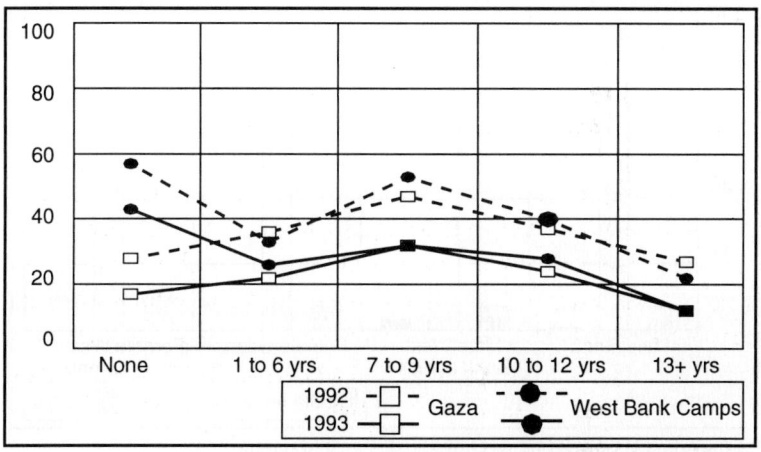

Figure 2.35 Employed males who worked mainly in Israel, by main geographical area and maritial status. Percentage of adult males in respective groups employed one week or more during a four-week period prior to the survey, (October/November 1993), and the corresponding period in 1992

55

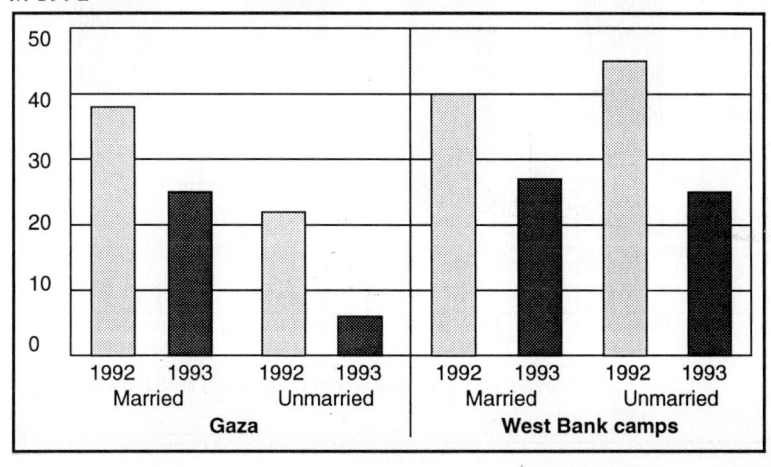

Even if the 20-29 and 30-39 age groups still are over-represented among Palestinian workers in Israel, variations by age are smaller in 1993 than in 1992. Regional comparisons of average age and years of education for workers employed in Israel in 1993 and 1992 show that

Figure 2.36 Main area of work in 1993 for persons who worked in the OT or abroad in 1992, by gender and main geographical area. Percentage of adults in respective groups

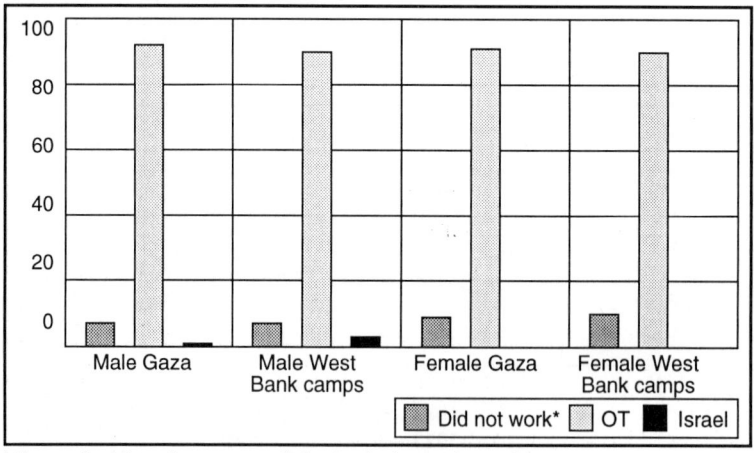

* I.e worked less than one week in the designated month

Figure 2.37 Employment situation in 1993 for persons who worked in the OT or abroad in 1992, by gender and main geographical area. Percentage of adults in respective groups

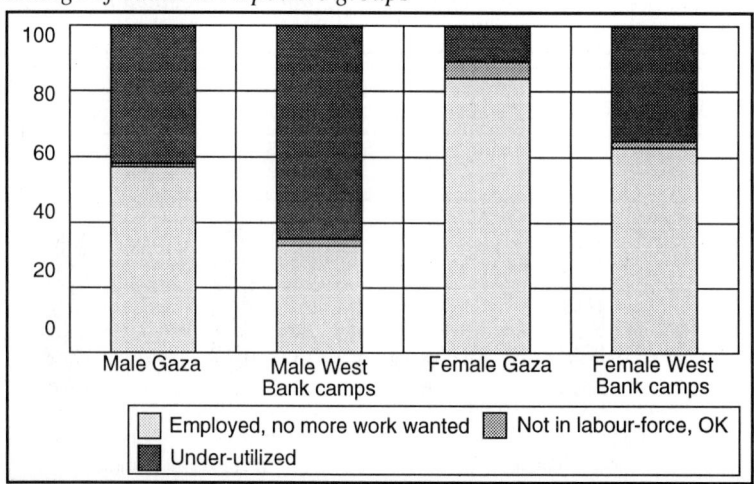

the average age of workers employed in Israel has increased by 1.6 years in both main regions.

The 1993 labour-force status and place of employment for workers who in 1992 were employed in the Occupied Territories illustrates the *gross indirect* employment effect of the border closure. Figure 2.36

Figure 2.38 Main area of work in 1993 for persons who did not work in 1992, by gender and main geographical area. Percentage of adults in respective groups

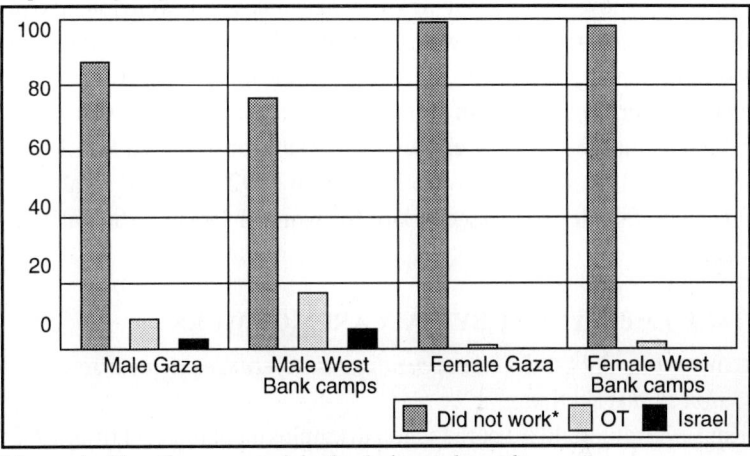

* I.e worked less than one week in the designated month

Figure 2.39 Employment situation in 1993 for persons who did not work in 1992, by gender and main geographical area. Percentage of adults in respective groups

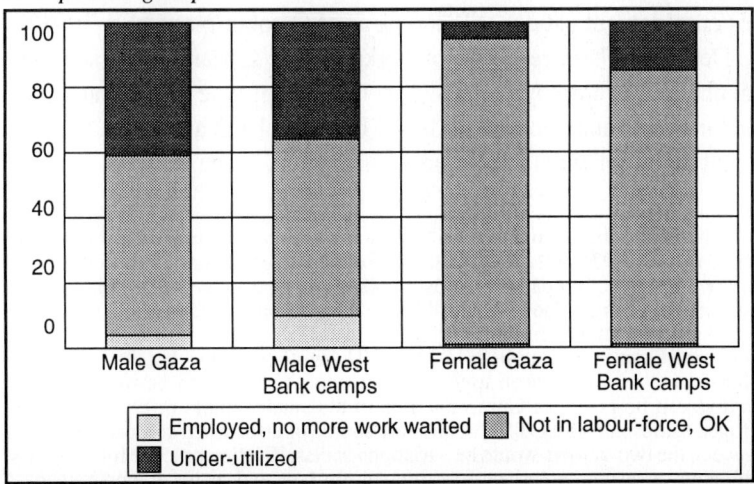

shows that 9 out of 10 of those who had been employed in the Occupied Territories in 1992 were still working there in 1993. Measured in this way the indirect effects of the border closure seem to be limited.

As shown by figure 2.37, there is, however, a widespread desire for more work among men in this group, particularly in the West Bank refugee camps. This may reflect a substantial drop in income from local employment after the border closure.

We finally turn to the persons with no labour activities in 1992. Figure 2.38 shows that almost 90% of Gaza males who were inactive in 1992 remained so in 1993 as well. In the West Bank refugee camps 1 out of 4 males inactive in 1992 started working in 1993, mostly in the Occupied Territories. In both main geographical areas, more than 1 out of 3 males inactive in 1992 expressed a desire for more work in 1993.

Almost all women who were inactive in 1992 remained so also in 1993. Few females expressed desire for work in 1993, particularly in Gaza.

MALE EMPLOYMENT BY MAIN AREA OF WORK

See tables 2.44 to 2.52 in appendix 3 as references to the discussion in this section.

Despite the almost 40% net reduction in employment in Israel from 1992 to 1993, 1 out of 4 employed men in the survey population were working in Israel in 1993. The FALCOT 92 report found that the vast majority of Palestinian workers in Israel perform unskilled, service and vocational work in the construction, service and agricultural sectors. Did this employment pattern still persist as of October/November 1993?[6]

Despite the large reduction of workers, there appear to be no substantial changes in employment patterns in terms of type of work and sector for Palestinian workers in Israel between 1992 and 1993. Professional employment is almost non-existent. As much as 9 out of 10 of

---

6 Comparisons between 1993 and 1992 are based mainly on questions concerning 1993 and 1992 employment patterns for the persons interviewed in the 1993 survey. As a result, comparisons across the 1993 survey data set may under-estimate the extent of changes due to a plausible tendency among respondents to report the same employment pattern for both years.

For the Gaza Strip, data from FALCOT 92 (*another* sample, but the same sampling frame) have also been used as a reference. Comparison between the two surveys can be made for Gaza only, due to the small sample of the West Bank refugee camps in FALCOT 92. A possible source of error when comparing results between the two surveys would be variations in classification practice for variables with many answer alternatives, in particular, for type and sector of employment.

these workers, the same figure as in the FALCOT 92 report, perform unskilled, service or vocational work. Construction is the dominant sector, providing employment for over half the workers.

Not surprisingly, job stability of Palestinians workers in Israel is found to be generally lower than for workers employed in the Occupied

Figure 2.40 Type of employment, by area of work and main geographical area of residence 1993. Percentage of persons working one week or more during a four-week period prior to the survey (October/November 1993)

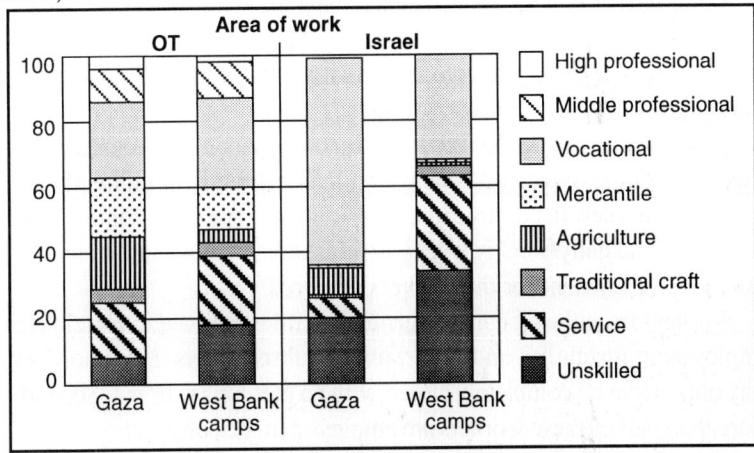

Figure 2.41 Sector of employment by area of work and main geographical area of residence 1993. Percentage of persons working one week or more during a four-week period prior to the survey (October/November 1993)

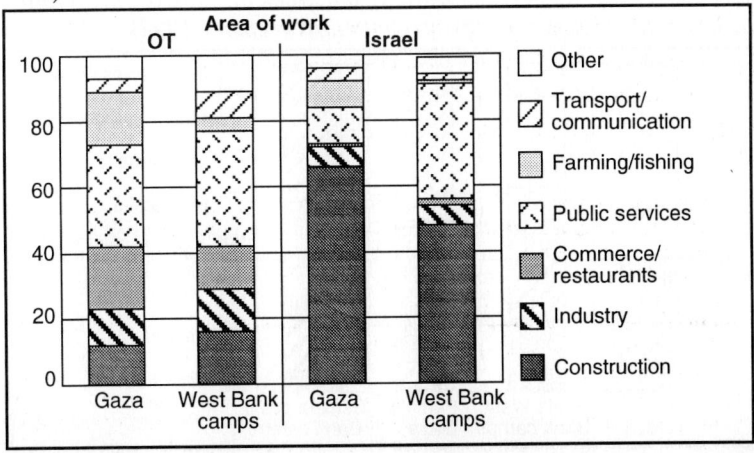

Territories. The same finding was noted in the FALCOT 92 report. A decrease in the number of working weeks, particularly concerning employment in Israel, was the only substantial change between 1993 and 1992 which was reported *within* the 1993 sample.

Nor for Palestinian workers employed in the Occupied Territories can any substantial change in employment types and sectors be found. Approximately half of these workers perform unskilled, service or vocational work. In Gaza, however, this group seems to have increased in size compared to the FALCOT 92 report.

Sub-contracting and piecework payment are widespread in the Occupied Territories. Among Palestinian workers employed in Israel, on the contrary, such arrangements are virtually non-existent. Instead these workers receive daily or weekly wages.

Many enterprises in the Occupied Territories using sub-contracting or piecework are owned by Israelis or produce directly or indirectly for the Israeli market. In contrast to monthly wages, both sub-contracting/piecework and daily/weekly wages are indicators of unstable and unpredictable employment for the workers involved.

Workers from the Occupied Territories still employed in Israel face employment instability and uncertainty on three levels. First, borders may once again be completely closed with no previous warning. Second, more than half of these workers are employed in the construction sector, which is characterized by even greater cyclical fluctuations than in most

Figure 2.42 Type of employment, by gender and main geographical area. Percentage of persons working one week or more during a four-week period prior to the survey (October/November 1993)

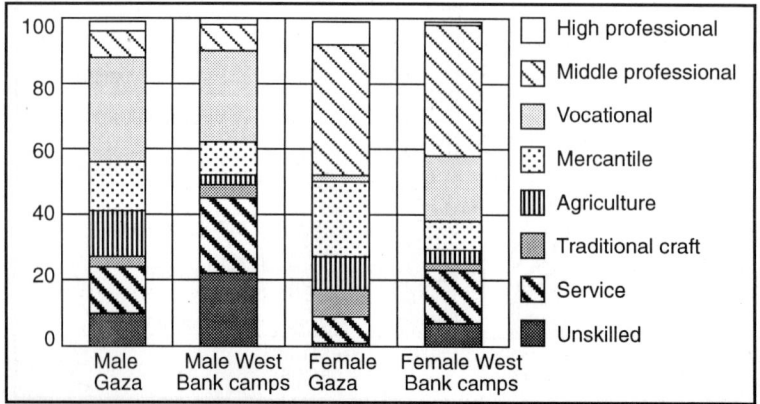

other countries, due to immigration from the former Soviet Union. Third, the majority of workers in Israel receive daily wages, indicating short employment horizons, with constant risk of being ousted by other workers.

EMPLOYMENT BY GENDER AND AREA OF RESIDENCE

See tables 2.53 to 2.56 in appendix 3 as references to the discussion in this section.

As in the FALCOT 92 report, the 1993 employment characteristics show large differences by gender but relatively small variations by area of residence. There are far more professional workers among women than among men; this is reflected both in the high share of female workers receiving wages on a monthly basis, and in the higher job stability for female than for male workers.

The total number of employed women in the survey is too small for detailed comparisons by sector and type of work. Due to the community of (land-owning) non-refugees in Gaza, male employment in agriculture is higher in Gaza than in the West Bank refugee camps. The number of male unskilled and service workers in the West Bank refugee camps, by contrast, is almost twice as high as in Gaza. Because most West Bank refugee camps are situated close to urban areas with relatively high purchasing power, a reasonable explanation is that these workers serve adjacent towns.

A breakdown of the results for Gaza men by refugee status and type of locality does not reveal any major differences in the average number of working weeks, status at the workplace or type of payment. There is some tendency towards lower work stability for camp refugees than for other groups in Gaza. As could be expected, the Gaza non-refugee community has a somewhat higher instance of (agriculture related) family labour, and a lower number of persons working for UNRWA.

INDIVIDUAL ENGAGEMENT IN INCOME-GENERATING HOUSEHOLD ACTIVITIES

See tables 2.57 to 2.62 in appendix 3 as references to the discussion in this section.

In the first part of this chapter, "income-generating household activities" were defined as activities that bring supplementary income to households. Such activities have both traditional and modern origins in the

Occupied Territories. Historically, elderly women played a pivotal role, passing their knowledge and skills on to daughters and daughters-in-law.

Even though many activities declined along with the process of modernization, the Intifada brought about a revival of income-generating household activities for political reasons, meant to reduce dependence on the Israeli economy, such income-generating activities symbolized the return to the land and rejection of Israeli dominance.

This sub-section will focus on the *employment* aspect of such activities, to the extent responsibility for them can be ascribed to *individual*, adult members of a household. Their significance for the household economy, and changes since the border closure, will be discussed in the subsequent chapter regarding household economy.

The proportion of households engaged in various income-generating household activities is, of course, higher than the corresponding figure for individuals. Except for poultry, crafts and in particular food processing, no activities are conducted by more than 5 per cent of the individuals in any area.

To simplify the discussion, the most common activity – food processing has been singled out separately and the remaining activities grouped together as "other" activities. Engagement in "other" activities indicates that a person is involved in at least one of the following activities:

Figure 2.43 Persons responsible for household production, by gender and main geographical area. Percentage of all adults in respective groups

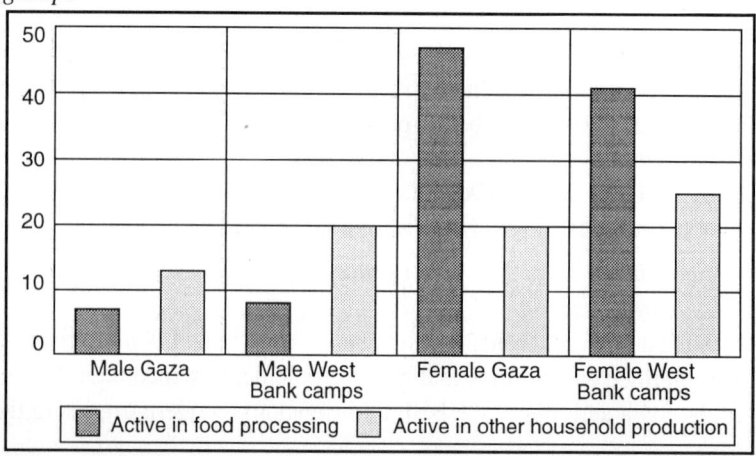

1) Growing vegetables/fruits/herbs
2) Raising poultry or other animals
3) Fishing
4) Producing crafts
5) Conducting services or trade from a mobile installation or on the street.

Figure 2.43 shows hardly any geographical variation in the regional prevalence of individual engagement in food processing or "other" activities. Nor can any significant variation by refugee status be found for the Gaza sample.

Are income-generating household activities still conducted primarily by elderly and middle-aged women? Figure 2.44 shows individual engagement in food processing and "other" income-generating household activities by gender, main geographical area and age.

Women seem to be the dominant agents in both groups of activities. Few men are engaged in food processing, irrespective of age. About 20-30% of men 30 years or older, however, report that they are involved in other income-generating household activities than food processing.

Figure 2.44 Persons responsible for household production, by gender and age. Percentage of all persons in respective groups

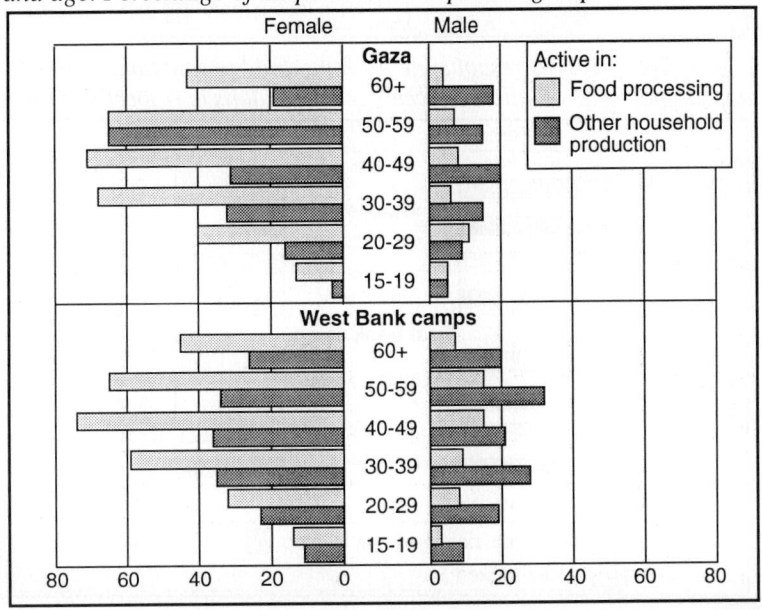

For women food processing is by far the most important activity, but female engagement in food production and in other activities varies greatly with age. Here we note that involvement is particularly high among middle-aged and to some extent old women.

Previous sections have documented a substantial drop in formal employment since the border closure. Have household income-generating activities provided alternative employment to persons outside the labour force?

Figure 2.45 Persons responsible for household production, by gender and labour-force status. Percentage of all adults in respective groups

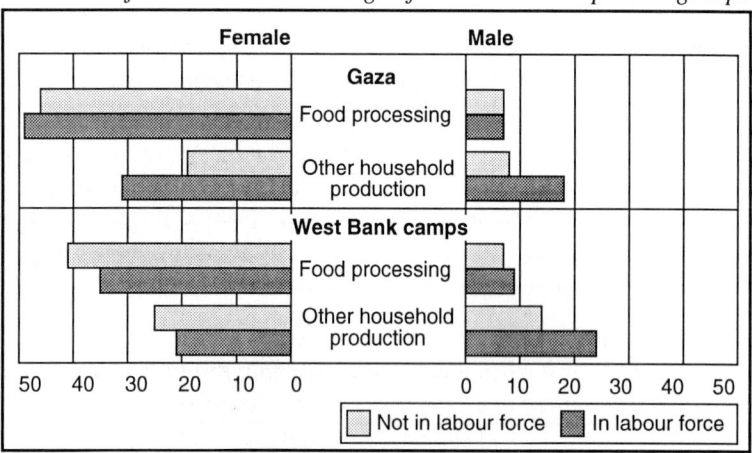

Figure 2.46 Persons responsible for household production, by gender and employment situation. Percentage of all adults in respective groups

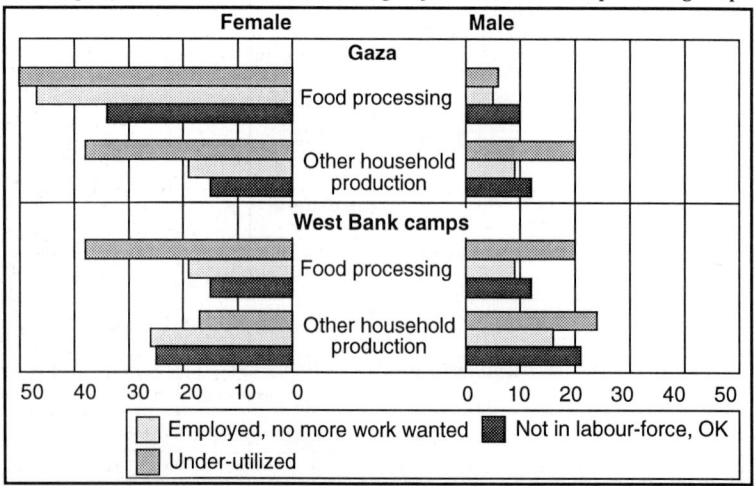

From figure 2.45 we see that the prevalence of food processing is roughly at the same level for both labour-force participants and non-participants. The proportion of males who perform "other" income-generating household activities is even higher among labour-force participants than non-participants. The same result is found for Gaza women. Rather than substituting for formal employment it would seem that activity leads to more activity.

Figure 2.46 confirms these findings, by comparing activity levels along the "employment situation" dimension used in the section regarding under-utilization of labour presented above. In general, engagement in income-generating household activities seems to be higher among labour-force participants who do not want additional employment, than among non-participants who do *not* want work, or among the "under-utilized".

Do we find more household production among persons who lost employment in Israel during the last year? Figure 2.47 does not lend support to this assumption, as income-generating household activities are not significantly more prevalent among these persons than among other males.

The use of merely one hour of weekly work as the standard criterion for labour-force participation indicates the wide scope of labour activities such definitions intend to cover. Would it be better to revise the labour-force status of persons involved in income-generating household

Figure 2.47 Participation in household production among men who lost employment in Israel from 1992 to 1993, by main geographical area. Percentage of adult men in respective groups

65

activities, but classified as "unemployed" or "outside labour-force" by standard labour-force surveys?

In our opinion a distinction should be made between food processing and other household activities. Because of an unclear distinction between "food processing" and "cooking", involvement in food processing as a supplementary criterion for labour-force participation would make interpretations even more difficult.

For other income-generating household activities, however, an expansion of the criteria for labour-force participation seems more reasonable. On the other hand, this is challenged by the fact that income-generating household activities seem to represent a supplement rather than an alternative to formal labour activity. We will return to the definitions and basis for labour-force participation in the next section.

FUTURE LABOUR-FORCE SCENARIOS

This section presents scenarios for future labour supply in Gaza based on results from the current data set. Alternative projections from the Work-Force and Labour Modules of the World Bank's macro-economic model for the Occupied Territories will also be presented.[7] Finally, we will sum up the findings of this chapter, focusing on the effects of the border closure and Palestinian adaptations to it.

LABOUR-FORCE SCENARIOS FOR GAZA

See table 2.63 in appendix 3 as reference to the discussion in this section.

The "Work-Force Module" (Module a), of the World Bank model projects population growth and demographic change with associated changes in labour-force participation. Here we will present scenarios for future labour supply using the World Bank's estimates for the future size of the labour force as a baseline.

In the Gaza Strip, our sample represents all types of localities in one coherent geographical entity. The sample from the West Bank refugee camps, by contrast, represents 19 separate refugee camps throughout the West Bank and in Arab Jerusalem. Many camps are situated adjacent to other localities, but all camps are physically separated from each other.

---

7 World Bank (1993), *Developing the Occupied Territories*,Volume 2, Chapter 5 and Annex module a) and c).

Thus there would be little point in presenting separate scenarios for the West Bank refugee camps. In the subsequent discussion we will present labour-force scenarios for the Gaza Strip only.

Mathematically, the size of the labour force may be calculated as the sum of population groups defined by age and gender, multiplied by the labour-force participation rate of each group. The size and composition of the population at any point in time will depend on the size of so-called "base population", and developments in fertility, mortality and migration.

The population figures used in the World Bank's labour-force projections are based on official Israeli population projections for the Occupied Territories.[8] According to the same source, fertility rates began to increase in the mid-1980s after showing a declining tendency in previous years. Mortality continued to decline throughout the period. Migration flows changed from net emigration in the 1970s and 1980s, to net immigration after the 1991 Gulf War.

Referring to these developments, the World Bank applied the highest CBS projection for natural population growth, assuming future fertility to remain at the 1982 level and net migration to be zero.

Most migration in previous years had economic motives.[9] A continuation of this tendency in the future may lead to two separate migration patterns, with opposite effects for Gaza. First, general economic development in Gaza may stimulate a return of Palestinians currently living abroad. Second, lifting current restrictions on internal migration may lead to substantial population movements from Gaza to the more prosperous West Bank and Arab Jerusalem.

At present it is hardly possible to assess which effect will dominate. A future net migration rate of zero in the Occupied Territories thus seems as reasonable as any other assumption.

Most independent researchers have argued that the official Israeli projections underestimate the true population. The population count in the 1967 census is said to be too low, and it is alleged that there has been an under-recording of (surviving) infants in the subsequent years.

---

8 Israeli Central Bureau of Statistics (1987), *Projections of Population in Judea, Samaria and Gaza Area up to 2002, Based on the Population in 1982*, Special Series No. 802.

9 World Bank (1993), *Developing the Occupied Territories*, Volume 6, Page 11. Tables from Abdel-Fattah Abu Shokor, «External Migration from the West Bank and Gaza Strip and its Economic and Social Impact». Arab Thought Forum, (1990), in Arabic, assembled by the World Bank.

Hence, the World Bank adjusted the 1992 level of population projections for the Occupied Territories upwards by 12%. This augmentation provides for the largest plausible estimate of the under-recording of the population. For Gaza, the size of the new 1992 "base population" amounts to 800,000 persons. The highest CBS population growth rate of 4% in Gaza is then applied, yielding a population level of 1,184,000 persons by the year 2002.

To simplify the discussion concerning future labour-force scenarios, FAFO originally desired to use the same base population and population growth rates as the World Bank's "Work-Force Module". Most regrettably, however, FAFO did not have access to adjusted population projections for Gaza broken down by gender and age.

For the Gaza labour-force scenarios, FAFO has thus used the World Bank's 1992 "base" population of 800,000 as a baseline. From this starting point, the Gaza population is assumed to increase at a constant annual rate of 4% towards the year 2000. The labour force scenarios are based on the assumption that the composition of the population by gender and age remains unchanged, as calculated by the FALUP 93 survey.

As for the *labour force participation rate*, most economic models for labour markets assume it to be endogenously determined. Further, this rate is assumed, at least at an aggregate level, to increase with increasing wage levels.

Much evidence indicates a highly segmented supply side in the labour market of the Occupied Territories, that is, the supply of labour for various groups of individuals is targeted to specific job types and job locations. In addition to the usual variations according to age and gender, the relation between supply of labour and wages also varies substantially across different socio-economic groups and regions. Except for the tendency of labour supply to increase with wages, it is not simple to assess the exact nature of the relationship between the supply of labour and wage rates for different groups.

The labour supply function in the Occupied Territories seems to depend heavily on gender and position in the household. Local cultural attitudes about "socially acceptable" work location and work types are crucial for female labour supply. Travel restrictions between Gaza and the West Bank/ Arab Jerusalem further allow for substantial geographical segmentation of the relations between labour supply and wages.

As elsewhere, the relationship between supply of labour and wages in the Occupied Territories can also be assumed to depend on the availability of alternative sources. Particularly important are non-labour income sources like public and private transfers. One hypothesis assumes that the labour supply function for (registered) refugees differs from that of other groups, due to the elements of a social security system provided by UNRWA.

Figure 2.49 presents four different scenarios for the development of the Gaza labour-force towards the year 2000. Let us now discuss some of the assumptions leading to these scenarios.

Despite of the considerations concerning the endogenously determined labour-force participation presented above, we have lowered our ambitions as to constructing such a complex model. The size of the

Table 2.2 Gaza labour-force participation rates, by gender and source

	Gaza FAFO 93	Gaza FAFO adj. 93	Gaza FAFO 92	Gaza CBS 92	Gaza WB/CBS 91
Estimates:					
Percentage of total population in LF	13	18	20	17,5	17,4
n	3535	3535	958	NA	NA
Percentage of total population, 15 years or more	49	49	50	49,7	50.7
n	3535	3535	958	NA	NA
Percentage of adults in labour force	26	38	39	35,3	34,3
n	3535	3535	958	NA	NA
Percentage of males in sample	49	49	50		50,3
n	3549	3549	*	NA	NA
Percentage of adult males in LF	47	52	72	70,3	68,4
n	1744	1744	477	NA	NA
Percentage of adult females in LF	6	24	7	1,7	1,7
n	1792	1792	481	NA	NA

NA = Not available (CBS figures partially calculated by FAFO from "Statistical Abstract of Israel"; 1993 using *unadjusted* population totals).

* The sex rate in the FALCOT 92 report was fixed to 50% male/ female. (The gender of the Randomly Selected Individual had to be pre-selected due to a number of questions which required female interviewers to interview female respondents.)

labour force for any given year is thus *exogenously* determined. Within each scenario, gender-specific products of population size and *constant* labour-force participation rates are added up, to give the total labour-force. The four scenarios vary substantially in terms of their assumptions about gender-specific labour-force participation rates. As a background for the scenarios, table 2.2 presents five gender-specific participation rates for Gaza from alternative sources.

The 1992 labour-force participation rates of FAFO and the CBS seem to be approximately the same. Higher female participation rates for the FAFO survey are most likely due to various aspects of survey implementation. To gain the confidence of female respondents, FAFO used female interviewer pairs for interviewing women. The FALCOT 92 report was also carefully designed to obtain more accurate statistics on women's activities.

Comparing 1993 FAFO results with FAFO and CBS/ World Bank figures for previous years, we note that the participation rate for adult males seems to have dropped dramatically. However, this rate for Gaza in 1993 is most likely a temporary rather than a permanent phenomenon. Heightened requirements as to formal education and productivity during an economic recovery period may, however, prevent future adult male labour-force participation rates from regaining their pre-closure levels.

For women, the CBS/ World Bank labour-force participation rate would seem implausibly low. Decreased fertility and/ or fewer cultural restrictions with regard to socially "acceptable" work locations and types of work for women could lead to a substantial increase in the future supply of female labour. One possible indication of such a development is the already high labour-force participation rate among the most highly educated women in the FAFO survey population.

FAFO's 1993 study found a relatively widespread engagement in household income-generating activities, in particular among middle-aged and older women. Most previous labour-force surveys in the Occupied Territories have not managed (or tried) to record this type of labour activities in statistical terms, even though it is formally covered by the ILO definitions for labour-force participation.

To cope with this challenge, FAFO experimented with an "expanded" labour-force definition applied to the 1993 FALUP data set. Following this definition the "labour-force" comprises all adults who are either labour-force participants according to answers to the "standard" employment module in the questionnaire, or who are engaged in household income-generating household activities (excluding food processing).

Using this expanded definition almost quadruples the size of the female labour-force. The male labour-force, however, increases by only 10%.

As can be seen from figure 2.48, the resultant inflation of the labour force is particularly dramatic for women between 30 and 60 years of age, and less so for younger women. A possible explanation is that many of these women are students or too occupied with child-bearing and rearing to engage in extra income-generating household activities.

Four different scenarios were elaborated for the development of the size of the Gaza labour-force until the year 2000. In the first and the most conservative scenario presented in figure 2.49, both male and female labour-force participation rates (using the "standard" definition) stay unchanged at the level of the FALUP 93 survey. In this case the Gaza labour-force will reach 142,000 by the year 2000, of whom 125,000 will be males. Applying the "expanded" labour-force definition to the

Figure 2.48 Labourforce in Gaza including those active in household production, by age. Percentage of all persons in Gaza

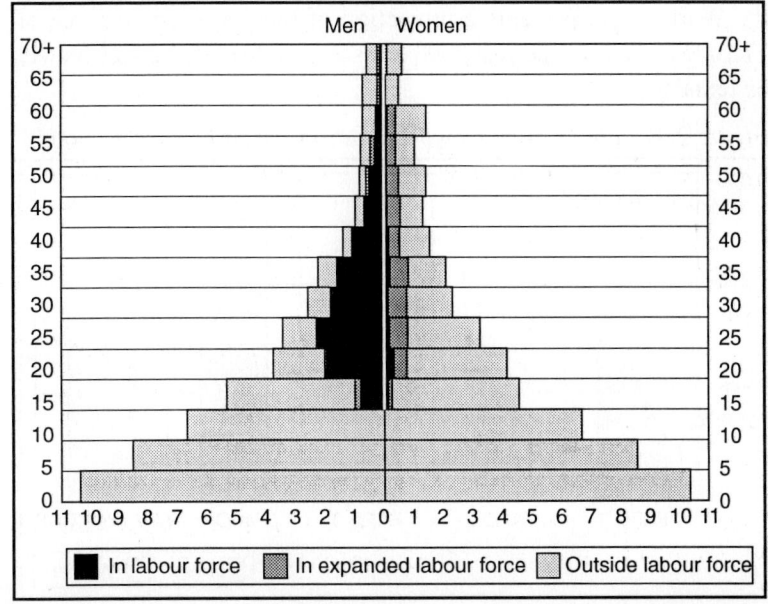

FALUP 93 data set scenario number two yields a Gaza labour-force of 204,000 by the year 2000, of whom 138,000 will be males.

A third projection based on labour-force participation rates from the FALCOT 92 report, but with the same population size as above, yields a Gaza labour-force by the year 2000 of 213,000. As many as 192,000 of these workers will be males. The third scenario consequently yields about the same total labour-force as scenario number two, but is radically different with regard to gender composition.

If the Gaza Strip experiences an economic recovery, the adult male participation rate may be expected to approach the FALCOT 92 report level rather than the level of the FALUP 93 survey. Let us now further assume that the "expanded" labour-force definition used in the FALUP 93 survey manages to picture a "reserve army" of potential female workers.

Combining the "expanded" FALUP 93 labour-force participation rate for females with that of males in the FALCOT 92 report yields the most radical scenario for the Gaza labour-force. Under these assumptions, by the year 2000 the Gaza labour-force may comprise as many as 259,000 persons, of whom 192,000 will be males.

How do the FAFO scenarios concerning the future size of the Gaza labour-force compare with the World Bank's Work Force Module? Assuming that no changes take place in labour-force participation rates, the World Bank presents a projection of the Gaza labour-force of 171,000 persons by the year 2000. Less than 5000 of these workers will be females.

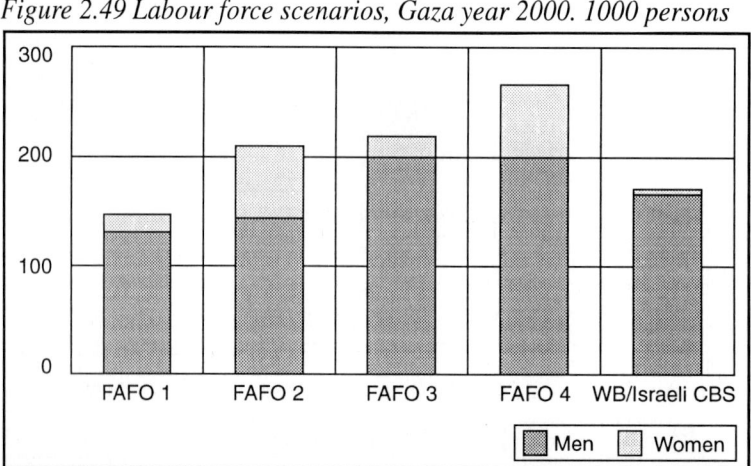

Figure 2.49 Labour force scenarios, Gaza year 2000. 1000 persons

What conclusions can be drawn from the comparison of future labour-force scenarios for the Gaza Strip? Based on constant labour-force participation rates, the FAFO labour-force scenarios show considerable variance with the World Bank figures. Our contention is thus that the future labour supply is a rather uncertain variable.

Secondly, if we assume that beliefs and behaviour emanate among the upper social strata and spread downward, a possible future scenario may be an increased desire for employment also among females with less education. This would imply a marked increase in the aggregate desire for employment among women in the future. For any total size of the future population, we thus believe that women will represent a greater share of the labour force than estimated by World Bank projections.

CONCLUDING REMARKS

The introductory chapter described the large and possibly permanent adverse change in household income which has hit the Occupied Territories after the March 1993 border closure. The employment situation was expected to deteriorate, due to the loss of jobs in Israel and to the decrease in the local demand for labour following the drop in income.

The two main aims of this chapter were: 1) to investigate and if possible document the loss of employment in Gaza and the West Bank refugee camps after the border closure; 2) to contribute to an understanding of the mechanisms at work among individuals and households with regard to response and adaptation to the post-closure situation. Our unit of analysis has been adult *individuals*.

First of all we saw a dramatic drop in the 1993 adult male labour-force participation rate compared to that of FALCOT 1992. The FALUP 93 survey has found that in Gaza this reduction amounts to 1/3 of the males in the 1992 labour-force. In the West Bank refugee camps the reduction amounts to 1/4.

We have showed that the reduction in male labour-force participation reflects widespread under-utilization of labour in the survey area. Regular unemployment rates do not capture the magnitude of labour under-utilization, and have remained roughly unchanged since 1992. These unemployment rates must consequently be supplemented with the number of "discouraged workers" and the number of employed persons who state that they want more work.

The indirect employment effects of the border closure on local employment do not emerge clearly with the indicators used in the survey. Many locally employed workers, however, have expressed a desire for more work, which may indicate that income levels (not measured by the survey) have dropped between 1992 and 1993.

The direct employment effects of the border closure are illustrated by the finding that only half the persons employed in Israel in 1992 were still working there in 1993. Of those who lost employment in Israel, two thirds now express a desire for more work.

Less than one fourth of those who lost their work in Israel have found new employment in the Occupied Territories. Their employment characteristics indicate a group of marginal workers, employed in low status jobs with high instability and insecurity. There are no indications that these workers have squeezed out other workers in local employment.

In Gaza, the border closure seems to have affected non-refugees more than refugees. The FALCOT 92 report showed that Greater Gaza City, where non-refugees are over-represented, had the least difficult employment situation at the time. The border closure has seemingly equalized regional differences in Gaza, bringing all localities in the Gaza Strip up to the same high levels of labour under-utilization.

Many Israeli restrictions following the border closure have specifically targeted young, unmarried men. Not surprisingly, the documented reduction in employment is also strongest among these individuals.

Most women in both areas are inactive in the labour market, and do not express the desire to work more or to start working because they are either housewives, students or old/ill. A breakdown by age and education however, indicates that women's desire for work may increase in the future.

All this shows that the loss of employment among Palestinians in Gaza and the West Bank refugee camps after the border closure can be clearly documented.

Our second goal in this chapter was to contribute to an understanding of the mechanisms with regard to post-closure responses and adaptation. Here we found that labour-force participation is primarily determined by factors such as gender, age, marital status and position within he household. This may indicate that individual response and adaptation strategies are closely coordinated with household coping strategies, at least with regard to labour activities.

Second, we found nothing to indicate that persons outside the labour force are more active in so-called household income-generating activities than labour-force participants. Neither the non-active nor the "under-utilized", nor those who lost employment in Israel between 1992 and 1993 were found to be more involved in household production than the average population. Household production seems to be a supplement rather than an alternative to formal labour activity; such activities do not seem to play any compensatory role with regard to individual adaptation to loss of formal employment.

Third, it seems misleading to take the low and comparably stable open unemployment rates as indicating that the labour market in the Occupied Territories has adjusted quickly to reduced labour demand through lower wages. We found that the reduction in formal employment is much larger if we take into consideration both unemployment rates *and* the large number of "discouraged workers".

Because the survey did not measure wages directly, we cannot tell whether the substantial reduction in employment is due to a greater decrease in the labour demand than has been assumed by the CBS/ the World Bank, or to a less pronounced downward change in workers' reservation wages (i.e. the lowest wage where employment is accepted) than could be expected.

The high number of "discouraged workers" may support the latter explanation. The reservation wage of these workers still seems to be above the wage level they can obtain in the Occupied Territories. Many persons can still "afford" to be inactive while looking for an "acceptable" job. The search for *any* kind of local employment at *any* wage level has not yet been launched.

One possible explanation for the apparently low downward change in workers' reservation wages would be that the population expects the employment situation to improve in the near future. The large proportion of male "discouraged workers" who cite "security" related reasons for not seeking work may support this assumption.

If the border closure is regarded as being temporary, then employment in Israel is expected to become available eventually, and workers may prefer to await developments. Such expectations have solid foundations in the experience of numerous fluctuations between tighter and more relaxed border restrictions in recent years. Another factor which may explain why workers' reservation wages do not seem to have declined very much is the expectation of an economic revival in the Occupied Territories through foreign aid.

In any case, the seemingly low downward change in of workers' reservation wages may be a temporary phenomenon. In the long term, minimum consumption expenditure requirements and depleted savings may force households to implement *all* possible compensatory measures. Sources of income other than formal labour activities and the household's access to capital will be crucial to the development in workers' reservation wages, and hence the supply of labour in the future.

CHAPTER 3
HOUSEHOLD ECONOMY

INTRODUCTION

In contrast to the previous chapter, the unit of analysis throughout chapter 3 will be *households*. In chapter 2 on employment we noted that under-utilization of labour in particular is manifested by a high number of "discouraged workers". Since many of them can still "afford" to be inactive while looking for an "acceptable" job, this indicates that their reservation wage is above the wage level they can obtain in the Occupied Territories.

We further noted that individual response and adaptation strategies with regard to labour activity seem closely coordinated with the coping strategies practised at the level of the household.

These findings would indicate that a possible reason for the seemingly minor downward shift in worker reservation wages may be found in the household's system for re-distributing economic resources among its members. In this model the reservation wage of a "discouraged worker" will depend largely on the income of *other* household members.

An alternative model could be that various kinds of non-labour income from public sources, like UNRWA and the Israeli Civil Administration, make it possible for households in the sample to survive at a minimum welfare level, without their being obliged to search for *any* kind of employment at *any* level of remuneration.

A third possible explanation might be that many households at present choose to draw on their net liquid wealth. Whether through sales of savings, or through accumulating debt or credit, such reduction of net liquid wealth can only be a short-term strategy. In the longer term, either consumption expenditures must be reduced, or households must implement *some* sort of compensatory measure on the income side.

A possible explanation for following short-term strategies is that people expect the employment situation to improve in the near future. Here we should recall that the fieldwork for this survey was conducted in October/ November 1993, less than half a year after the border closure.

This chapter is divided into three main parts. The first part will investigate income-generating household activities on the *household* level. The corresponding section in chapter 2 found no indication that involvement in household production plays a compensatory role with regard to *individual* adaptation to the loss of formal employment. It might well be, however, that *other* household members (with lower reservation wages), have increased their involvement in household production to compensate for the overall loss of formal labour income.

The second part will discuss the relationship between types of household income, an index for household possession of consumer durables, and employment. Here we are particularly interested in finding out whether an explanation for the seemingly low downward change in worker reservation wages may be found in the household's system for re-distributing economic resources among its members.

Finally, the third part of this chapter will discuss net liquid household wealth, as measured through sales of savings, or through the accumulation of debt or credit. The role of net liquid wealth as a household coping strategy will be discussed, in particular whether the fact that households draw on their net liquid wealth may help explain the seemingly downward shift in worker reservation wages.

HOUSEHOLD INCOME-GENERATING ACTIVITIES AS ADAPTATION STRATEGY

See table 3.1 to 3.18 in appendix 4 for references to this section.
The relation between household income-generating activities and individual *labour activity* has already been discussed in the employment chapter. We will now complete the picture by turning to the *economic* significance of such activities.

Household income-generating activities are, as we noted, characterized by their essentially supplementary nature, rather than for example by the fact that they are usually carried out in a domestic setting. Such activities may still yield important economic benefits for households, through sale or barter of products, and in particular through saving on household consumption expenditures.

It is reasonable to expect households to try to increase their income-generating activities to compensate for the reduction in income from formal employment after the border closure. Contrary to expectations, we found that neither persons outside the labour force, nor the "under-utilized", nor those who lost employment in Israel between 1992 and 1993 are more involved in household production than the average population. For *individuals*, engaging in household production thus seem to be a supplement rather than an alternative to formal labour activity.

One explanation could be that the reservation wage of many of those who fail to obtain formal employment is higher than the income level which can be expected from household activities. The employment chapter showed that income-generating household activities primarily are conducted by middle-aged or elderly women. Because formal labour activity among these groups is very low, their reservation wage may be expected to be lower than for those (males) who aspire to formal jobs. One possible hypothesis is thus that *other* household members (with lower reservation wages) have increased their involvement in household production so as to compensate for the overall loss of formal labour income in the household.

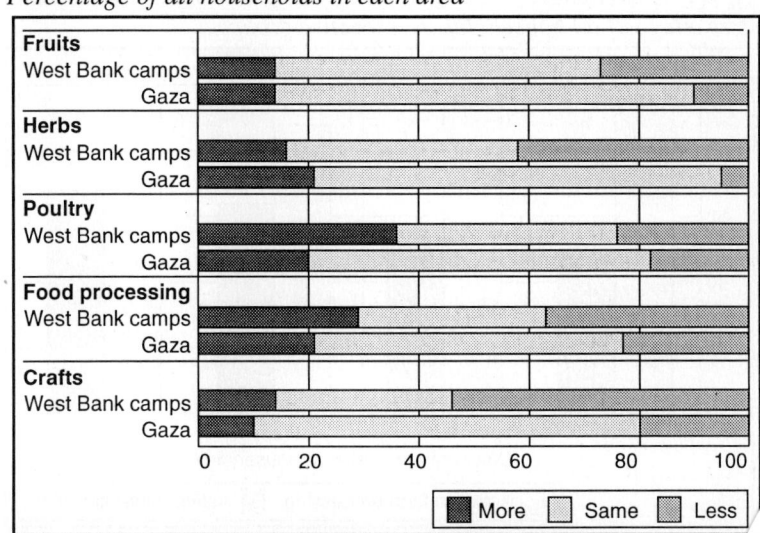

To investigate this *"intra-household compensation"* hypothesis, we asked respondents about changes in the household's output of various income-generating activities since the summer of 1992. Figure 3.1 presents a regional picture of changes in the output of those activities conducted by at least 5% of the households in the sample.

Figure 3.1 Household production changes, by main geographical area. Percentage of all households in each area

Figure 3.1 does *not* support the "intra-household compensation" hypothesis. On the contrary, activities even show a declining tendency with regard to activity for crafts, and especially in the West Bank refugee camps. (There may, however, be a tendency for respondents to report "no change".)

Breaking down results for Gaza by refugee status and type of locality does not reveal significant differences in this pattern. Nor could we find any systematic influence from household size or the household head's individual characteristics (gender, age and education).

Investigation of prevalence of income-generating activities specifically in households comprising "discouraged workers", under-utilized workers, or households where the head or other members lost employment in Israel, further confirms that the "intra-household compensation" hypothesis can be rejected.

Figures 3.2, 3.3 and 3.4 do not show a higher prevalence of income-generating activities in households including "discouraged workers" or members who lost employment in Israel, or under-utilized workers.

Figure 3.8 (concerning household size and production) shows that the share of households engaged in such production increases with increasing household size. As shown by figure 3.5 the share of households with one or more discouraged or under-utilized worker(s), or person(s) who lost employment in Israel do, however, also increases with house-

Figure 3.2 Household production, by discouraged workers in household. Percentage of all households in respective groups

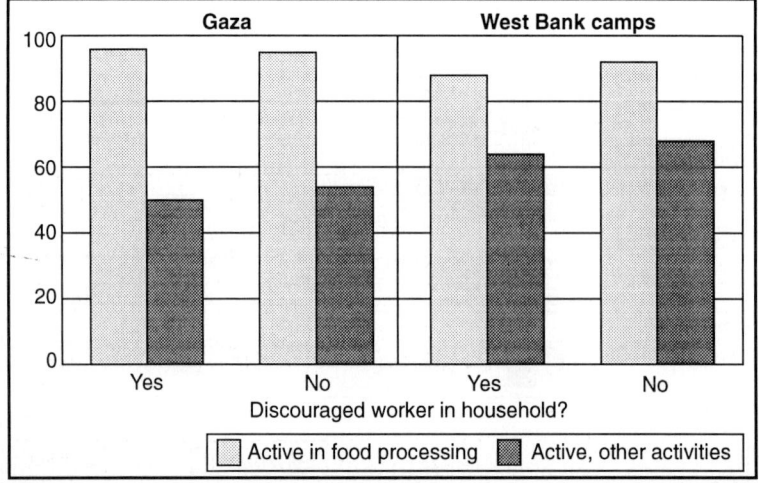

hold size. The somewhat higher prevalence of household production in households with under-utilized workers is most likely due to effects of household size.

Household production thus does not seem to play any (short-term) compensatory role, *neither* at the individual *nor* at the household level. The "intra-household compensation" hypothesis must be rejected.

Figure 3.3 Household production, by workers who lost employment in Israel in household. Percentage of all households in respective groups

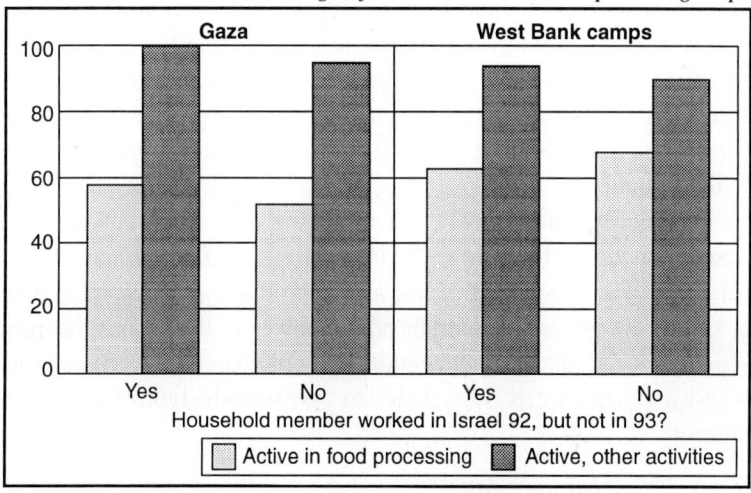

Figure 3.4 Household production, by under-utilized workers in household. Percentage of all households in respective groups

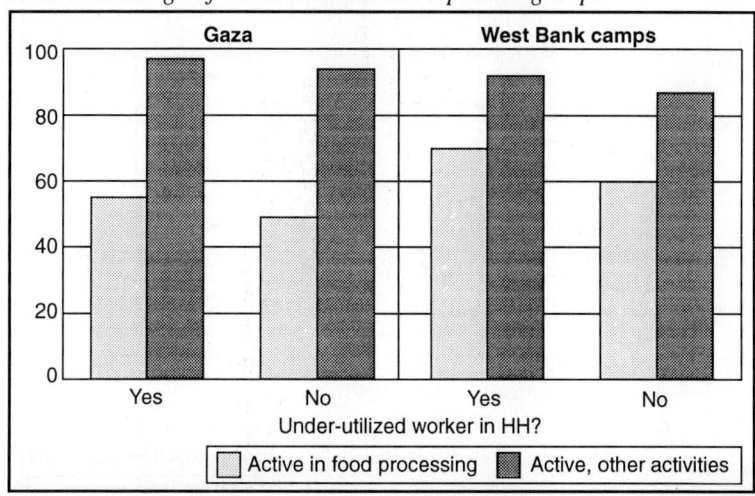

Why have household income-generating activities not shown an increase in response to the drop in income after the border closure? Rejection of the "intra-household compensation" hypothesis does not, after all, necessarily imply that the primary agents in household activities, middle aged and older women, also have too high reservation wages for this kind of production.

Bearing in mind that formal labour activity, and hence reservation wages, are low among these persons, meagre revenues from household production may only partly explain the lack of increase in output. Non-labour income, e.g. support from UNRWA, could have been expected to raise the reservation wage threshold for initiating low productivity production. Much UNRWA support, however, is provided in kind; this means it may be used as input in for example food processing, making it complementary rather than alternative to at least some types of household production.

Another possible explanation for the lack of increase in household production may be found in the *"constraints in production"* hypothesis. This hypothesis assumes that household production is constrained by lack of land, water, raw materials or manpower, or that some time must elapse before production can be initiated or increased. The constraining factors must, of course, be expected to vary with the type of activity in question.

Figure 3.5 Labour force categories of household members, by household size. Percentage of all households in respective groups

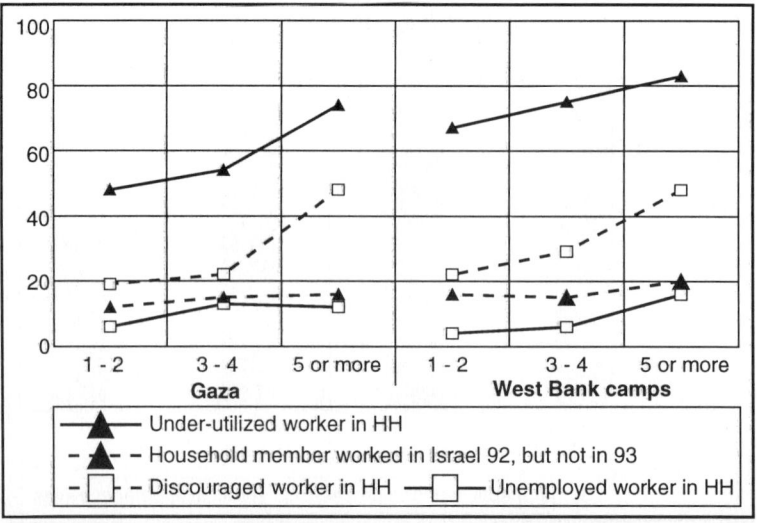

To simplify the discussion, the various types of household activities have been categorized into 5 groups: namely plant production, raising poultry or other animals, food processing, crafts, and services and trade. Figure 3.6 shows the prevalence of each of the 5 groups by main geographical area. (As mentioned in the chapter 2, the share of *households* engaged in a specific activity is generally higher than the corresponding share of individuals.)

For many activities the limiting factor in production may be access to raw materials. Most agricultural activities – plant or animal production, for example – require land, and are thus less suitable in overcrowded refugee camps. Not surprisingly, figure 3.7 shows that the (land-owning) community of Gaza non-refugees is more involved in agricultural production than the (usually landless) camp refugees.

Food processing is to a significant degree dependent on raw materials from agricultural production. Because some food processing is carried out in almost all households, and because the absolute level of output is not measured, factors that may possibly limit food processing cannot be identified. Both food processing and plant production may be expected to show strong seasonal variations.

In contrast to agricultural-related activities, craft production requires little space or land, and may thus be better suited to refugee camp households. Figure 3.7 shows that both craft production and trade and services are more prevalent in West Bank refugee camps than in the Gaza Strip.

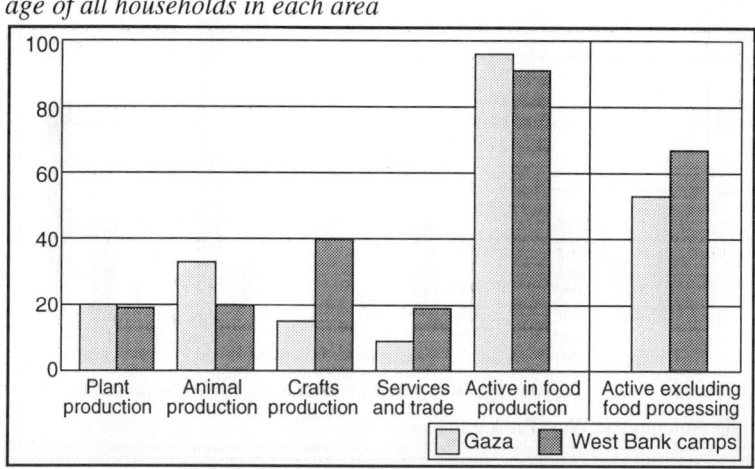

Figure 3.6 Household production, by main geographical area. Percentage of all households in each area

While craft production is more common among refugee camp households, locality of residence and refugee status do not seem to affect the prevalence of trade and services in Gaza. Because many non-agricultural household activities are dependent on raw materials bought in markets, UNRWA support in training and in the provision of raw materials may help to explain the higher level of craft production in the refugee camps.

Does the amount of available manpower constrain household production? Figure 3.8 shows that household income-generating activities (except plant production and food processing) tend to increase with household size. On the other hand, this may equally well be due to the fact that the potential for saving consumption expenditures increases with total household size, because large households include more potential producers.

The prevalence of food processing is high regardless of household size. For plant production, the lack of increase with increasing household size may indicate that land rather than manpower is the limiting factor.

A final variant of the "constraints in production" hypothesis is that some activities can, by their very nature, be initiated or substantially increased only over a period of time. Aiming to capture such effects, we asked households about their *plans* to initiate various household income-generating activities. Figure 3.9 shows the regional proportions of

Figure 3.7 Household production, by refugee status. Percentage of all households in respective groups

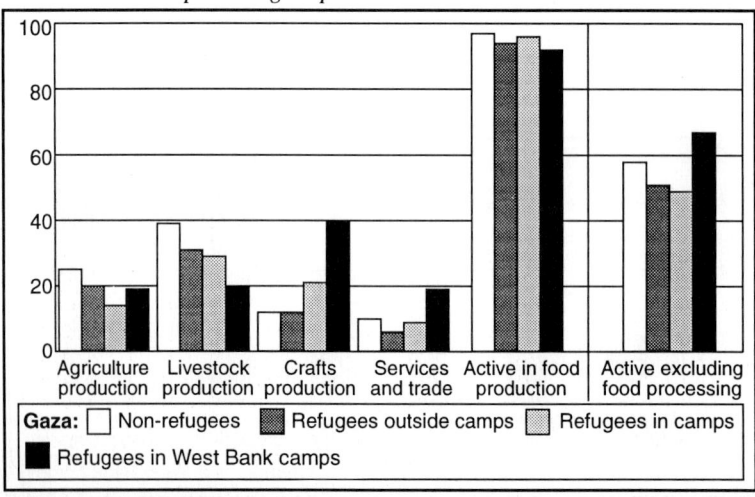

households that answered that they planned to initiate at least one activity within the five main groups of activities noted above, and the proportion of these planning to initiate *some* kind of household income-generating activity.

In Gaza only 1 out of 8 households stated that they plan to start up new household income-generating activities, while the corresponding figure in West Bank refugee camps is 1 out of 3 households.

A regional break-down of plans for new activities reveals only minor differences by refugee status, region and locality of residence in Gaza. In West Bank refugee camps, however, almost twice as many households in the Northern camps as in the Southern camps plan to start up new activities. Many of these households plan to start up services and

Figure 3.8 Household production, by household size. Percentage of all households in respective groups

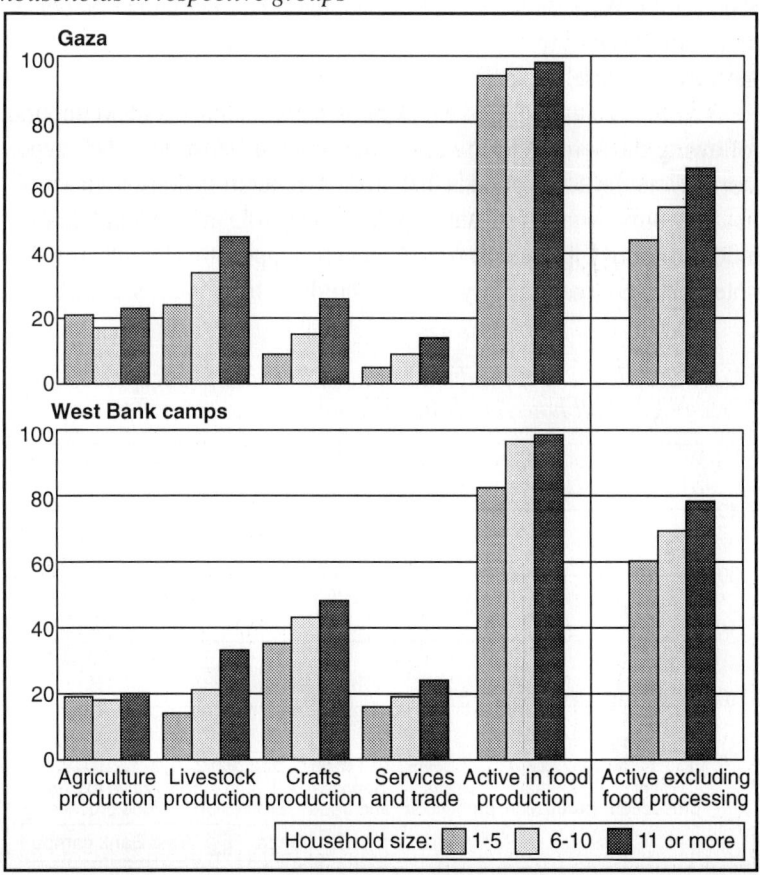

trade, activities already more prevalent in this region than elsewhere in the survey population.

Neither household size and composition nor individual characteristics of the head of household seem to affect plans for starting up new household income-generating activities.

The distributional pattern of income-generating household activities across socio-economic groups facing various limiting factors does *not* give us reason to discard the "constraints in production" hypothesis to explain the lack of change in household production.

The time-lags necessary for changing the level of production may be particularly important. Because the duration and magnitude of the negative effects from the border closure on the Palestinian economy became apparent on the household level only after some time, initiating compensatory measures like household production may have been delayed. At least for the West Bank refugee camps, the relatively large number of households planning to start up such activities may indicate a possible increase of household activities in the long term.

A final explanation for the lack of increase in household production following the border closure can be termed the *"marginal role"* hypothesis. Here the assumption is that income-generating household activities play only an insignificant, supplementary role in the overall household economy. Figure 3.10 would seem to support this hypothesis: We note that the large majority of households in both main survey areas

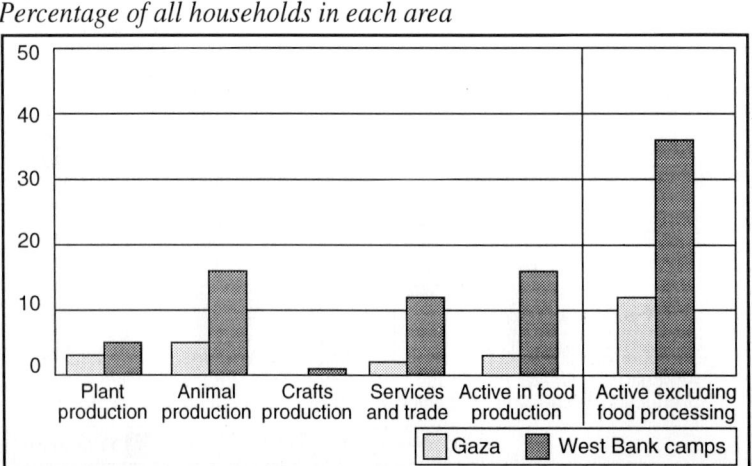

Figure 3.9 Household production plans, by main geographical area. Percentage of all households in each area

neither sell nor give away their products, but produce exclusively for own consumption.

There are, however, two reasons for rejecting the "marginal role" hypothesis. Firstly, the strong correlation between increase in household production and increasing household size indicates that the principal economic significance of household income-generating activities is saving on consumption expenditures, rather than involvement in market transactions.

Furthermore actual marketing of household production may be related to the locality of the household. The higher prevalence of services and trade in the West Bank refugee camps may be due to higher demand for such services in the West Bank and Arab Jerusalem than in Gaza. Thus, lack of purchasing power, just as much as features of the households or low value of household production, may explain why so few households market their products.

Summing up, income-generating household activities do not seem to play any compensatory role in the short term, *neither* at the individual *nor* at the household level. Because of the low level of formal labour activity, and hence reservation wages among the primary agents in household activities, middle-aged and older women, meagre revenues from household production may only to a limited extent explain the lack of increase in production output.

The prevalence of household production increases with household size. This finding indicates that these activities may play an important

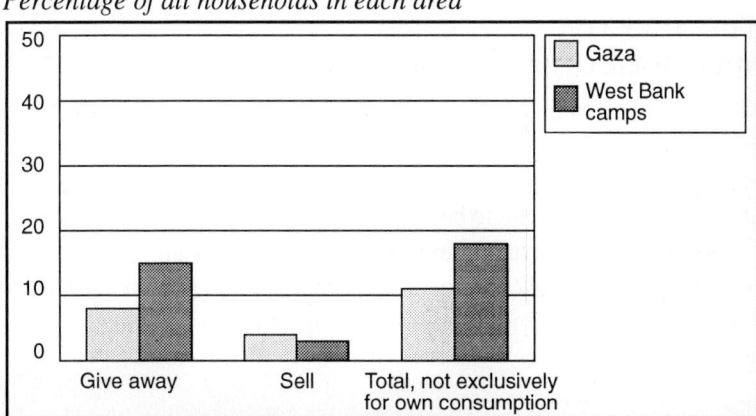

Figure 3.10 Household production use, by main geographical area. Percentage of all households in each area

role in household economy by reducing consumption expenditures, despite of low involvement in market transactions. The survey interviewing was conducted in October/ November 1993, only about half a year after the border closure. We cannot rule out various constraints in initiating or increasing household production as an explanation of its apparent stability.

Changes in household production are also obviously linked to expectations about future employment prospects. At the time of the interviewing there were relatively high expectations about an imminent Israeli withdrawal from Gaza and Jericho. As such withdrawal was expected to be followed by considerable foreign aid to all of the Occupied Territories, this may have acted to restrain an augmentation of household production.

HOUSEHOLD INCOME TYPES AND EMPLOYMENT

See table 3.19 to 3.41 in appendix 4 for references to this section.
This section will investigate the relationship between types of household income, the index for household possession of consumer durables and employment within the household context. We are especially interested in seeing whether an explanation of the seemingly low downward shift of worker reservation wages may be found in the household's system for re-distributing economic resources among its members.

We begin by presenting two of the main devices to be used in the discussion: the index for household possession of consumer durables, and the classification system for household income types.

THE INDEX FOR
HOUSEHOLD POSSESSION OF CONSUMER DURABLES

Measuring economic resources is problematic in most countries. First, the popular understanding of the concept "income" is usually far more narrow than definitions used by social scientists. In particular, women's and children's work tend to be neglected in most developing countries.

Second, fear of taxation and lack of trust in national and local authorities lead to scepticism towards strangers asking about economic affairs. The result is intentional under-reporting and concealment of assets.

In the Occupied Territories, the problem of under-reporting of economic resources is reinforced by two factors. First, as these areas are under military occupation, public trust in local authorities is close to naught. Second, the relatively large number of local and foreign organizations providing material support to the population encourages under-reporting of actual economic resources.

To cope with the measurement problems likely to occur if crude questions asked about household income, we chose to take household wealth as the principal point of reference for measuring differences in household economic resources, as in FALCOT 92.

Most items included in the index for household possession of consumer durables are verifiable, which reduces the problem of memory problems and under-reporting. The residual character of wealth, leading to greater variation in household wealth than in household income, makes it useful as an indicator for identification of households which suffer economic deprivation.

Finally, because household wealth is less vulnerable to short-term economic fluctuations than various kinds of income, one could argue that it largely reflects the distribution of economic resources in the households in the sample *prior* to the border closure, thus providing a baseline for subsequent changes.

Resembling the approach used in FALCOT 92, the index for possession of consumer durables divides the households in Gaza and the West Bank refugee camps into three equal-sized groups, yielding a low, a middle and a high wealth group. In contrast to FALCOT 92, this index for possession of consumer durables is based on a *simple* addition of a household's consumer durables and other items. A region or socio-economic group may be characterized as "under-privileged", relative to the survey population on average, when its proportion of households in the lowest wealth group exceeds 1/3 *and* its proportion in the upper wealth group is less than 1/3.

It is worth emphasizing that even if this index for possession of consumer durables allows a ranking of households according to wealth, it does not aspire to measure the absolute level of household economic resources or economic deprivation for any region or socio-economic group. This means that absolute measures of economic deprivation, such as "poverty lines", cannot be constructed on the basis of this index.

Furthermore in contrast to FALCOT 92, the 1993 index for possession of consumer durables is constructed exclusively from the sample of households in Gaza and the West Bank refugee camps. It thus presents the relative distribution of wealth in *these* areas, *not* in the Occupied Territories as a whole. This point is particularly important because the low score of Gaza and the West Bank refugee camps in the FALCOT 92 index for possession of consumer durables was the principal reason for conducting the FALUP survey in these areas.

DISTRIBUTION OF THE INDEX FOR HOUSEHOLD POSSESSION OF CONSUMER DURABLES BY REGION AND SOCIO-ECONOMIC GROUP

Household wealth is accumulated over time, and is thus less vulnerable to sudden changes in the economic environment than income. Despite the border closure, we would expect only relatively minor short-term changes in the relative distribution of wealth across regions and socio-economic groups.

And indeed, the relative distribution of the 1993 index for possession of consumer durables seems to correspond roughly to the findings of FALCOT 92, taking into consideration differences in the base population and the construction of the two indices. Figure 3.11 presents the distribution of the 1993 the index for household possession of consumer durables by Gaza refugee status and for the West Bank refugee camps.

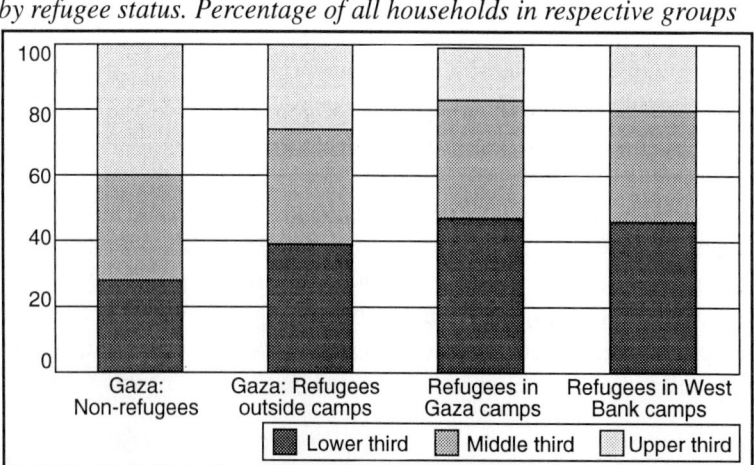

Figure 3.11 1993 index for household possession of consumer durables, by refugee status. Percentage of all households in respective groups

For the *1993* sample, the highest household score is found among Gaza non-refugees. Gaza refugees outside camps score clearly below non-refugees, but still higher than camp refugees in both Gaza and the West Bank. A possible explanation for this last finding is that refugee households that rich, can afford to prefer to move out of the camps.

While regional variations within Gaza seem to be correlated with variations in refugee status and type of locality, no significant regional variation was found among the West Bank refugee camps. We have not applied a conventional rural-urban classification of localities, because the Gaza Strip is highly urbanized.

The distribution of the index for household possession of consumer durables with regard to individual characteristics of the head of household like age and education is similar to findings from FALCOT 92 and will consequently not be further discussed here.

TYPES OF HOUSEHOLD INCOME

In FALCOT 92 only the prevalence of various types of household income was recorded. FALUP 93 included more income types, and respondents were also asked to assess the relative importance of the various types, as well as any changes since 1992. We are particularly interested in the income types of households where members face employment problems after the closure.

No attempts have been made to record exact levels of household income. As already noted, absolute measures of economic deprivation such as a "poverty line" can consequently not be constructed.

Our working hypothesis, the *"family employment network"* hypothesis, is that individuals with employment problems primarily rely on the labour activity of other household members for economic support. The reservation wage of unemployed and discouraged workers must thus be assumed to depend largely on the labour activity of *other* household members.

The "family employment network" hypothesis will be further examined below. First let us present the regional pattern of income types in the sample as of 1993. Second, some results concerning changes in income since 1992 will be discussed. Finally, we turn to the question of correlations between the various income types and the index for household possession of consumer durables.

PREVALENCE AND IMPORTANCE OF HOUSEHOLD INCOME TYPES

Table 3.1 presents the various types of income by main geographical area. For each socio-economic group, the upper rows illustrate the *prevalence* of various income types for all households in the group. The lower rows reflect the *importance* of various income types defined as the proportion of all households in the group where these types are of "main importance". (The sums of these proportions vary in the range 105-115% across different areas and socio-economic groups.)

For each type of income the relative difference between the two rows illustrates whether it is a primary or supplementary component in the household economy of that socio-economic group. Income types of "main importance" for *less* than half of the households in a particular group are defined as "supplementary" for that group.

By far the most significant type of income, both with regard to prevalence and importance, is wages. Central and Southern Gaza have the lowest proportion of households receiving various types of labour income, a finding also made by FALCOT 92. The highest prevalence of wages is found in the Central/ Southern West Bank refugee camps, close to the *relatively* prosperous labour market in the Greater Jerusalem Area.

Agricultural income has some importance in Gaza, but is, as could be expected, virtually absent in the densely crowded West Bank refugee camps. In Gaza, agricultural income and self- employment/ household production play a more important role for the non-refugee community than for refugees, probably because most agricultural land is owned by the original Gaza inhabitants.

UNRWA support is, of course, received almost exclusively by refugee households. Because of the relatively high proportion of original inhabitants living in Greater Gaza City, geographical variations in UNRWA support can be explained mainly by differences in the regional proportions of the population constituted by refugees.

Among the West Bank refugee camps, Northern camps have more business income, the highest proportion of households selling properties, and more persons receiving UNRWA support and zaqat money than the Southern/ Central camps. The Northern camps, however, receive less wages and social benefits. For social benefits, this is possibly because 20% of households in the Southern/ Central camps live in Jerusalem.

The types of household income in table 3.1 can be crudely divided in three. The first, and generally most important group, is income from labour activity (in the Occupied Territories), especially in the form of wages.

Table 3.1 Household income types, by main geographical area[1]

	Gaza	West Bank camps
Labour income		
Wages	59	75
Main importance	54	69
Agricultural income	9	2
Main importance	5	1
Income from self employement and home prod.	10	7
Main importance	4	3
Income from trade establishments	7	12
Main importance	6	7
Income from industry and service establishments	3	3
Main importance	2	2
Non-labour income from private sources		
Remittances	12	8
Main importance	5	3
Pensions	2	2
Main importance	1	1
Sale of possessions	12	11
Main importance	3	3
Rent revenues	3	2
Main importance	1	0
Other income	21	18
Main importance	8	8
Non-labour income from public sources		
UNRWA support	57	84
Main importance	13	14
Receive social benefits	11	4
Main importance	3	0
Receive Zaqat money	6	8
Main importance	0	1
n	949	498

1 The sums of income types of "main importance" vary from 105 to 115% across different areas and socio-economic groups.

The second group is "non-labour" income from private sources, like pensions and remittances. This group also includes "other" income, even if such income in many cases refers to various kinds of casual work not reported in the questions about individual employment.

The third group is non-labour income from public sources, like zaqat money and support from UNRWA and the Israeli Civil Administration.

Except for income from home production/ self-employment, all types of labour income are "primary" components in the household economy. Non-labour income from both private and public sources *generally* has a "supplementary" character. All the same, as shown by figure 3.12, these two types of non-labour income were primary sources of income in approximately one third of the households in both main regions.

CHANGES IN INCOME SINCE 1992

Respondents were asked explicitly about changes in these income types since summer 1992, (i.e. the time of interviewing for FALCOT 92). However, many income types are received by so few households as to make it meaningless to construct any sub-division here. The March 1993 border closure in effect represented a negative shift in demand for labour; and this, according to economic theory, should lead to a reduction in both wages and the volume of employment. Being the product of

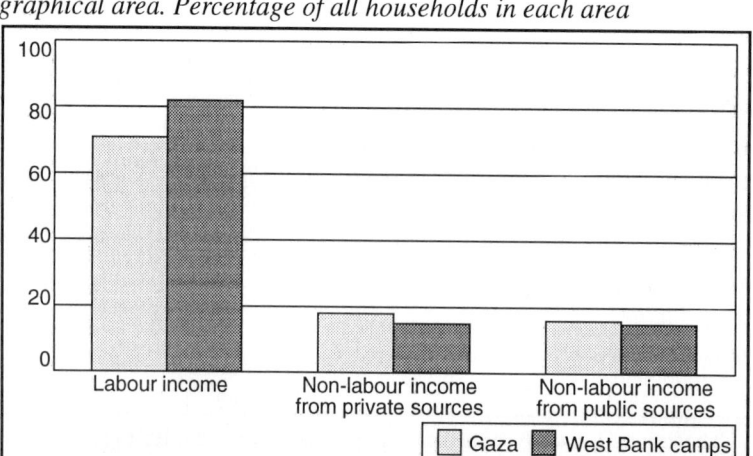

Figure 3.12 Household income types of main importance, by main geographical area. Percentage of all households in each area

these factors, a substantial decrease in income from labour activity should thus be expected.

However, for all types of labour income, the majority of households in the sample reported "no change" in income since 1992. In the West Bank refugee camps there seem to have been a downward shift in wages, in particular in the Northern camps. In Gaza, on the other hand, the size of the group reporting more wages almost equals that reporting less wages. Figure 3.13 presents a regional overview of reported changes in wages from 1992 to 1993.

The pattern of changes in wages may in part reflect the fact that comprehensive restrictions on employment migration to Israel had troubled Gaza ever since the 1991 Gulf War, while the economic shock in the West Bank refugee camps occurred primarily after the March 1993 border closure. Still, the proportion of households reporting substantial downward shifts in labour income in Gaza from 1992 to 1993 is surprisingly small.

Chapter 2 clearly documented the decrease in volume of employment from 1992 to 1993. Assuming that hourly wages have also declined, the lack of reported change in household income from wages may be due to a tendency among respondents to give the most "easy" / "neutral" answer: simply "no changes".

It is difficult to find any systematic pattern of regional changes for non-labour income types from private and public sources. Remittances, which dropped substantially immediately after the Gulf War, still show a falling tendency in both main geographical areas.

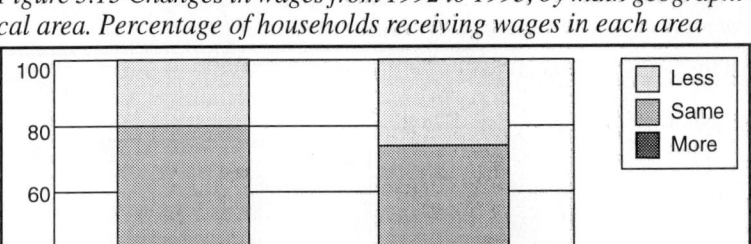

Figure 3.13 Changes in wages from 1992 to 1993, by main geographical area. Percentage of households receiving wages in each area

Social support from public organizations, (UNRWA and others) generally seems unchanged in Gaza, but displays a slightly falling tendency in the West Bank refugee camps, as illustrated by figure 3.14.

INCOME TYPES AND THE INDEX FOR HOUSEHOLD POSSESSION OF CONSUMER DURABLES

Here we discuss the relationship between household wealth and the three main groups of family income. We are particularly interested in the relationship between non-labour income from public sources and household wealth. Are, for example, various social support arrangements from UNRWA, the Israeli Civil Administration, etc., received primarily by poor and presumably needy households?

Figure 3.15 shows the relationship between household wealth and the three main groups of family income. If the proportion of households receiving one group of income types increases with household wealth, these income types may be said to be associated with high status.

The proportion of households receiving labour income tends to increase with household wealth. For the dominant labour-income type – wages – the increase is particularly marked from the lowest to the middle wealth group. In Gaza, agricultural income is also associated with (relatively) high wealth.

In dealing with household income-generating activities no indications were found that these activities had increased so as to compensate for lost income from formal employment, neither at the individual nor

Figure 3.14 Changes in non-labour income from public sources, by main geographical area. Percentage of households receiving non-labour income from public sources in groups

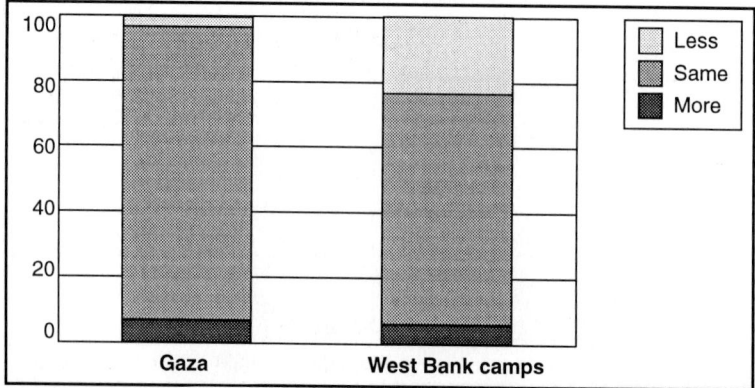

at the household level. If household income-generating activities had played a compensatory role, higher proportions of income from home production and self-employment could have been expected in the lower household wealth groups. Here we see that the proportion of households receiving income from home production and self-employment *increases* with household wealth, which confirms our findings in the section about household income-generating activities.

The types of labour income most clearly associated with "high" household wealth are income from trade, industry and service establishments. Similar findings were made in FALCOT 92. This observation does, however, not necessarily reflect a favourable climate for such establishments in the Occupied Territories. Because of the virtual absence of non-personal financial institutions for capital supply, high wealth may be a pre-condition for starting up trade, industry and service establishments, rather than a result of such activity.

Non-labour income types from private sources are somewhat overrepresented in the lowest household wealth group. This is due largely to the high number of households in this group reporting "other income" as being of "main importance". This finding is in line with the observation that poor households usually pursue multiple economic strategies.

Remittances and pensions are not found to be associated with any particular wealth group. As could be expected, the few households

Figure 3.15 Household income types, by index for possession of consumer durables. Percentage of the income types reported as having "main importance" within respective groups of households

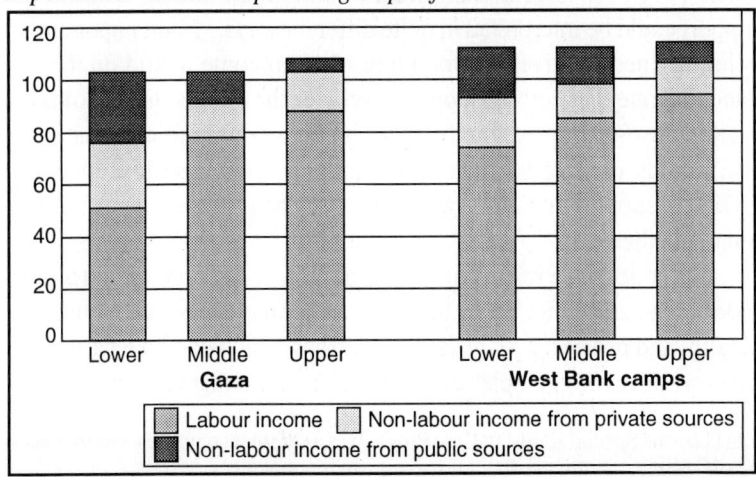

receiving rent revenues are over-represented in the upper wealth group. Sale of possessions is not particularly associated with the lowest wealth group, probably because the poorest households also have the fewest assets to sell. (Many household often have only a used fridge or radio).

Are various social support arrangements from UNRWA, the Israeli Civil Administration, etc., received primarily by the poor and presumably needy households? For all three types of support, the proportion of recipient households decreases with increasing wealth. The only exception here is UNRWA support among households in the West Bank refugee camps.

Also many households in the "highest" wealth group receive UNRWA support. However, this finding does not necessarily indicate "incorrect" priorities within the UNRWA support system.

First, it should be remembered that all areas to be included in our survey population were selected on the basis of having *below* average scores (relative to the Occupied Territories) on the index for household possession of consumer durables in FALCOT 92.

Second, the index is *relative*; belonging to the "highest" household wealth group does not necessarily imply a satisfactory level of material welfare for households in this group.

Third, UNRWA runs various relief programmes. Some of them distribute support to all refugee households. Other programmes, like the "Special Hardship Cases", are means-tested and thus distribute support only to particularly needy refugee households.[2]

Because we do not know the absolute level of support, the high proportion of households in the lowest wealth group relying on UNRWA support could be interpreted in quite different ways. "Main importance", being defined relatively to total household income, could on the one hand indicate that current support levels for the poorest households are high in absolute terms. On the other hand, it could indicate that these households receive so little other income that even low levels of UNRWA support constitute a major component of total household income for them.

As a conclusive remark it should be stressed that figure 3.15 illustrate *correlations* between household income types and household wealth, and not necessarily casual relations which can take various directions. It is for example reasonable to assume that receiving wages,

[2] In Gaza the Special Hardship Case Program as of present comprises approximately 12 000 refugee families.

and hence holding employment, may yield a higher score on the index for household possession of consumer durables. Receiving economic support from UNRWA on the contrary, is obviously the condition for, rather than the reason behind, a low household wealth score.

THE "FAMILY EMPLOYMENT NETWORK" HYPOTHESIS

We will now proceed with the investigation of income types of households whose members face employment problems after the closure. The "family employment network" hypothesis stipulated that individuals facing employment problems primarily rely on the labour activity of other household members for economic support. The reservation wage level of unemployed and discouraged workers must thus to a large extent be assumed to depend on the labour activity of *other* household members.

To test this hypothesis we have singled out three groups of households. First, households with at least one unemployed member. Second, households with at least one "discouraged worker". Third, and partially included in the two first groups, households where at least one member lost employment in Israel from 1992 to 1993.

Neither figure 3.16 nor 3.17 seems to contradict the "family employment network" hypothesis. In the households with unemployed and discouraged workers, the majority rely primarily on labour income – which

Figure 3.16 Income types of main importance, by main geographical area and unemployed worker in household. Percentage of all households in respective groups

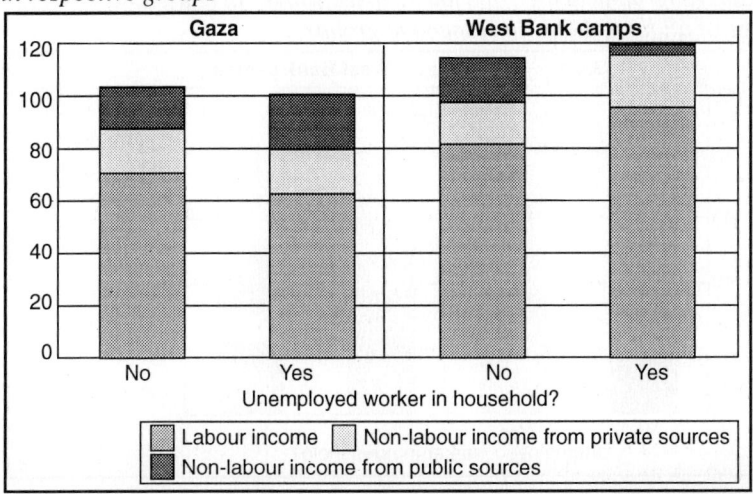

must be assumed to stem from the labour activity of other household members.

Non-labour income from public sources is not systematically more important in households with unemployed and discouraged workers than in other households. In the West Bank refugee camps, the proportion of

Figure 3.17 Income types of main importance, by main geographical area and discouraged worker in household. Percentage of all households in respective groups

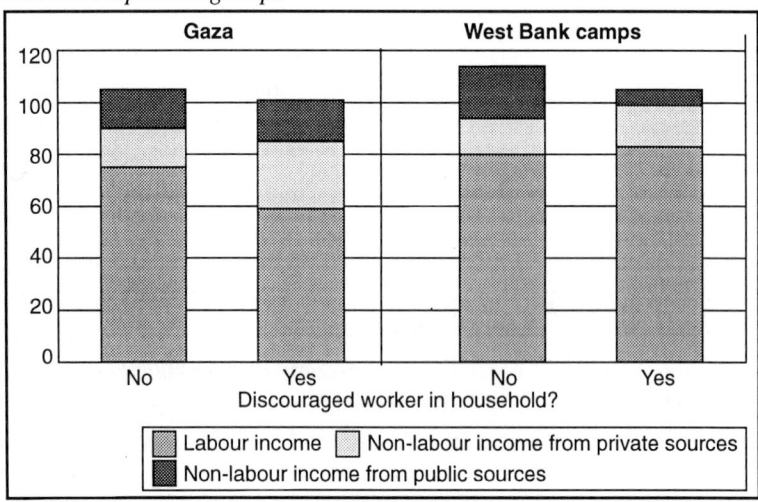

Figure 3.18 Household index for possession of consumer durable, by main geographical area and unemployed worker in household. Percentage of all households in respective groups

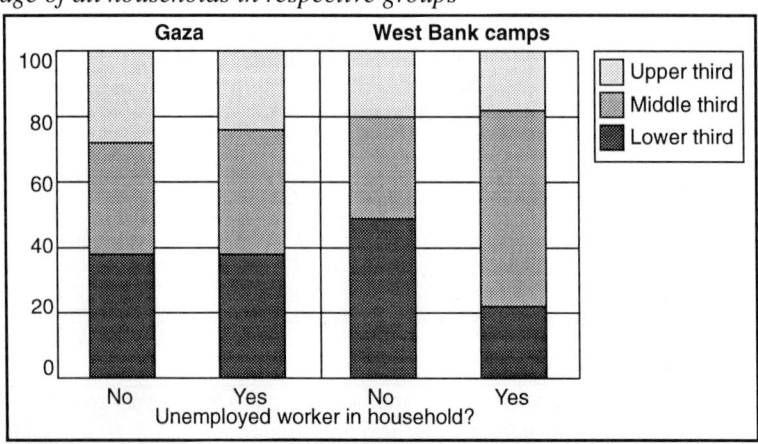

households relying on non-labour income from public sources is even lower among households with unemployed and discouraged workers than among other households. These results do not lend support to claims that non-labour income from public sources – for example, UNRWA – is the main factor halting a decline in the reservation wages of unemployed and discouraged workers.

Figures 3.18 and 3.19 provide further support to the "family employment network" hypothesis. In both main geographical areas the distribution of the index for household possession of consumer durables across households with unemployed and discouraged workers is hardly different from the distribution in other households.

Because income from labour activity is the main source of income for these households. labour income from *other* household members seems to explain why (at least one) member(s) in these households can "afford" to stay unemployed, or be a "discouraged worker" while waiting for an "acceptable" job.

The findings above are confirmed by figure 3.20 which shows income types of "main importance" in households where at least one member lost employment in Israel from 1992 to 1993. In both main geographical areas, more than 2/3 of this group of households rely on labour income as their primary source of income. Non-labour income from public sources seems even less important than among other households.

Figure 3.19 Household index for possession of consumer durable, by main geographical area and discouraged worker in household. Percentage of all households in respective groups

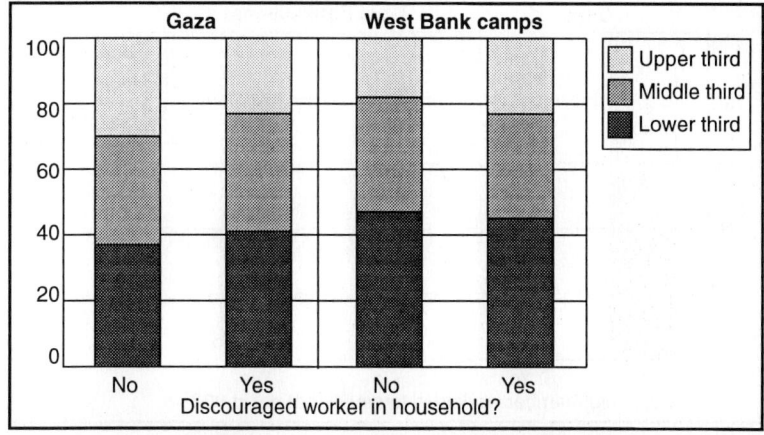

Figure 3.21 shows no difference in the distribution of the index for household possession of consumer durables in households where at least one member lost employment in Israel from 1992 to 1993, as compared with other households. Here we should recall, however, that the index for household possession of consumer durables represents economic re-

Figure 3.20 Income types of main importance, by main geographical area and workers who lost employment in Israel in household. Percentage of all households in respective groups

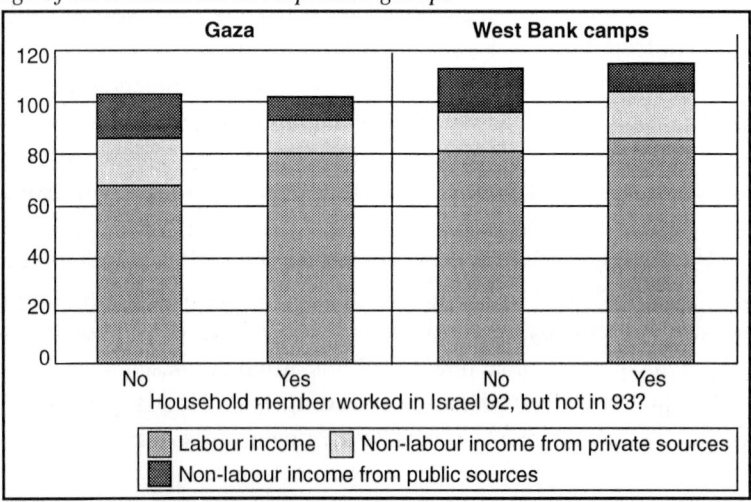

Figure 3.21 Household index for possession of consumer durables, by main geographical area and workers hwo lost employment in Israel in household. Percentage of all households in respective groups

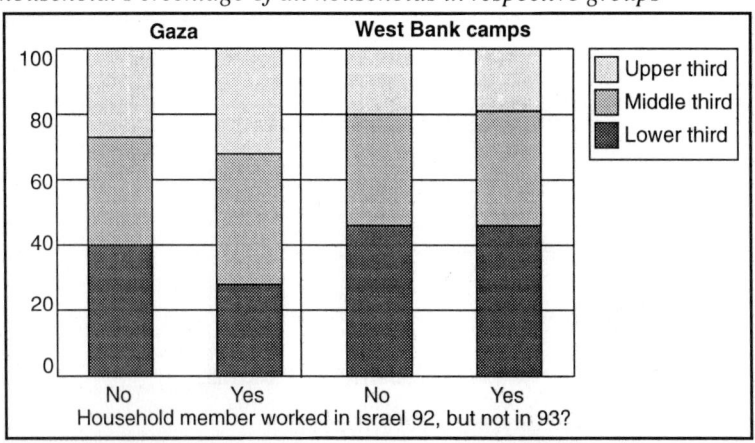

sources accumulated over time, and does not necessarily give an exhaustive picture of the post-closure economic situation.

DEPENDENCE ON PUBLIC SUPPORT, EMPLOYMENT AND HOUSEHOLD WEALTH

The previous section found no reason to reject the "family employment network" hypothesis, which suggests that individuals facing employment problems rely primarily on the labour activity of other members of the household for economic support. In households with one or more unemployed and "discouraged workers", we found no indications that non-labour income from public sources was more important than in other households, nor any sign that these households scored lower on the index for household possession of consumer durables.

If the "family employment network" hypothesis holds, then the presence of other income-earners in the household is of critical importance for the economic welfare of those who lose employment. It seems reasonable to assume that the chances of other household members being employed are positively correlated with household size, and in particular increasing with the number of adult males, who constitute more than 90% of the labour force.

Because the number of adult males, adult females and children in a household all are highly correlated, we have compared the importance of the main income groups across total household size. Figure 3.22

Figure 3.22 Household income types of main importance, by household size. Percentage of all households in respective groups

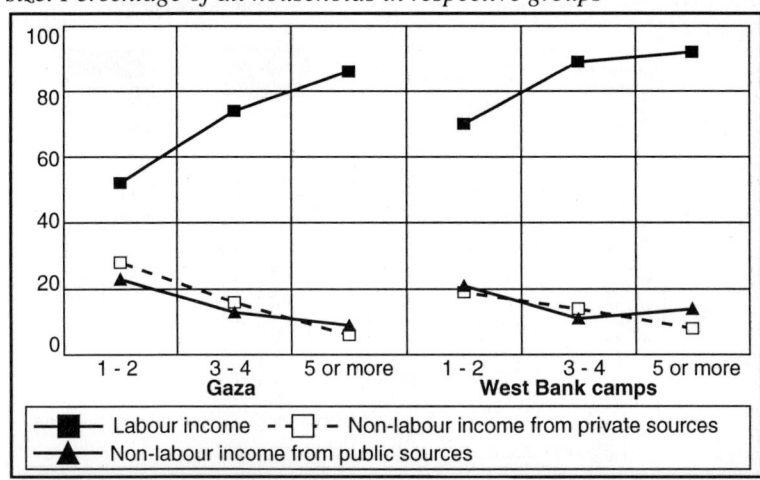

shows, as expected, that the importance of labour income tends to increase with the number of household members, whereas the importance of both private and public non-labour income decreases with household size. The positive correlation between labour income and household size is particularly marked for wages, and in Gaza also for agricultural income.

Figure 3.23 Index for household possession of consumer durables, by household size. Percentage of all households in respective groups

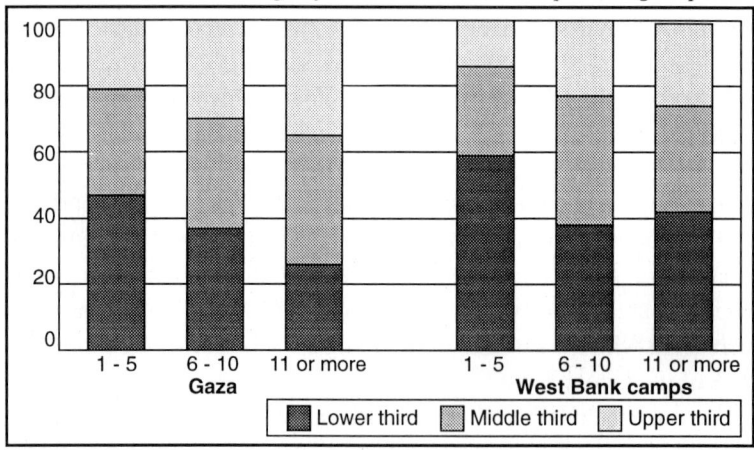

Figure 3.24 Income types of main importance, by main geographical area and full-time worker in household. Percentage of all households in respective groups

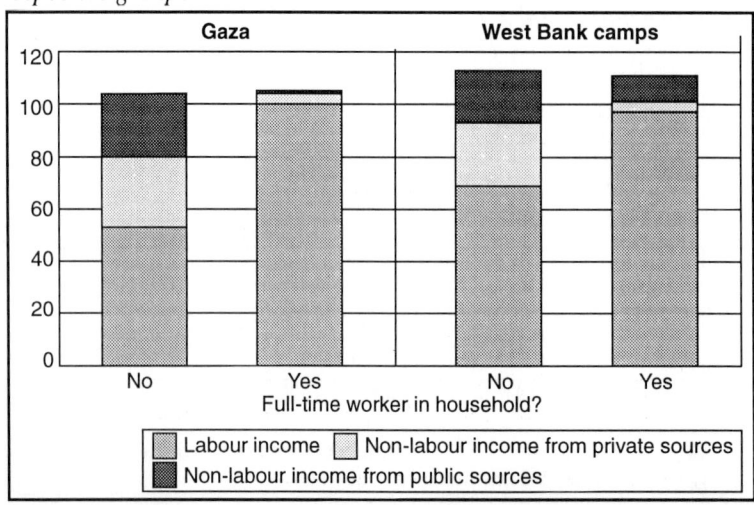

Household wealth clearly seems to increase with household size in both main geographical areas. Figures 3.23 show that particularly small households are over-represented in the lower, and under-represented in the upper wealth group.

Large households are thus less dependent on public support than small households are; financially, they rank above average as measured by the index for household possession of consumer durables. Summing up, large households form a private "social security system" on the micro-level, offering their members a kind of collective insurance against sudden economic shocks. The higher chance that at least one household member will be employed may help to explain why worker reservation wages do not seem to have fallen sharply after the border closure.

Let us now turn to the role played by various types of non-labour income from public sources, and assess their importance for the different socio-economic groups. Highlighting the importance of employment for the (total) household economy, figure 3.24 demonstrates that households with at least one full-time employed member rely almost exclusively on labour income for survival. The role of non-labour income from public sources is consequently marginal here.

Even though the labour force classification of household members refers to the week immediately prior to the survey, we may assume that

Figure 3.25 Household index for possession of consumer durables, by main geographical area and full-time worker in household. Percentage of all households in respective groups

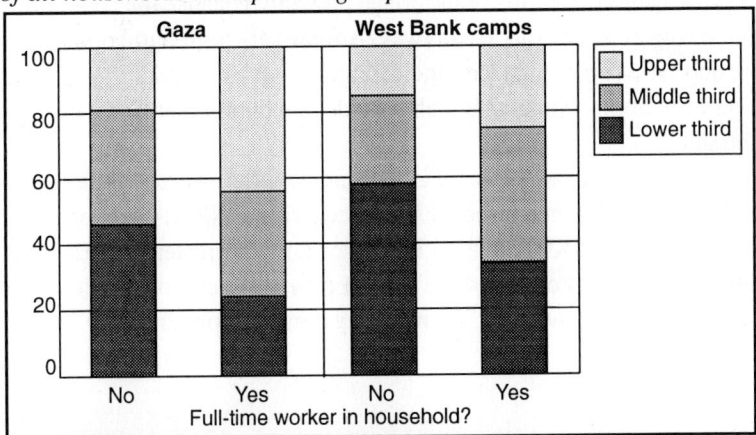

most of the households with at least one full-time worker have been in this situation since before the border closure.

Using the index for household possession of consumer durables to describe the relative economic position of households with at least one full-time worker, we find that the importance of stable labour activity is once more demonstrated (see figure 3.25.) Households with at least one full-time worker are under-represented in the lower, and over-represented in the upper wealth group.

The "family employment network" hypothesis cannot, of course, hold for households where all members are out of work. Here non-labour income from public sources seems likely to enter the picture. What kinds of income do these households rely on? (See table 3.2.)

The classification "no labour force member" in table 3.2 refers to the last week prior to the survey, while prevalence and importance of income types refer to a somewhat longer time period, "at the time of the survey". The reason labour income still holds "main importance" in at least one fourth of the households with no labour-force members is thus (casual) labour activity among household members prior to the week in question.

The high number of households receiving "other" income is in many cases also due to various kinds of casual work in the reference week, not reported in the questions about individual employment. Income from trade and business establishments, which tend to reflect more permanent employment, is virtually absent from the households with no labour-force members.

Households without labour-force members do not rely more on sale of possessions than other households, probably because they own little in the way of salable goods anyway. A relatively high number of them are dependent on remittances, indicating that the household nevertheless lives off labour income, although provided by family members working abroad.

In contrast to zaqat money and social benefits, there is little variation in the *prevalence* of households receiving UNRWA support. The *importance* of UNRWA support is, however, much greater in households without labour-force members than in other households, while zaqat money and social benefits seem to play a more supplementary role.

Table 3.2 Income types, by main geographical area and labour-force participant in household. Percentage of all households in respective groups

	Gaza		West Bank camps	
	\multicolumn{4}{c}{Labour-force member in household?}
	No	Yes	No	Yes
Labour income				
Wages	24	75	35	86
Main importance	19	69	28	80
Agricultural income	5	11		3
Main importance	3	6		1
Income from self employement and home production	3	13	4	8
Main importance	1	5	3	2
Income from trade establishments	1	10	4	14
Main importance	1	8	2	8
Income from industry and service establishments	0	4		4
Main importance		3		3
Non-labour income from private sources				
Remittances	20	9	11	7
Main importance	13	2	8	2
Pensions	2	2	3	1
Main importance	1	1	3	1
Sale of possessions	12	12	9	12
Main importance	5	2	6	3
Rent revenues	3	2	1	2
Main importance	1	0	1	0
Non-labour income from public sources				
UNRWA support	65	53	89	84
Main importance	28	6	27	10
Receive social benefits	23	5	5	4
Main importance	6	1	2	0
Receive Zaqat money	14	3	17	6
Main importance	0	0	1	0
Other income	43	11	43	11
Main importance	23	2	26	3
n	293	655	106	388

Figure 3.26 sums up the importance of the three main groups of household income for households with and without labour-force members. We see that in both Gaza and West Bank refugee camps, households without labour-force members rely primarily on non-labour income from private sources.[3]

Even though two out of three households without labour-force members rely mainly on income originating from various private sources, it seems that it is difficult for private arrangements like family and other personal social support networks to cover the needs of all households in this situation. In the West Bank refugee camps three times, and in Gaza five times as many of these households rely mainly on public transfers like UNRWA support, social benefits and zaqat money than on private arrangements.

As was the case with households with at least one full-time worker, we may also assume that many households without labour-force members have been in this situation for some time. Comparing how these households on the index for household possession of consumer durables with other households yields a picture quite the opposite as for households with at least one full-time worker. From figure 3.27 we see that in both main geographical areas households without labour-force mem-

Figure 3.26 Income types of main importance, by main geographical area and labour-force participant in household. Percentage of all households in respective groups

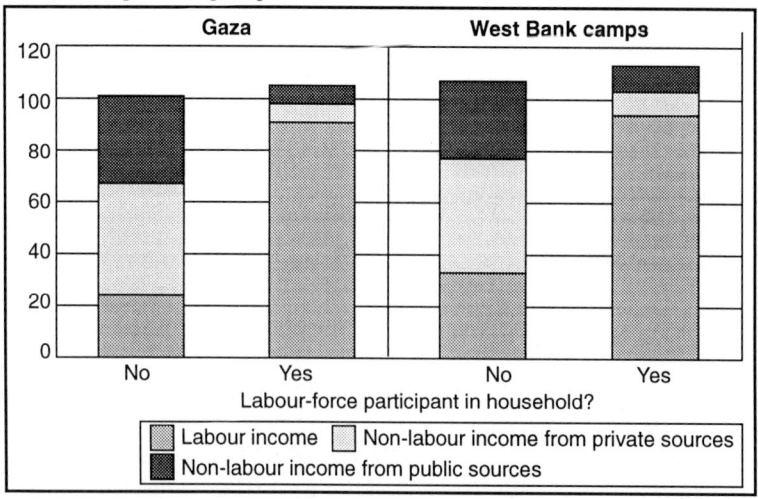

---

[3] The classification "no labour-force member" refers to the last week prior to the survey, while main income types refer to a somewhat longer time period.

bers are over-represented in the lower, and under-represented in the upper wealth group.

Are there any other socio-economic groups where the family and social network system fails to provide sufficient mutual support among household members? Particularly vulnerable in this context seem to be households headed by women. This group scores very low on the index for household possession of consumer durables, particularly in Gaza (see figure 3.28).

Figure 3.27 The index for household possession of consumer durables, by main geographical area and labour-force member in household. Percentage of all households in respective groups

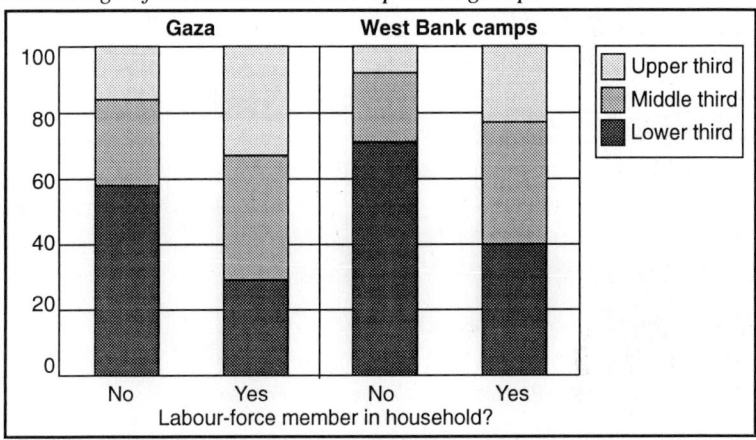

Figure 3.28 The index for household possession of consumer durables, by main geographical area and gender of head of household. Percentage of all households in respective groups

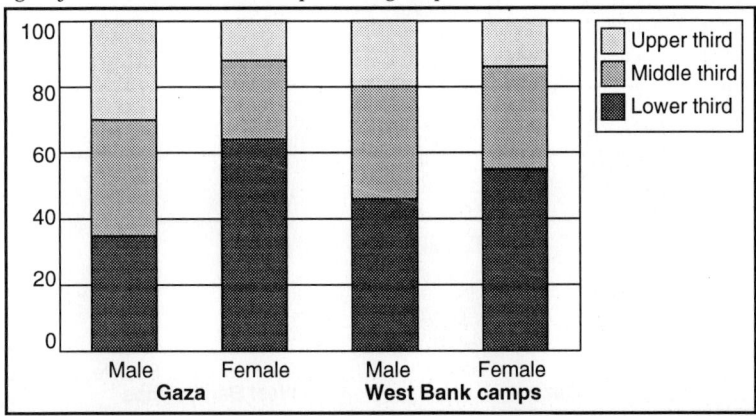

The "family employment network" hypothesis assumes that employment problems among household members are absorbed by the labour activity of *other* household members, at least to some extent. As shown by figures 3.29 and 3.30, households with female heads are, however, both small and frequently without any labour-force members at all.

Because of their small size and low labour activity, many female headed households to a large extent fall outside the private "social security system" formed by large households on the micro level. Instead they must often rely on public transfers for survival.

Figure 3.29 Household size, by main geographical area and gender of head of household. Percentage of all households in respective groups

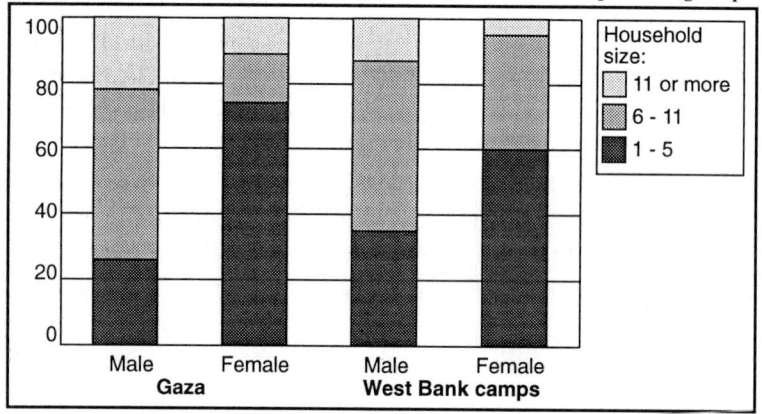

Figure 3.30 Labour-force member in household, by main geographical area and gender of head of household. Percentage of all households in respective groups

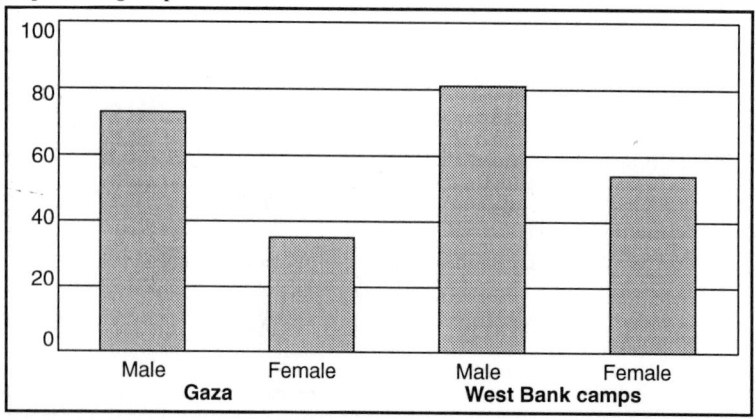

In female-headed households in Gaza, the proportions of labour and non-labour income types having "main importance" are 29% and 75% respectively, whereas in male-headed households in Gaza, the corresponding proportions are 75% and 28%. Non-labour income from public sources – like UNRWA support, social benefits and zaqat money are of "main importance" to only 12% of Gaza's male-headed households, but to as many as 47% of its female-headed households.

SUMMING UP
HOUSEHOLD INCOME TYPES AND EMPLOYMENT

We have found no reason to reject the "family employment network" hypothesis, which suggests that individuals facing employment problems rely primarily on the labour activity of other household members for economic support. In households with one or more unemployed and "discouraged workers", we found no indications that non-labour income from public sources is more important than in other households, nor any sign that these households score lower on the index for household possession of consumer durables.

If the "family employment network" hypothesis holds, the presence of other income earners in the households is of critical importance for the economic welfare of those who lose employment. This makes *large* households less dependent on public support than small households, and place them economically above average as measured by the index for household possession of consumer durables.

Large households seem to form a private "social security system" on the micro level, offering their members a kind of collective insurance against sudden economic shocks. The greater chance that at least one household member will have work, may help to explain why worker reservation wages do not seem to have fallen sharply after the border closure.

The "family employment network" hypothesis cannot, of course, apply to households where no members have employment. Because of their small size and low labour activity, households headed by women tend to fall outside the micro level "social security system" described above. Many of these households rely on public transfers for survival.

THE ROLE OF NET LIQUID WEALTH AS HOUSEHOLD COPING STRATEGY

See table3.42 to 3.53 in the appendix 4 for references to this section.

In this section we will discuss changes in net liquid wealth among households in the sample. Reduction in net liquid wealth – whether through use of savings, or through taking up debt or credits – allows households to break the immediate link between household income and consumption expenditures. Drawing on net liquid wealth may thus be yet another adaptation strategy vis-à-vis the drop in income from formal employment after the border closure.

Even during economic crises households *must* uphold a certain minimum level of consumption expenditures. Use of savings, or taking up debt or credits, may provide a household with some leeway before adapting compensatory measures on the income side of the household economy. That households may choose to reduce their net liquid wealth rather than compel their members to engage in *any* kind of income-generating activity, could explain what seems to be the low downward shift in worker reservation wages.

As already mentioned, reduction of net liquid household wealth can only be a short-term strategy. In the longer term, households without public social security must either reduce their consumption expenditures, or implement *all* possible compensatory measure on the income side to meet their minimum consumption requirements.

Drawing on net liquid wealth as a household coping strategy is consequently closely linked to expectations about future income possibilities. The more optimistic the expectations about future developments, the more will utilization of net liquid wealth appear as an attractive temporary solution, compared to a more painful reduction in household consumption expenditures.

Reducing net liquid wealth is, however, not a strategy available to all households. Some households possess no savings, and have restricted access to loans and credits. Households that use their savings may thus be less deprived than households which have nothing to sell.

The previous section found no reason to reject the "family employment *network*" hypothesis, according to which individuals facing employment problems rely primarily on the labour activity of other household members for economic support. Another possible coping strategy within the household support system may be labelled the *"family capital network"* hypothesis, whereby individuals facing employment problems also rely on reduction in net liquid household wealth for survival.

Before looking into this hypothesis, we need to present the indicators for net liquid wealth to be used. Second, we will discuss their distribution across socio-economic groups, and third, consider how they should be interpreted.

INDICATORS FOR NET LIQUID HOUSEHOLD WEALTH

In addition to the index for household possession of consumer durables presented in the previous section, the survey has used four indicators to measure the level of net liquid household wealth, and any changes in it.

The two first indicators are possession and sale of *gold* (jewellery) and use of other *"savings"*. Gold and "savings" are used as labels for real or finance capital of high liquidity, i.e assets which can be quickly transformed into legal tender without losing substantial value. Most real capital assets included in the index for household possession of consumer durable described above have low liquidity, and are consequently not considered as "savings".

Many Palestinian households, in particular those who became refugees, lost all or most of their gold and other such savings in the 1948-49 war. Because savings are frequently obtained through inheritance, we would expect the number of households with savings to be generally low, since there are many refugee households in our sample.

Gold has been singled out as a separate asset, for two main reasons. First, as we shall see, possession of gold is quite widespread.

Second, the patriarchal tradition in Palestinian households implies that final decision-making authority in economic affairs usually rests with the (male) head of household. Gold is, however, most often the personal property of women, obtained as dowry at marriage, or upon the birth of a child. This practice is supported by Shari'a law in which a woman's dowry is specified as her sole property.

Historically, dowry in the form of jewellery has been the main mechanism to ensure women some form of independent economic resources. The type of jewellery sold in the Occupied Territories and the fact that it is sold by weight, attest to its recognized significance as liquid capital comparable to other types of savings.

The third and fourth indicators which we used for measuring net liquid household wealth are use of credits for daily consumption and taking up loans for various purposes. Through the use of credits or borrowed money, even households with no gold or other savings can break the immediate link between household income and consumption expenditures.

The need to break this link is not necessarily rooted in a permanent decline in household income. Some households – for example those living from agriculture – have unstable income, and thus take up loans or use credits to keep consumption expenditures stable in the face of large fluctuations.

The practice of taking up debt differs in several ways from using credits. While credits are taken up primarily for daily consumption purposes, debt is commonly taken up for other reasons, such as for investments in housing, sales or production.

The sources of loans are far more diverse as well. While credits are provided primarily by local grocery stores, loans can be obtained from family, relatives, friends or various institutions. Those providing loans may be classified as personal or non-personal; among personal providers, whether they represent kinship relations or not.

INDICATORS FOR NET LIQUID HOUSEHOLD WEALTH BY SOCIO-ECONOMIC GROUP

In general we found only small regional variations in the possession of gold and other savings. As shown by figure 3.31, about two in ten households report having no gold, while as many as two out of three households report that they have no savings.

The proportion of households reporting no savings *may* be exaggerated because fear of taxation by the Israeli Civil Administration often leads to under-reporting and concealment of assets. Among the households which reported *selling* gold and using of other savings, roughly half had done so to obtain money for consumption purposes, and one third for investments.

Within Gaza we found little variation in the possession and selling of gold and use of other savings, with regard to geography and refugee status. Households in the Northern West Bank refugee camps reported more savings and less gold than in the Central/ Southern camps.

Also for indicators for debt and credits regional variations are relatively small. Two out of five households in Gaza have loans, compared to three out of five in the West Bank refugee camps; loans for housing and consumption purposes are typical of West Bank refugee camps.

Among the households in both regions *who have taken up loans*, roughly 75% report increased debt since the border closure. About the same proportion say their loans are so large that they cannot easily repay them.

About half of the households in both main geographical areas buy their daily consumption on credit. The most important reasons cited are "No regular salary" in Gaza and "Cannot pay" in the West Bank refugee camps.

As for gold and other savings, we hardly found any variation in the indicators for loans and credits within Gaza, neither for geography nor for refugee status. In the West Bank refugee camps, the Northern camps have more debt, in particular for consumption purposes. More households in the Northern camps report increased debt since the border closure and that their loans cannot be easily repaid.

The single most prevalent source of capital in both areas is friends. In general, access to capital seems to be more dependent on kinship structures (family and relatives) in Gaza than in the West Bank refugee camps. The proportion of non-personal capital providers ("other than above") on the contrary, is highest in the West Bank refugee camps, possibly because of the lack of such institutions in Gaza.

Variations in sources of capital according to purpose for taking up loans are generally small. Money for house building comes from a mixture of sources, to a larger extent than other types of debt, probably because of the relatively large amounts involved.

The sources of debt among the group of households with increased debt since the border closure do not differ much from other households, and variations in capital sources according to changes in debt are generally smaller than between the two main geographical areas. The same goes for the group of households with payment problems.

INTERPRETING INDICATORS FOR NET LIQUID HOUSEHOLD WEALTH

How should we interpret these indicators for net liquid wealth? Are for example households that sell their gold and using savings, or take up loans and credits, particularly deprived? To answer these and other similar questions, we have correlated the indicators for net liquid wealth with the index for household possession of consumer durables.

Because of its relative stability, the index for household possession of consumer durables may serve as an indicator for household economic resources before the border closure. In table 3.3, this index has been correlated with the proportion of households possessing gold and other

Table 3.3 Net liquid household wealth, by index for household posses-sion of consumer durables. Percentage of all households in respective groups

	Gaza			West Bank camps		
	\multicolumn{6}{c}{Household consumer durables by thirds}
	Lower	Middle	Upper	Lower	Middle	Upper
Sold savings for daily consumption	12	16	18	8	13	9
No savings	81	66	49	71	65	64
Sold gold for daily consumption	22	23	15	15	13	18
No gold	15	9	7	29	23	11
Have debt for:						
Any purpose	41	44	42	57	58	61
Consumption	21	18	10	34	27	21
Debt change since border closure						
Greater	29	32	24	45	40	49
Same	6	7	8	10	11	6
Smaller	2	1	7	1	3	6
Not applicable	4	4	3	1	3	1
No loans	59	56	58	43	42	39
Can loans not be repaid						
Yes	31	33	25	45	46	44
No	10	11	17	11	12	17
No loans	59	56	58	43	42	39
Reason for credits						
Cannot pay	31	14	10	42	28	16
Long-time practice	5	6	8	7	8	5
No regular salary	19	27	24	14	11	12
Other	1	5	10	1	3	3
No credits	44	48	48	36	50	63
n	365	323	267	231	168	98

savings, and the proportion of households which have sold these assets for consumption purposes.

The proportion of households possessing gold and other savings naturally increases with the score on the index for household possession of consumer durables. However, we find no systematic variation concerning the households selling gold and using other savings for consumption purposes. Such sales are thus possible but not indisputable indicators for particular economic deprivation. The poorest households seem to be characterized by having neither gold nor savings, rather than by selling gold and using savings for consumption purposes.

As shown by table 3.3, taking up debt is in itself not necessarily a sign of *particularly* serious economic deprivation. Taking up debt for consumption purposes, however, seem to be a coping strategy used especially by the poorest households.

Table 3.3 also shows that the vast majority of households with loans have increased their debt after the border closure, regardless of their score on the index for household possession of consumer durables. There is also little correlation between having repayment problems, source of loans, and score on index.

That also a high proportion of households in the upper wealth group reports repayment problems may be because the index for household possession of consumer durables reflects *both* former and present income levels. It may also indicate that the economic crisis has hit all types of households, but until now has not compelled those households which are *relatively* best off to sell their consumer durables.

Finally, does taking up credits for daily consumption indicate particular economic deprivation? Table 3.3 shows that in Gaza there is little variation in the prevalence of households using credits, in terms of the index for household possession of consumer durables. In the West Bank refugee camps, however, the proportion of households using credits decreases rather sharply with the index.

The proportion of households taking up credits because they "cannot pay" decrease with increasing household wealth in both main geographical areas. That also some households in the upper wealth group report taking up credits for this reason is most probably because the index for household possession of consumer durables reflects *both* former and current income levels.

Neither in Gaza nor in the West Bank refugee camps does taking up credits because of irregular salary seem particularly associated with low wealth. The same goes for households taking up credits as a long-time practice or for other reasons. In contrast to households taking up credits because they "cannot pay", taking up credits as such is thus not necessarily a sign of particular economic deprivation.

Investigating the typical time-sequence involved in selling gold and using other savings or taking up debt and credits is an alternative way of finding out which measures indicate particular deprivation. Figure 3.31 presents two examples of typical time-sequences for sale of gold, use of other savings, taking up loans for consumption purposes and using credits for consumption purposes.

The underlying assumption is that all households may take up debt and credits for consumption purposes, but that many households do not possess gold or other savings.

The typical time-sequence in reducing net liquid wealth among households which *do* possess gold or other savings is to start using savings, then to take up credits for consumption purposes, third to sell gold, and finally to take up debt for consumption purposes.

Among *all* households, taking up debt for consumption purposes is still the last measure to be implemented. Because many households do not possess gold or other savings, taking up credits for consumption purposes comes first.

The finding that taking up debt for consumption purposes is the last measure to be implemented – both among households with gold or other savings, and among all households – is in line with our earlier finding that the proportions of households using this measure increases with

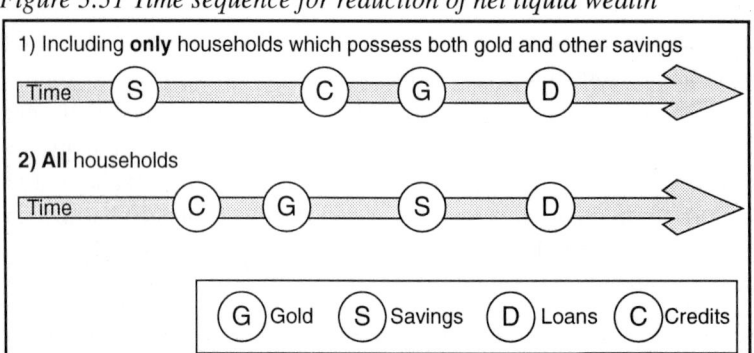

Figure 3.31 Time sequence for reduction of net liquid wealth

1) Including **only** households which possess both gold and other savings

Time — S — C — G — D →

2) **All** households

Time — C — G — S — D →

G) Gold   S) Savings   D) Loans   C) Credits

decreasing score on the index for household possession of consumer durables.[4]

NET LIQUID HOUSEHOLD WEALTH AND EMPLOYMENT PROBLEMS AMONG HOUSEHOLD MEMBERS

Let us now return to the "family capital network" hypothesis which, as mentioned, concerns the relationship between changes in net liquid household wealth and employment problems among household members.

Do individuals facing employment problems also rely on a reduction in net liquid household wealth for survival? May this adaptation strategy further help to explain the seemingly low downward shift in worker reservation wages?

We have compared the indicators for net liquid household wealth between households with at least one "discouraged" or unemployed worker, and other households.

Table 3.4 shows that households with "discouraged workers" have more debt, in particular for consumption purposes, than other households. It can further be seen that as many as 80% of these households have increased their debt since the border closure, an even higher figure than for other households. Finally, table 3.4 shows that more households with "discouraged workers" use credit for consumption purposes, and that these households more often cite "cannot pay" as the primary reason for taking up credits.

For possession of gold and other savings, and sale of these assets for consumption purposes, households with "discouraged workers" have the same scores as the overall average for the sample. The (much smaller group of) households with unemployed workers show roughly the same distribution with regard to indicators for net liquid household wealth as do households with "discouraged workers".

These results give no reason to reject the "family capital network" hypothesis. Many households in the sample seem to use reduction of net

---

4 It should be noted that the investigation of the typical time sequence for selling gold and other savings, or taking up debt and credits have been made from 6 *pair vise* relations between the four measures.

Variations in disposition rights between the elements of net household wealth (for example women's role in disposition of jewelry) have not been taken into account. Finally we assume that the basic conditions for using the various measures, e.g. the interest rates, or the price of gold, have not been dramatically changed since the Gulf War.

liquid wealth as a strategy for adapting to the effects of the border closure. Households with "discouraged" and unemployed workers tend to reduce their net liquid wealth even more than other households.

Individuals facing employment problems thus also seem to rely on reduction in net liquid household wealth for survival. This may help explain why there has been so little of evidence a downward shift in the reservation wages of "discouraged" and unemployed workers.

REDUCING NET LIQUID WEALTH AS COPING STRATEGY: HOUSEHOLD PROTOTYPES

Most households with "discouraged" or unemployed workers may be assumed to be more adversely affected by the border closure than other households. Below we will use these and other groups of households as prototypes in discussing the role of net liquid wealth in household adaptation strategies.

The various prototypes will be grouped rather *crudely* according to assumptions about their economic situation prior to the border closure, and how much they are assumed to be affected by the closure. Figure

Table 3.4 Net liquid household wealth, by main geographical area and discouraged worker in household. Percentage of all households in respective groups

	Gaza		West Bank Camps	
	Discouraged worker in household?			
	No	Yes	No	Yes
Have debt for:				
Any purpose	41	47	53	69
Consumption	15	22	26	35
Debt change since border closure				
Greater	25	37	39	56
Same	7	7	10	9
Smaller	4	1	3	2
Not applicable	5	1	1	2
No loans	59	53	47	31
Reason for credits				
Cannot pay	15	29	30	37
Long-time practice	6	6	6	10
No regular salary	22	26	12	14
Other	6	3	2	3
No credits	50	36	50	37
n	681	268	337	157

3.32 gives an overview of theoretical prototypes, and the groups of households which will be used as empirical indicators.

As noted before, the labour force classification of household members refers to the week immediately prior to the survey, but we assume that both many of the households without labour-force members, and many of those with at least one full-time worker, have been in this situation for some time.

In the section about household income types, we found that female headed households tended to rely more on non-labour income from public sources than other households. This type of income has been relatively little affected by the border closure. Households with female heads have thus been classified together with households without labour-force members and households with at least one full-time worker, into a group of households where the affects of the border closure are assumed to be *less* than average.

On the other hand we have the three partially overlapping groups of large households, households with "discouraged" or unemployed workers, and households with members who lost employment in Israel from 1992 to 1993. These are assumed to have been *more* adversely affected than the average by the border closure.[5]

Figure 3.32 Reduction of net wealth as coping strategy, household prototypes

| | | Assumed change since border closure ||
		More than average	Less than average
Assumed relative economic level before the border closure	Above average	II "Large households" Households where member lost work in Israel from 1992 to 1993 Households with "discouraged" or unemployed worker	I Full-time worker in household
	Below average		III Households without labour-force members Households with female household head

5 See figure 3.5 (page 82) for relation between number of «discouraged» and unemployed workers and household size.

Additionally, the various household groups have been classified according to assumptions about their level of economic resources prior to closure. The index for household possession of consumer durables has been the main tool utilized here.

Large households and households with at least one full-time worker both have *above* average scores on the index for household possession of consumer durables. Households with "discouraged" or unemployed workers score close to average, while households without labour-force members, or with female head of household, have *below* average scores on the index.

These two dimensions – *pre-closure economic level* and *degree of adverse influence by the border closure* – together form a matrix of four theoretical prototypes of households. We have, however, no empirical indicator for the prototype of households with a below-average pre-closure economic level and which are more adversely affected by the closure than the average ones.

It should further be noted that these groups of households are heterogenous, and that they thus only partially satisfy empirical indicators for the theoretical prototypes of households outlined in our classification table. (Some households headed by women, or households without labour-force members, must for example be assumed to belong to the now empty group noted above.

Given these initial reservations, we now turn to the role of net liquid household wealth as coping strategy among households in each of the three remaining theoretical prototypes.

The first prototype, characterized by above-average pre-closure economic level and by being less adversely affected by the closure than average, is represented by households in which there is at least *one full-time worker*.

These households more frequently possess gold and other savings than do other households. The proportion that has taken up loans is about the same as for other households, but relatively more of these loans has been obtained for housing purposes, and less for consumption purposes. Finally, these households do not use credits to a smaller degree for daily consumption purposes than others do, and they do not cite "cannot pay" less often as the primary reason for taking up credits.

The second prototype consists of households with above-average pre-closure economic level and which are more adversely affected by the closure than average. Here we find large households, households with members who lost employment in Israel from 1992 to 1993, and households with one or more "discouraged" or unemployed workers. As can be seen from table 3.5, the distribution of indicators for net liquid household wealth among *large households* resembles the distribution among households with *"discouraged" or unemployed workers.*

Relative to small households, more large households have debt for consumption purposes, and a higher proportion have debt which they now find difficult to repay. Further, these households tend to use credits for daily consumption purposes, and more often cite "cannot pay" as the primary reason for taking up credits.

In Gaza, "large" households also have more gold and savings than small households. In the West Bank refugee camps, there is little variation in possession of gold and savings in terms of household size,

Table 3.5 Net liquid household wealth, by main geographical area and no. of persons in household. Percentage of all households in respective groups

	Gaza			West Bank camps		
	Total number of persons in household?					
	1 - 5	6 - 10	11 or more	1 - 5	6 - 10	11 or more
Debt change since border closure						
Greater	21	30	36	38	45	59
Same	5	7	9	8	10	12
Smaller	2	3	5	4	2	4
Not applicable	6	3	2	2	2	
No loans	66	57	48	48	42	25
Difficulty repaying loans						
Yes	26	30	36	38	46	63
No	8	13	17	14	12	12
No loans	66	57	48	48	42	25
Reason for credits						
Cannot pay	16	20	22	27	34	40
Long-time practice	7	6	6	5	8	6
No regular salary	17	25	28	11	14	13
Other	3	4	10	1	1	8
No credits	58	44	34	55	43	33
n	297	462	195	186	248	62

perhaps because the most "wealthy" households have moved out. The profile of net liquid wealth indicators among households with *members who lost employment in Israel* resembles that of large households, but there seem to be even greater adverse changes in net liquid household wealth. This group has the largest proportion of households possessing gold and other savings, reflecting the *relatively* high remuneration of employment in Israel.

The third and final prototype is constituted by households with pre-closure economic level below average, assumed to be less than average adversely affected by the Closure. It is here we find the households *without labour-force members* and households *headed by women*.

Relative to other households, a lower proportion in these two groups of households possess gold and other savings. Further, these households have less debt, in particular for consumption purposes; they less often use credits for daily consumption purposes, and less often cite "cannot pay" as the primary reason for taking up credits than other households

Table 3.6 Net liquid household wealth, by main geographical area and head of households gender. Percentage of all households in respective groups

	Gaza		West Bank camps	
	Male	Female	Male	Female
No savings	66	84	66	86
No gold	0	29	20	51
Have debt for:				
Any purpose	44	26	59	47
Consumption	18	7	30	24
Debt change since border closure				
Greater	30	16	47	24
Same	7	6	9	16
Smaller	3	1	2	6
Not applicable	4	4	1	2
No loans	56	74	41	53
Reason for credits				
Cannot pay	19	22	32	39
Long-time practice	7	3	8	
No regular salary	25	10	13	8
Other	6	1	2	
No credits	44	65	45	53
n	848	97	444	48

do. Finally, fewer households without labour-force members, or with female heads, have greater debt now than before the border closure, or loans which are difficult to repay.

A possible explanation for the samll use of debt and credits among households with female heads may be found on the supply side of the capital market. Many households which take up credits as a long-standing practice, or because they have irregular salary incomes, have close family or social connections with shop owners. Many female-headed households have less comprehensive family connections, and their access to credits in shops may be more restricted.

Table 3.6 shows the net liquid wealth indicator profile of the most "extreme" of the two groups of households of the third theoretical prototype, households with female heads.

Let us now sum up the role played by net liquid household wealth in coping strategies in each of the three theoretical prototypes.

Among the first prototype, empirically represented by households with at least one full-time worker, relatively stable labour income reduces the need to draw on net liquid household wealth. These households are *relatively* well off, and their best "adaptation strategy" is to uphold the income flow from labour activity.

Households of the third prototype, empirically represented by those without labour-force members or households headed by females, may in general be assumed *already to have adapted* to a minimum level of consumption expenditures. Relatively few of these households possess gold or other savings. Their use of (and possibly access to) loans and credits is further constrained because of their more limited access to capital, compared to households from larger family structures. Thus, the situation of these households illustrates that reducing net liquid household wealth may be used as a short-term coping strategy only.

The second prototype, empirically represented by large households, those with "discouraged" or unemployed workers, and those with members who lost employment in Israel from 1992 to 1993, would seem to rely most heavily on reducing net liquid wealth as a household coping strategy. These households do not yet seem to have adjusted consumption expenditures down to the lower level found among households in the third prototype. For large households, such reductions may also be extremely difficult, because they have a higher minimum level of consumption expenditures.

Reducing net liquid wealth represents, as stated above, only a short-term household coping strategy. Households of this prototype are thus crucially dependent on improved income opportunities in the near future. If such an improvement fails to materialize, their drift towards the situation characterizing households headed by females, can hardly be stopped.

CHAPTER 4
REPORT CONCLUSION

The general aim of FALUP 93 is a better understanding of the mechanisms at work among individuals and households in Gaza and the West Bank refugee camps with regard to adaptation to economic shocks. As mentioned, we are not measuring merely the short-term effects of the border closure, but also the long-term effects of occupation and Intifada and the medium-term effects of the Gulf War.

Using as a baseline the pre-closure FALCOT 92 living conditions survey, FALUP 93 has documented a dramatic drop in adult male labour-force participation from 1992 to 1993. In Gaza this reduction amounts to one third of the males in the 1992 labour force; in the West Bank refugee camps, one fourth.

This reduction in labour-force participation is particularly marked among young, unmarried men, and among Gaza non-refugees. Some indications were found that the Northern West Bank refugee camps were more affected than the Central/ Southern camps. One possible explanation is that, of the population in the Central/ Southern camps, 20% are less affected by the closure because they live in Arab Jerusalem, where there is a generally stronger local economy. The sample in FALCOT 92 is, however, too small to permit direct comparisons.

The discussion has further showed that the reduction in male labour-force participation reflects widespread under-utilization of labour in the survey area. Open unemployment rates cannot capture the magnitude of labour under-utilization, and have stayed roughly unchanged since 1992. Such unemployment rates must consequently be supplemented with the number of "discouraged workers" and the number of employed persons who, although employed, state that they want more work.

Only half the persons employed in Israel in 1992 were still working there in 1993. Two-thirds of those who lost employment in Israel express a desire for more work. Less than one fourth of those who lost employment in Israel have found new employment in the Occupied Territories. Employment characteristics of these workers indicate a group of marginal workers, employed in low-status jobs with high instability and insecurity. There are no indications that these workers have "squeezed out" other workers in local employment.

It seems misleading to take the low and comparably stable open unemployment rates as indicating that the labour market in the Occupied Territories has quickly adjusted to reduced labour demand through lower wages. The reduction in formal employment is much larger if we take the unemployment rates *as well as* the high number of "discouraged workers" into consideration.

Because the survey did not measure wages directly, we cannot tell whether the large reduction in employment is due to a greater decrease in labour demand than assumed by the Israeli Central Bureau of Statistics/ the World Bank, or the downward shift in worker reservation wages is less than expected.

The high number of "discouraged workers" may support the last explanation. The reservation wage of these workers (i.e. the lowest wage for which they offer employment), still seems to be above the wage level they can obtain in the Occupied Territories. Many persons can still "afford" to be inactive while looking for an "acceptable" job. The search for *any* kind of local employment at *any* wage level has not yet been launched.

Labour-force participation is found to be primarily determined by gender, age, marital status and position in the household. This observation may indicate that individual response and adaptation strategies are closely coordinated with the coping strategies practised on the household level. One possible explanation for the apparently low downward shift in worker reservation wages may thus be found in household systems for re-distributing economic resources among their members.

In the chapter on household economy we found no reason to reject the "family employment network" hypothesis, which stipulates that individuals facing employment problems rely primarily on the labour activity of other household members for economic support. The reservation wage of unemployed and discouraged workers seems to depend primarily on the labour activity of *other* household members. The presence of other income-earners in the households is of decisive importance for the economic welfare of individuals who lose employment. The larger the household, the greater the chance that at least one household member will be full-time employed. Large households thus seem to form a private "social security system" on the microlevel, offering their members a kind of collective insurance against sudden economic shocks.

Non-labour income from public sources is not more important in households with one or more unemployed and "discouraged workers" than in other households. Support from UNRWA and various social benefits does not seem to have any strong influence on the reservation wage of unemployed and discouraged workers.

The "family employment network" hypothesis cannot, of course, apply to households where no members are labour-force participants. Because of their small size and low labour activity, most female-headed households fall outside the private "social security system". Small households thus seem to be particularly vulnerable; many of them must, in contrast to large households, rely on public transfers for survival.

The second major household adaptation strategy seems to be that of *drawing on net wealth*, which allows them to break the immediate link between income and consumption expenditures. The vast majority of households with loans have increased their debt after the border closure, regardless of how they score on the index for household possession of consumer durables. Particularly poor households are characterized by having no gold or other savings, by taking up debt for consumption purposes, and by using credits for daily consumption because they "cannot pay".

The degree of reliance on reducing net household wealth, however, varies with the type of households. Both households with at least one full-time worker, and households without labour-force members or with female heads, seem to rely less than average on this strategy - albeit for different reasons.

For households with at least one full-time worker, the *need* for adaptation is less pressing, and the best "adaptation strategy" is simply to uphold the income flow from labour activity. In contrast, households without labour-force members, or with female heads, in general seem already to have adapted to a minimum level of consumption expenditures *before* the closure.

Households which at present seem to rely most strongly on reducing net liquid wealth as a household coping strategy are large households, households with members who lost employment in Israel from 1992 to 1993, and households with one or more "discouraged" or unemployed workers.

These households do not yet seem to have adjusted their level of consumption expenditures down to the new lower level of income. For large households, this may also be extremely difficult, because of a higher minimum level of consumption expenditures.

Relying on net liquid household wealth can only be a short-term strategy. In the long term, households without public social security must either reduce their consumption expenditures, or implement *some* compensatory measures on the income side to meet their minimum consumption requirements. Reducing net liquid wealth as household coping strategy is consequently closely linked to expectations about future income possibilities.

One possible explanation for the apparently low downward shift in worker reservation wages may be expectations of an improvement in the employment situation in the near future. The high proportion of male "discouraged workers" who cite "security" related reasons for not seeking work at present may support this assumption.

Expectations of a future improvement in the employment situation may also help explain why income-generating household activities (at least in the short term) have not increased to compensate for the reduction in formal labour activity, *neither* at the individual *nor* at the household level. It must also be remembered that the field work was conducted in September/ October 1993, and that the survey thus reflects the situation only *six months* after the border closure.

If the border closure is regarded as temporary, then employment in Israel is eventually expected to be available, and workers may well prefer to await developments. Such expectations have solid foundations in the experience of numerous fluctuations between tighter and more relaxed border restrictions in recent years.

"Discouraged" and unemployed workers aspiring to get permission to obtain relatively well-paid work in Israel, may be described as participants in a "lottery". Economic activity, and hence employment opportunities, in the Occupied Territories are also characterized by unpredictability and sudden changes in fundamental factors.

The apparently low downward shift in worker reservation wages and the tendency for households to rely on short-term strategies may thus be interpreted as an effect of the lack of overall control stemming from prolonged occupation, and a high degree of vulnerability towards outside factors.

For large parts of the population, the economic situation depends as much on "high policy" and political events outside their control as on their own efforts and actions. In the present state of occupation, living conditions are thus not only threatened by adverse effects on income and employment, but also by the fact that the population has been deprived of control over basic factors that influence its situation.

If there is no improvement in the employment situation in the near future, the majority of households may drift into a situation of worsening poverty, typical of very poor Less Developed Countries and presently found among households in the FALUP sample without labour-force members, or with female household heads.

Minimum consumption expenditure requirements and depleted savings may oblige households to implement *any and every possible* compensatory measure on the income side. Alternative sources of income, other than formal labour activity and access to capital, will be crucial to the development of worker reservation wages, and hence the supply of labour.

Another factor critical for worker reservation wages is expectations of an economic revival in the Occupied Territories through foreign aid. Donors may face a dilemma between giving priority to the poorest segments - small households and households with female heads, on the basis of poverty criteria – and trying to moderate social frustration and political turmoil by targeting households with young and middle-aged under-utilized male workers, which are, however, not those worst off.

The question of expectations poses parallel dilemmas for a Palestinian self-governing authority. On the one hand, expectations of rapid improvements may have to be met to avoid political turmoil. On the other hand, expectations of rapid improvements may raise worker reservation wages above realistic levels, which in turn could encourage short-term, less rational adaptation strategies.

APPENDIX 1 THE SAMPLE OF THE FALUP STUDY

By Jon Pedersen

The sample design of the FALUP study follows closely that of the FALCOT 92 study. The interested reader should therefore also consult the appendix on sampling strategy in the report "Palestinian Society" (Heiberg & Øvensen 1993). Here we will only outline the sampling strategy and point out the main differences in design between the two surveys.

The first, and main, difference between the FALUP 93 and the FALCOT 92 sampling strategies lies in the coverage of the sample. In FALCOT 92, the sampling plan covered the whole Palestinian population in the Occupied Territories, whereas FALUP has been based on samples drawn from two domains only, namely Gaza and refugee camps on the West Bank. The main reason for the FALUP approach was that it was assumed that Gaza and the West Bank Camps would be most affected by the border closure, as they were the areas found to be worst off in the FALCOT 92 survey. An important corrollary of the design of the present study is that pooled statistics for the whole of the Occupied Territories cannot be given.

A second difference between the FALUP and FALCOT sampling lies in the final stages of the sample. In FALCOT, a household was chosen, and the household head was interviewed about household variables. Then a person was selected at random within the household, and posed questions relating to his or her personal experience. If the randomly selected person turned out to be a woman (which in fact was determined before the interview, to ease allocation of field workers), she was also asked questions from a separate questionnaire.

In FALUP a household was chosen, and the household head interviewed about household variables as well as selected activities of the household members. There was no randomly selected person, and no special questionnaire for women.

THE GAZA SAMPLE

The Gaza sample totalled 960 households. The sampling *strategy* was the same as that of the FALCOT survey down to the household level. Thus, the sample had the following stages:

* Stratification, consisting of 8 strata of PSUs defined according to type of locality.
* Selection of PSUs by simple random sampling within each stratum.
* Each of the selected PSUs were divided into cells, by using maps provided by the local statistical office. Cells were selected with equal probability within each PSU. The number of cells to be selected from each PSU was chosen so that the product of the probability of selection of a PSU and cells was constant across all cells and PSUs.
* Within each cell, housing units were selected. A housing unit was defined as a group of households sharing a common entrance. The reason for this stage in the sampling was that households could not be directely identified, while housing units could easily be identified. The actual selection was made through specified 'enumeration walks' in which every third housing unit was selected until a full subsample had been obtained. Random starting points were chosen, and each walk entailed four to six selected housing units. On average, ten housing units were selected from each cell, but the actual number for a given cell was determined by allocation a number of households proportionate to the total number of households in the cell.
* Finally, a single household was selected by simple random sample from the households constituting a household unit. This was done by first constructing a list of households in the housing unit, and then making the selection by drawing from a list of random numbers prepared for the purpose.

As the FALCOT and FALUP survey used the same strategy, and because the enumeration walk had a predetermined fixed pattern, rather than a random one, the FALUP study could have had exactly the same respondents as the FALCOT study. However, respondents in the FALCOT study were promised that reinterviewing would not take place. This was found to be important in order to ease anxiety about future misuse of the original material. Therefore, in the present survey it was decided to choose the next housing unit in the enumeration walk, rather than the same one.

Because of the last stage of the sample, i.e. the choice of households from housing units, the sample is not self-weighting, but the household weights and the individual weights are identical.

THE WEST BANK SAMPLE

The West bank sample included households from all the refugee camps in the West Bank. The sample had the following stages:

* Selecting a number of huseholds to be interviewed in each camp with an allocation proportionate to the number of persons in the camp.
* In each camp, using the random walk to select housing units as described above.
* From each housing unit selecting a household, also as described above.

As was the case for the Gaza sample, the West Bank sample is not self-weighting because of the final stage of selecting households from housing units.

Because the samples have multi-stage designs, tests of significance or confidence intervals based on the assumption of a simple random sample design are not appropriate. The design of a sample influences the variance of statistical measures, such as percentages or means. The influence of the sample design on the variance is commonly measured by the 'design effect', DEFF, which is the ratio between the actual variance of the measure and the variance the measure would have had with simple random sampling. Although experience suggests that the DEFF for the type of sample design used here will be around 1.5, one cannot assume that this will be the case for any specific measure, variable or table. The effect of a DEFF of 1.5 will be to increase the confidence interval around a percentage with about 20 per cent compared to simple random sampling.

To estimate empirically the variances or DEFFs of the present designs is exceedingly complicated. Nevertheless they may be approximated by the use of the so-called 'ultimate cluster'-method (Hansen, Hurwitz & Madow 1953). With the aid of the computer program CENVAR (US Bureau of the Census 1994), we have thus calculated confidence intervals and design effects for some of the variables in the Gaza sample. As may be seen from the table which details design effects of some individual level variabeles, the design effects are generally quite acceptable.

Response Rates and Errors in the Data Files

Of the 960 households selected in Gaza, only 5 households were not interviewed, giving a response rate of 99.5% In the West Bank Camps 504 households were selected, and 498 interviewed, corresponding to a response rate of 98.8%. Hence, selected households that were not interviewed, cannot be said to bias the sample in any significant manner. In addition to omissions that occurred in the field work process, the match between households and individuals could not be achieved in the data files in 26 cases because of errors during entry of identification numbers. These errors afffect only the analysis of the link between household activities and individual activities, but are far too few to influence the analysis.

Conclusion

The results of all surveys based on probability samples are subject to uncertainty resulting from the nature of the sampling process and from errors due to imperfections in the execution in the design. In the case of FALUP the uncertainties, or sampling errors, due to the sampling process do not pose any problems for the analyses reported here. The response rates are also insignificant as a source of error. For the discussion of non-sampling errors, i.e. errors due to the wording or questions or conduct of the interviews, etc, the reader should consult the section on field work procedures and the discussions in the main text.

Estimates of sample variability for some individual level variables
The table furnishes estimates of individual level variables. Percentages are always based on the total population.

Gender	Labour force participation	Estimate	Standard error	C.V.	95% Confidence interval Lower	95% Confidence interval Upper	Design effect	n
Male	Full time	11.3	0.5	4.86	10.2	12.4	1.94	427
Male	Part-time	9.0	0.3	3.27	8.5	9.6	0.68	337
Male	Temporarily absent	0.2	0.1	41.50	0.0	0.3	1.81	7
Male	Not in labour force	25.9	0.6	2.34	24.7	27.0	1.23	958
Male	Unemployed	2.7	0.6	20.49	1.6	3.8	7.65	93
Female	Full time	1.1	0.4	33.48	0.4	1.8	7.97	34
Female	Part-time	1.2	0.2	12.73	0.9	1.5	1.31	48
Female	Temporarily absent	0.3	0.1	35.73	0.1	0.5	2.31	10
Female	Not in labour force	47.5	0.7	1.47	46.1	48.9	1.26	1755
Female	Unemployed		0.1	17.41	0.3	0.7	1.00	21

Worked in Israel 1992	Worked in Israel 1993	Estimate	Standard error	C.V. (%)	95% Confidence interval Lower	95% Confidence interval Upper	Design effect	n
Male								
Not worked 1992	Not worked in 1993	40.3	1.1	2.79	38.1	42.5	3.40	1513
Not worked 1992	Worked in 1993	1.0	0.2	16.57	0.7	1.3	1.81	40
Worked 1992	Not worked in 1993	4.1	0.3	6.41	3.6	4.6	1.13	134
Worked 1992	Worked in 1993	3.8	0.6	15.24	2.7	5.0	5.94	139
Female								
Not worked 1992	Not worked in 1993	50.7	0.5	0.97	49.7	51.6	0.63	1870
Not worked 1992	Worked in 1993	0.0	0.0	75.52	0.0	0.1	0.86	1
Worked 1992	Not worked in 1993	0.0	0.0	75.52	0.0	0.1	0.81	1
Worked 1992	Worked in 1993	0.0	0.0		0.0	0.0		

Worked in Israel 1993	Estimate	Standard error	C.V. (%)	95% Confidence interval Lower	Upper	Design effect	n
Not worked in 1993	95.2	0.7	0.74	93.8	96.5	6.99	3519
Worked in 1993	4.8	0.7	14.58	3.5	6.2	6.99	180
	0.0	0.0		0.0	0.0		
Worked in Israel 1992	0.0	0.0		0.0	0.0		
Not worked 1992	92.1	0.8	0.86	90.5	93.6	5.53	3425
Worked 1992	7.9	0.8	9.96	6.4	9.5	5.53	274

Expanded labour force member (without food production)	Estimate	Standard error	C.V. (%)	95% Confidence interval Lower	Upper	Design effect	n
Male							
Not active	40.5	1.1	2.80	38.3	42.7	3.46	1487
Active	8.7	1.1	12.04	6.7	10.8	8.95	339
Female							
Not active	25.7	0.9	3.53	24.0	27.5	2.80	989
Active	25.0	0.9	3.43	23.3	26.7	2.52	883

Expanded labour force member	Estimate	Standard error	C.V. (%)	95% Confidence interval Lower	Upper	Design effect	n
Male							
Not active	42.9	0.6	1.32	41.8	44.0	0.84	1577
Active	6.3	0.4	6.89	5.5	7.2	2.06	249
Female							
Not active	40.6	0.8	1.94	39.0	42.1	1.65	1507
Active	10.2	0.5	4.93	9.2	11.1	1.77	365

Labour force participation	Estimate	Standard error	C.V. (%)	95% Confidence interval Lower	Upper	Design effect	n
In labour force	26.4	0.8	318.0	24.8	28.1	2.34	978
Not in labour force	73.3	0.9	127.0	71.5	75.2	2.87	2713

	Estimate	Standard error	C.V. (%)	95% Confidence interval Lower	Upper	Design effect	n
Male							
Employed, not under-utilized	11.8	0.4	3.68	11.0	12.7	1.17	438
Not in labour force	16.8	0.7	4.27	15.4	18.2	2.36	624
Under-utilized	20.5	0.7	3.31	19.2	21.9	1.83	760
Female							
Employed, not under-utilized	2.0	0.4	20.59	1.2	2.8	5.57	70
Not in labour force	46.2	0.8	1.80	44.6	47.9	1.79	1705
Under-utilized	2.4	0.3	13.10	1.8	3.0	2.69	93

APPENDIX 2 THE FIELD WORK

By Neil Hawkins

The field work for the FALUP study took place within the general context of FAFO activities in the Middle East. An important aspect of those activities is institution building and training. During the FALCOT 92 survey, FAFO had created a core group of local staff, which served as supervisors. After the establishment of the Palestinian Bureau of Statistics, it was decided that the FAFO staff should be transferred to the new institution, in order to strengthen the capacity to carry out surveys. Therefore, FAFO decided that it would be an opportunity for the local staff to design and run as many areas of the survey work as possible. The aim was that next time they could cover all aspects of survey management and organisation themselves. In the event they handled nearly all aspects of this survey with a minimum of supervision which, was extremely impressive.

The organisation and implementation of the field work for this particular survey greatly benefited from the experiences gained by FAFO in the FAFO Living conditions Survey in 1992 (FALCOT 92). This was particularly useful as there was considerable pressure to implement the field work as soon as possible. The situation was further complicated by the closure of the Occupied Territories by the Israeli authorities which led to some staff having to «smuggle» themselves in to work in particular areas. The signing of the peace accord in Washington led to high expectations as well as wariness over anything new. Field workers often faced respondents who thought the survey was intended to resettle them or demolish their shelter.

Nevertheless the team that worked on this survey was experienced and well trained, and managed to overcome such problems. It was the hard work and dedication of the local staff that ensured the success of this survey, which took place in very difficult circumstances.

RECRUITMENT

Despite having contacts with experienced data collectors from previous surveys, FAFO decided to advertise openly for the required data collectors, as FAFO did not want to be seen to be making appointments without giving all a chance to apply.

Adverts were placed in the local press and a short-list was made of all applicants after they had been screened and graded by both the Office

Coordinators, and the in-field coordinator. Interviews were held in Jerusalem, Gaza and Nablus and out of the seventy-five applicants, six data collectors were chosen for the West Bank and twelve for Gaza. It must be remembered that the West Bank sample was half the size of Gaza. The majority were female and nearly all had worked with FAFO in the previous survey.

FAFO supervisors were involved both in the screening of the candidates as well as setting up and conducting the interviews.

TRAINING

It was decided that the most efficient way to conduct the training was to have a number of parallel courses running at the same time and led by the supervisors. The alternative was to run them consecutively (travel restrictions prevented the possibility of holding only one course for all areas) and taken by FAFO experts. This would have been time consuming and impractical. Therefore the supervisors were invited to design a course for the data collectors as well as go through the proposed questionnaire. The latter task was performed with a FAFO expert.

Meetings had already been held where the questionnaire was openly discussed in detail and the many comments of the supervisors were registered. This is a vital stage for any survey, as not only do the supervisors criticise the questionnaire based on their experience but it also is an important factor in motivation, since it is they who will have to defend the questionnaire to the data collectors. Their comments are based on field experience and contribute to preventing misunderstandings and confusion in the field work.

The questionnaire was repeatedly tested out in the field by the supervisors at this stage in order to check for any mistakes and irregularities.

Together the supervisors and in-field coordinators developed a training course. Papers were represented on the theme of training, covering the aims and various methods, and subsequently discussed in detail. Training styles and techniques were discussed and practised and a course schedule and plan was put together.

In addition to this supervisors produced a small booklet for the data collectors which gave an overview of the project, the role of the data collector, confidence building, dealing with refusals, being objective, avoiding giving the respondent expectations of help as well as interview techniques.

It was decided to use small discussion groups in the training course as this gave more opportunity for data collectors to have their say and was a more efficient use of time. The classroom section of the course would last three days. Then they would spend two days testing the questionnaire in the field to give the data collectors practice.

This stage instilled an effective feeling of teamwork as well as pride in their work, and as a result of their extensive involvement at all stages, the supervisors began to regard it more as their survey.

The training of the data collectors went smoothly and the supervisors were easily able to establish their authority through the fact that they were running the course.

The course used both the booklet and the questionnaire as a starting point but it also used role playing techniques to make the data collectors used to the various problems they would meet in the field.

Data entry operators were also trained along with the data collectors, as it was important that they understand the context of what they were doing. They also had a training course of two days given by both a FAFO expert and one of the administrative assistants. A booklet outlining how to organise and save their files, etc., was also prepared for them.

By the end of the training course FAFO were confident that the teams were ready for the field work stage.

SAMPLING

Preparations for the survey differed between Gaza and the West Bank. In Gaza we used the same cells as the FALCOT 92 survey but seeing as we gave a commitment to the households we visited that no one would be able to use this survey to make a revisit (to avoid people worrying about having visits by the tax men), we could not go back to them. Instead we chose their neighbours as this meant we could use the basic maps again, which would save a great deal of time.

In Gaza the maps were therefore re-done based on the old ones but this was not without problems. Seeing as it was not desirable to identify houses by the names of the inhabitants, the only other way of identifying houses was by physical characteristics as there is no numbering system. Naturally, in the space of a year changes take place such as a new coat of paint, an extension or even building into the alley with the result of closing it. Nevertheless these were the exceptions and most houses were successfully identified first time round.

In the West Bank the sample population in this survey was refugee camps whereas in FALCOT 92 they were a small proportion of the total population of the West Bank sample. Therefore, FAFO had to select a new sample. Maps were obtained of the camps with the help of UNRWA and they were divided into identifiable localities (based on a road or path). A starting point was taken at random in each of the districts and marked on a map. The supervisors then went back into the field with the data collectors, found the starting point and implemented a set walking pattern to identify the selected houses. Data collectors were distributed to these houses as they walked. This method was decided upon in order to save time as the mapping had to be done prior to the collection of data, otherwise there would have been considerable delay.

For statistical aspects of the sampling, see appendix 1.

ORGANISATION AND FIELD WORK

The supervisors decided that it would be better to hire the data collectors on a monthly basis instead of paying them per questionnaire. The arguments revolved around control and incentive. Being paid per questionnaire would, it is argued, lead to the data collector finishing more questionnaires, whereas if they were paid by the month there would be no incentive to finish or fill in a questionnaire well. The problem with that system is that if you need to have meetings to review questionnaires, the data collector sees that he is not getting paid for it, so he has no incentive to attend. Furthermore the system could also encourage them to work too quickly. The supervisors felt that a mixture would be best.

It was decided to pay a set salary for a month with a bonus of 18% of the total salary upon completion, depending on the quality of their work and the consistency of keeping the required records plus their attendance of meetings. This system worked very well and fostered team-work as people did not feel that a colleague was trying to do more questionnaires than anyone else, but it still left room for an incentive for good work as well as underlining the supervisors' authority.

In Gaza there were three teams each with a supervisor as well as one trouble shooter supervisor. In addition there was a sampler who played a crucial role in ensuring the accuracy of the maps. The office was headed by the Gaza coordinator and helped by her assistant who oversaw the two data enterers.

The data enterers were trained to run cleaning passes on their questionnaires and the print out was given to the respective office coordinator. They would then return the inconsistent questionnaires to the supervisors for clarification and they in turn would approach the data collector. These questionnaires were corrected and subsequently re-entered at the end of the field work.

Forms were devised by the supervisors to keep track of expenditure and to organise the field work. Three forms were devised;

a) One where the data collector had to record the questionnaire number, date of receipt and completion, the cell and map number and the random number of the household if they had to make a selection from a number of households.

b) One which recorded the data collectors transport costs.

c) A form for the supervisors that recorded where each questionnaire was, when they gave it out and when it was returned, and who filled it in.

The aim was to have the maximum amount of control using the minimum amount of paper work.

The accounts were divided up between the three field offices with each office keeping their own accounts. They had been trained to use a computerised accounting system that greatly facilitated the control of the financial side of the survey.

They were then handed in to the in-field coordinator who joined all the accounts together.

The supervisors ran most aspects of the field work. They decided on the speed, which depended on the quality, they checked the questionnaires in the office before submitting them to the data entry and they had regular meeting to discuss the problems and to help clear up any misunderstandings as exceptions to the rules always occur. Approaches to difficult respondents were discussed and they were aided in their task by the use of a prepared leaflet that outlined the aims of the survey and gave a telephone number to call. Data collectors were also issued with ID cards, which they were required to show in each house.

Field work itself took a month (October 1993) to complete and this was followed by an evaluation firstly by the data collectors themselves, then a more thorough one by the supervisors jointly from Gaza and Jerusalem, which led to them writing a report summarising their recommendations.

APPENDIX 3 TABLES TO CHAPTER 2

LABOUR-FORCE PARTICIPATION

Table 2.1 International comparison of crude labour-force participation rates. Percentage of all persons in respective populations

	Gaza FALUP 93	West bank camp FALUP 93	Israel Jews 92*	Israel "Non-Jews"*	Syria 91**	Egypt 91**
Crude labour-force participation rate	13	18	38,4	24,5	24	27
n	3535	1865	NA	NA	NA	NA

NA = Not available
* Source: "Statistical Abstract of Israel 1993, Tables 12.1, 12,8, Main Series A.
** Source World Bank "An Investment in Peace"; book 6 page 12.

Table 2.2 Gaza labour-force participation, by gender and sub-region. Percentage of all adults in respective groups in Gaza

	Male			Female		
	North	Central	South	North	Central	South
FALUP 93	50	40	47	5	4	9
n	883	272	588	920	285	586
FALCOT 92	80	64	63	8	-	4
n	247	20	210	254	21	206

Table 2.3 Gaza labour-force participation, by gender and refugee status. Percentage of all adults in respective groups in Gaza

	Male			Female		
	Non-refugees	Refugees outside camps	Camp-refugees	Non-refugees	Refugees outside camps	Camp-refugees
FALUP 93	51	47	44	6	5	7
n	641	374	702	625	382	763
FALCOT 92	84	63	64	7	9	3
n	169	147	158	172	150	152

Table 2.4 Gaza labour-force participation, by gender and number of adult males in household. Percentage of all adults in respective groups in Gaza

	Male			Female		
Adult men in household:	0 - 1	2 - 3	4 or more	0 - 1	2 - 3	4 or more
FALUP 93	64	45	37	6	7	5
n	458	767	519	710	720	362
FALCOT 92	85	67	68	8	4	7
n	174	202	101	230	174	77

Table 2.5 Gaza labour-force participation, by gender and age. Percentage of all persons in respective groups in Gaza

	15-19	20-29	30-39	40-49	50-59	60+
Male FALUP 93	15	58	68	72	51	21
n	388	522	351	171	116	195
Male FALCOT 92	34	83	96	86	71	34
n	90	142	107	63	26	49
Female FALUP 93	3	7	7	9	7	5
n	330	536	320	206	177	222
Female FALCOT 92	1	5	8	16	8	2
n	82	117	130	70	30	52

Table 2.6 Gaza labour-force participation, by gender and education. Percentage of all adults in respective groups in Gaza

Years of education	0	1-6	7-9	10-12	13+	Still student
Male FALUP 93	24	57	61	62	72	4
n	173	371	294	397	193	318
Male FALCOT 92	38	84	76	67	82	**
n	48	100	82	160	87	**
Female FALUP 93	6	4	4	4	35	1
n	475	221	343	470	113	169
Female FALCOT 92	9	1	2	1	42	**
n	113	79	104	143	42	**

Table 2.7 Gaza labour-force participation, by gender and marital status. Percentage of all adults in respective groups in Gaza

	Male		Female	
	Unmarried	Married	Unmarried	Married
FALUP 93	24	60	8	6
n	581	1149	372	1235
FALCOT 92	50	80	6	6
n	140	333	73	356

COMPOSITION OF THE LABOUR FORCE

Table 2.8 Average age, by main geographical area, gender and labour-force status. Percentage of all adults in respective groups

	Average age	n
Gaza male		
Non-participants	33.1	917
Participants	34.7	825
Gaza female		
Non-participants	34.6	1685
Participants	36.3	110
West Bank camps male		
Non-participants	32.8	391
Participants	33.2	512
West Bank camps female		
Non-participants	33.3	871
Participants	31.7	91

Table 2.9 Labour force, by main geographical area, gender, age, education and occupation. Percentage of labour-force participants in respective groups

	Gaza	West Bank camps
Male	88	85
Female	12	15
Age intervals used by CBS		
15-17	3	3
18-24	22	27
25-34	35	35
35-44	23	19
45-54	11	8
55-64	6	6
65 or more	1	1
Age in 10-year intervals		
15-19	7	8
20-29	37	42
30-39	29	26
40-49	16	13
50-59	8	8
60+	4	4
Education intervals used by CBS (FAFO results)		
0	6	4
1-4	6	6
5-8	26	31
9-10	17	19
11-12	26	19
13 or more	20	21
Grouped years of education		
0	6	4
1-6	24	23
7-9	21	27
10-12	29	25
13+	20	21
Occupation		
High professional	6	4
Middle professional	11	16
Business administration	1	0
Skilled worker	25	28
Sales worker	6	1
Farmer/fisher	5	2
Traditional craftsman	4	6
Other training	6	17
No training/housewife/student	36	26
n	901	590

Table 2.10 Gaza labour force, by gender, age, education and occupation. Percentage of labour-force participants in respective groups in Gaza

	Male	Female	Total
Age intervals used by CBS			
5-17	3	4	3
18-24	21	26	22
25-34	37	21	35
35-44	23	23	23
45-54	11	13	11
55-64	5	13	6
65+	1	1	1
Age in 10-year intervals			
15-19	7	8	7
20-29	37	34	37
30-39	30	22	29
40-49	16	17	16
50-59	7	12	8
60+	3	9	4
Education intervals used by CBS (FAFO results)			
0	4	24	6
1-4	6	1	6
5-8	28	10	26
9-10	17	10	17
11-12	27	17	26
13 or more	17	37	20
Years of education			
0	4	24	6
1-6	26	9	24
7-9	22	13	21
10-12	31	17	29
13+	17	37	20
Occupation			
High professional	6	6	6
Middle professional	8	30	11
Business administration	1	1	1
Skilled worker	27	10	25
Sales worker	7	4	6
Farmer/fisher	5		5
Traditional craftsman	4	3	4
Other training	7	1	6
No training/housewife/student	35	43	36
n	794	106	901

Table 2.11 Labour force in the West Bank refugee camps, by gender, age, education and occupation. Percentage of labour-force participants in respective groups in West Bank refugee camps

	Male	Female	Total
Age intervals used by CBS (FAFO results)			
15-17	3	5	3
18-24	26	35	27
25-34	35	33	35
35-44	19	16	19
45-54	9	4	8
55-64	7	4	6
65+	1	3	1
Age in 10-year intervals			
15-19	7	15	8
20-29	42	44	42
30-39	26	24	26
40-49	14	6	13
50-59	8	5	8
60+	3	5	4
Education intervals used by CBS			
0	3	11	4
1-4	7	5	6
5-8	32	23	31
9-10	20	15	19
11-12	20	11	19
13+	18	36	21
Years of education			
0	3	11	4
1-6	24	15	23
7-9	28	19	27
10-12	26	19	25
13+	18	36	21
Occupation			
High professional	4	3	4
Middle professional	12	39	16
Business administration	0		0
Skilled worker	28	27	28
Sales worker	1		1
Farmer/fisher	2	1	2
Traditional craftsman	7		6
Other training	19	8	17
No training/housewife/student	27	22	26
n	501	88	590

UNDER-UTILIZATION OF LABOUR

UNEMPLOYMENT

Table 2.12 Full-time/part-time and unemployment rates, by gender and main geographical area(ILO definitions). Percentage of labour-force participants in respective groups

	Male Gaza	Male West Bank camps	Female Gaza	Female West Bank camps	Total Occupied territories
FALUP 93					
Full-time employed	49	52	35	47	
Part-time employed	38	38	39	28	
Unemployed	12	6	17	21	
n	807	504	107	88	
FALCOT 92					
Full-time employed	27	42	42	s.s.	43
Part-time employed	52	44	39	s.s.	48
Unemployed	12	s.s.	Occ. Terr: 6		6
n	341	32	32	7	1123

s.s. = too small sample size

Table 2.13 Male full-time, part-time and unemployed rates, by main geographical area and age. Percentage of male labour-force participants in respective groups

	15-19	20-29	30-39	40-49	50-59	60+
Gaza						
Full-time employed	38	47	57	47	46	41
Part-time employed	29	36	38	41	46	51
Unemployed	29	15	5	12	8	9
n	58	304	240	124	59	22
West Bank refugee camps						
Full-time employed	49	55	54	63	59	57
Part-time employed	47	42	42	30	33	43
Unemployed	5	3	4	7	8	
n	33	187	127	70	40	17

Table 2.14 Male full-time, part-time and unemployed rates, by main geographical area and education. Percentage of male labour-force participants in respective groups

	Years of education				
	0	1-6	7-9	10-12	13+
Gaza					
Full-time employed	42	53	43	43	67
Part-time employed	53	39	42	39	24
Unemployed	5	7	15	17	9
n	30	204	179	244	139
West Bank refugee camps					
Full-time employed	58	46	51	55	58
Part-time employed	42	46	37	35	31
Unemployed		2	5	9	9
n	16	122	141	130	92

Table 2.15 1993 and 1992 employment in Israel, by gender and main geographical area of residence. Percentage of adults in respective groups employed one week or more during a four-week period prior to the survey (October/November 1993), and the corresponding period in 1992

	Male		Female	
	Gaza	West Bank camps	Gaza	West Bank camps
1993	23	26	1	7
n	760	501	65	67
1992	37	41	1	8
n	768	469	61	56

Table 2.16 1993 and 1992 male employment in Israel, by sub-area of residence. Percentage of men in respective groups employed one week or more during a four-week period prior to the survey (October/November 1993), and the corresponding period in 1992

	Gaza			West Bank camps	
	North	Central	South	North	South/Central
1993	26	19	19	20	33
n	422	101	237	243	258
1992	39	33	34	38	43
n	431	97	240	228	241

Table 2.17 1993 employment situation of men who worked in Israel in 1992, but not in 1993, by main geographical area of residence. Percentage of men in respective groups employed in Israel one week or more during a four-week period in October/November 1992, but not in the corresponding period in 1993

	Gaza	West Bank camps	Total
Full-time, OK	9	4	7
Full-time, more work wanted	8	20	13
Part-time, OK	3	4	3
Part-time, more work wanted	20	15	18
Temporarily absent		3	1
Unemployed	11	5	8
Discouraged worker	45	45	45
Other persons outside LF	5	5	5
n	146	92	238

"DISCOURAGED WORKERS"

Table 2.18, Discouraged workers, by gender and main geographical area. Percentage of adults in respective groups who are outside the labour force

	Male Gaza	Male West Bank camps	Female Gaza	Female West Bank camps	FALCOT 92 OT Male and female
Discouraged workers	38	36	3	13	4
Other outside LF	62	64	97	87	96
n	815	348	1592	827	1315

Table 2.19 Persons outside the labour force who do not want to start working, by gender and main geographical area: reasons cited. Percentage of adults in respective groups who are outside the labour force and not discouraged workers

	Male Gaza	Male West Bank camps	Female Gaza	Female West Bank camps	Total
Housewife	3	2	80	63	56
Old/ill	42	44	9	17	20
Student	53	48	10	15	22
Live from pensions etc.	0	1	0	0	0
Other reasons	2	4	0	5	2
n	591	266	1637	763	3258

Table 2.20 Discouraged workers, reasons for not working or seeking jobs, by gender and main geographical area. Percentage of adult "discouraged" workers in respective groups

	Male		Female	
	Gaza	West Bank camps	Gaza	West Bank camps
Given up hope for work	7	6	55	9
No work for my training	4	9	41	31
Security/no permission	89	85	4	61
n	307	124	41	107

Table 2.21 Discouraged workers, by main geographical area, gender and age. Percentage of persons in respective groups who are outside the labour force

	15-19	20-29	30-39	40-49	50-59	60+
Gaza						
Male	12	73	76	53	18	0
n	328	209	106	47	56	69
Female	0	6	2	2	0	0
n	324	498	296	187	165	121
West Bank refugee camps						
Male	17	56	61	65	24	4
n	130	128	20	20	20	30
Female	15	21	11	4	1	2
n	195	270	150	76	89	47

Table 2.22 Discouraged workers, by main geographical area, gender and education. Percentage of adults in respective groups who are outside the labour force

	Years of education					
	0	1-6	7-9	10-12	13+	Student
Gaza						
Male	14	52	68	76	84	1
n	76	130	111	147	46	30
Female	0	0	0	2	45	0
n	360	210	330	452	71	168
West Bank refugee camps						
Male	12	35	67	82	63	2
n	26	57	73	49	16	127
Female	2	9	18	20	40	5
n	148	157	209	151	43	119

VISIBLE AND INVISIBLE UNDER-EMPLOYMENT

Table 2.23 Employed persons wanting/ not wanting more work, by gender and main geographical area. Percentage of adults in respective groups who worked at least one hour the week prior to the survey

	Male		Female	
	Gaza	West Bank camps	Gaza	West Bank camps
Full-time, OK	36	26	45	47
Full-time, more work wanted	19	32	2	16
Part-time, OK	22	14	33	19
Part-time, more work wanted	23	28	20	18
n	723	460	83	69

Table 2.24 Employed males wanting/ not wanting more work, by main geographical area and age. Percentage of men who worked at least one hour the week prior to the survey

	15-19	20-29	30-39	40-49	50-59	60+
Gaza						
Full-time, OK	41	32	37	40	46	31
Full-time, more work wanted	16	25	23	12	4	7
Part-time, OK	12	15	21	24	36	54
Part-time, more work wanted	31	28	19	23	14	8
n	39	255	227	108	54	40
West Bank refugee camps						
Full-time, OK	28	23	20	30	46	30
Full-time, more work wanted	23	34	36	38	18	22
Part-time, OK	19	14	12	6	23	28
Part-time, more work wanted	29	30	32	26	14	20
n	31	182	122	65	37	23

Table 2.25 employed males wanting/ not wanting more work, by main geographical area and education. Percentage of men who worked at least one hour the week prior to the survey

	Years of education					
	0	1-6	7-9	10-12	13+	Student
Gaza						
Full-time, OK	25	42	32	30	48	11
Full-time, more work wanted	14	15	18	21	26	7
Part-time, OK	54	23	23	18	14	25
Part-time, more work wanted	8	20	26	30	12	57
n	40	195	152	202	126	9
West Bank refugee camps						
Full-time, OK	24	30	28	22	19	31
Full-time, more work wanted	25	21	29	39	46	33
Part-time, OK	43	22	13	7	9	
Part-time, more work wanted	8	26	30	32	27	35
n	19	116	123	117	82	3

Table 2.26 Employed persons with 10 or more years of education, by gender, main geographical area and type of job. Percentage of employed adults in respective groups with at least 10 years of education

	Male		Female		Total OT
	Gaza	West Bank camps	Gaza	West Bank camps	Male and female
FALUP 93					
High professional	6	4	13	3	
Middle professional	17	19	76	74	
Other	77	77	11	23	
n	358	207	34	34	
FALCOT 92					
High professional	4	s.s	s.s	s.s.	5
Middle professional	17	s.s	s.s	s.s	24
Other	79	s.s	s.s	s.s	71
n	137	27	13	4	501

s.s. = too small sample size

Table 2.27 Employed persons with 13 or more years of education, by gender, main geographical area and type of job. Percentage of employed adults in respective groups with at least 13 years of education

	Male Gaza	Male West Bank camps	Female Gaza	Female West Bank camps	Total OT Male and female
FALUP 93					
High professional	12	10	15	4	
Middle professional	42	40	81	93	
Other	46	50	4	3	
n	135	85	28	22	
FALCOT 92					
High professional	9	s.s	s.s	s.s.	12
Middle professional	44	s.s	s.s	s.s	49
Other	47	s.s	s.s	s.s	39
n	51	18	13	3	216

s.s. = too small sample size

THREE TYPES OF LABOUR UNDER-UTILIZATION

Table 2.28 Types of under-utilization of labour, by gender and main geographical area. Percentage of under-utilized adults in respective groups

	Male Gaza	Male West Bank camps	Female Gaza	Female West Bank camps
Unemployed	13	7	21	12
Discouraged worker	44	28	53	71
Employed, more work wanted	42	65	26	17
n	729	447	84	151

Table 2.29 Employment situation, by gender and main geographical area. Percentage of adults in respective groups

	Male Gaza	Male West Bank camps	Female Gaza	Female West Bank camps
Employed, no more work wanted	24	21	4	5
Not in LF, OK	34	29	91	79
Under-utilized	42	49	5	16
n	1747	903	1800	962

Table 2.30 Employment situation, by gender and sub-region. Percentage of adults in respective groups

	Gaza			West Bank camps	
	North	Central	South	North	South/Central
Male					
Employed, no more work wanted	28	20	21	20	22
Not in LF, OK	33	39	33	28	30
Under-utilized	39	41	46	51	48
n	885	272	590	435	468
Female					
Employed, no more work wanted	4	2	5	4	6
Not in LF, OK	93	93	88	89	71
Under-utilized	3	5	7	7	23
n	927	285	588	459	503

Table 2.31 Employment situation, by gender and refugee status. Percentage of adults in respective groups

	Refugee status					
	Gaza Non-refugee	Refugee outside camps	Refugee in camps	Refugee in West Bank camps	Non-registere refugee	Non-refugee in camps
Male						
Employed, no more work wanted	28	23	21	21	12	48
Not in LF, OK	33	34	35	29	41	21
Under-utilized	39	43	44	50	47	31
n	643	374	704	874	30	24
Female						
Employed, no more work wanted	4	4	4	5	3	0
Not in LF, OK	93	93	89	80	87	78
Under-utilized	2	4	7	15	10	22
n	630	384	764	937	28	19

Table 2.32 Employment situation, by gender and age. Percentage of persons in respective groups

	15-19	20-29	30-39	40-49	50-59	60+
Gaza male						
Employed, no more work wanted	5	23	38	40	39	17
Not in LF, OK	74	11	7	13	40	79
Under-utilized	20	66	55	46	21	4
n	389	523	351	172	116	195
West Bank camps male						
Employed, no more work wanted	10	20	27	28	43	15
Not in LF, OK	65	17	5	8	24	74
Under-utilized	26	63	68	64	33	11
n	168	338	149	90	61	96
Gaza female						
Employed, no more work wanted	1	3	5	6	5	5
Not in LF, OK	97	87	90	88	93	94
Under-utilized	2	9	4	5	2	0
n	334	536	320	209	177	224
West Bank camps female						
Employed, no more work wanted	3	6	7	3	3	4
Not in LF, OK	80	69	78	89	94	92
Under-utilized	17	25	14	8	4	5
n	208	309	172	82	94	97

Table 2.33 Employment situation, by gender and education. Percentage of adults in respective groups

	\multicolumn{6}{c}{Years of education}
	0	1-6	7-9	10-12	13+	Student
Gaza male						
Employed, no more work wanted	18	34	28	24	41	1
Not in LF, OK	69	24	13	9	4	95
Under-utilized	13	42	58	66	55	4
n	173	371	295	398	193	319
West Bank camps male						
Employed, no more work wanted	18	32	25	19	22	1
Not in LF, OK	69	27	11	5	5	96
Under-utilized	13	41	64	76	72	3
n	69	202	214	180	107	130
Gaza female						
Employed, no more work wanted	5	2	2	2	25	1
Not in LF, OK	94	95	95	95	35	99
Under-utilized	1	3	3	4	40	
n	478	222	347	470	113	170
West Bank camps female						
Employed, no more work wanted	3	5	5	6	18	
Not in LF, OK	92	84	76	72	35	95
Under-utilized	5	12	19	22	47	5
n	202	172	227	168	74	119

EMPLOYMENT PATTERNS: CHANGES IN EMPLOYMENT FROM 1992 TO 1993

Table 2.34 Main area of work in 1993 of those working in Israel in 1992, by main geographical area of residence. Percentage of adults in respective groups

	Gaza	West Bank camps
Persons who worked in Israel in 1992		
Did not work *	32	24
Occupied Territories	20	24
Israel	48	52
n	279	194
Persons who lost employment in Israel from 1992 to 1993		
Did not work *	62	50
Occupied Territories	38	50
n	145	93

* i.e worked less than one week in the designated month

Table 2.35 Employment situation in 1993 of those working in Israel in 1992, by main geographical area of residence. Percentage of adults in respective groups

	Gaza	West Bank camps
Persons who worked in Israel in 1992		
Employed, no more work wanted	34	29
Not in LF, OK	3	3
Under-utilized	62	68
n	279	194
Persons who lost employment in Israel from 1992 to 1993		
Employed, no more work wanted	12	8
Not in LF, OK	4	4
Under-utilized	83	88
n	145	93

Table 2.36 1993/1992 male employment in Israel, by refugee status. Percentage of males employed one week or more during a four-week period prior to the survey (October/ November 1993), and the corresponding period in 1992

	Refugee status					
	Non-refugee	Gaza Refugee outside camps	Refugee in camps	Refugee in West Bank camps	Non-registere refugee	Non-refugee in camps
1993	29	18	18	26	44	26
n	300	166	279	484	14	17
1992	40	29	38	41	33	27
n	312	170	274	457	11	14

Table 2.37 Employed males who worked mainly in Israel, by main geographical area of residence and age. Percentage of males employed one week or more during a four-week period prior to the survey (October/November 1993), and the corresponding period in 1992

	15-19	20-29	30-39	40-49	50-59	60+
Gaza						
1993	3	25	28	18	17	9
n	40	274	244	111	54	37
1992	28	47	39	31	11	14
n	41	274	244	117	51	41
West Bank camps						
1993	25	28	19	33	26	35
n	32	200	132	74	39	25
1992	57	48	30	41	29	43
n	21	192	119	76	40	21

Table 2.38, Employed males who worked mainly in Israel, by main geographical area of residence and education. Percentage of males employed one week or more during a four-week period prior to the survey (October/November 1993), and the corresponding period in 1992

	0	1-6	7-9	10-12	13+	Student
Gaza						
1993	17	22	32	24	12	13
n	37	194	161	223	135	10
1992	28	36	47	37	27	70
n	42	212	167	209	137	2
West Bank refugee camps						
1993	43	26	32	28	12	
n	20	127	145	121	85	3
1992	57	33	53	40	22	68
n	18	120	144	112	69	5

Table 2.39 Employed males who worked mainly in Israel, by main geographical area of residence and marital status. Percentage of males employed one week or more during a four-week period prior to the survey (October/ November 1993), and the corresponding period in 1992

	Unmarried	Married
Gaza		
1993	6	25
n	95	660
1992	22	38
n	77	688
West Bank refugee camps		
1993	25	27
n	117	382
1992	45	40
n	98	368

Table 2.40 Main area of work in 1993 for persons working in the OT or abroad in 1992, by gender and main geographical area of residence. Percentage of adults in respective groups

	Male		Female	
	Gaza	West Bank camps	Gaza	West Bank camps
Occupied Territories	92	90	91	90
Israel	1	3		
Abroad		0		
Did not work *	7	7	9	10
n	471	275	60	50

* i.e worked less than one week in the designated month

Table 2.41 Employment situation in 1993 for persons working in the OT or abroad in 1992, by gender and main geographical area of residence. Percentage of adults in respective groups

	Male		Female	
	Gaza	West Bank camps	Gaza	West Bank camps
Employed, no more work wanted	57	33	84	63
Not in LF, OK	1	2	5	2
Under-utilized	41	65	11	35
n	471	275	60	50

Table 2.42 Main area of work in 1993 for persons who did not work in 1992, by gender and main geographical area of residence. Percentage of adults in respective groups

	Male		Female	
	Gaza	West Bank camps	Gaza	West Bank camps
Occupied Territories	9	17	1	2
Israel	3	6		0
Did not work *	87	76	99	98
n	894	388	1649	861

* i.e worked less than one week in the designated

Table 2.43 Employment situation in 1993 for persons who did not work in 1992, by gender and main geographical area of residence. Percentage of adults in respective groups

	Male		Female	
	Gaza	West Bank camps	Gaza	West Bank camps
Employed, no more work wanted	4	10	1	1
Not in LF, OK	55	54	94	84
Under-utilized	40	35	5	15
n	894	388	1649	861

MALE EMPLOYMENT, BY MAIN AREA OF WORK

Table 2.44 Type, sector and place of employment, by area of work and main geographical area of residence, males 1993. Percentage of persons working one week or more during a four-week period prior to the survey (October/November 1993)

Main area of work: Main area of residence:	Occupied Territories Gaza	West Bank camps	Israel Gaza	West Bank camps
Work-place in main job last month				
Gaza, own locality	93			
Gaza, other village	2			
Gaza, other town	4			
WBC, own camp		31		
WB, other village		6		
WB, other town	0	53		
Arab Jerusalem	0	10		
Israel including West Jerusalem			100	100
Type of work in main job last month				
High professional	4	2		
Middle professional	10	11	0	
Vocational	24	27	63	33
Mercantile	18	13	1	1
Agriculture	16	4	8	1
Traditional craft	4	4	1	3
Service	17	21	6	29
Unskilled	8	18	20	34
Sector of work in main job last month				
Construction	12	16	66	48
Industry	11	13	6	6
Commerce/restaurants	19	13	1	2
Public services	31	35	11	35
Farming/fishing	16	4	8	1
Transport/communication	4	8	4	2
Other	7	11	4	5
n	587	368	171	133

Table 2.45 Type, place and sector of employment, by area of work and main geographical area of residence, males 1992. Percentage of persons working one week or more during a four-week period in October/ November 1992

Main area of work: Main area of residence:	Occupied Territories		Israel	
	Gaza	West Bank camps	Gaza	West Bank camps
Work-place in main job last year:				
Gaza, own locality	92			
Gaza, other village	3			
Gaza, other town	4	0		
WBC, own camp		27		
WB, other village		8		
WB, other town	0	56		
Arab Jerusalem	1	9		
Israel including West Jerusalem			100	100
Type of work in main job last year				
High professional	4	3		
Middle professional	12	13	0	0
Vocational	24	21	59	36
Mercantile	19	14	2	1
Agriculture	17	6	9	3
Traditional craft	2	5	2	2
Service	13	20	9	25
Unskilled	9	18	19	32
Sector of work in main job last year				
Construction	11	11	62	48
Industry	11	13	10	10
Commerce/restaurants	19	14	2	2
Public services	29	37	11	31
Farming/fishing	17	6	9	3
Transport/communication	5	8	4	1
Other	8	11	3	5
n	486	274	281	191

Table 2.46 Number of work weeks, status and type of pay, by area of work and main geographical area of residence, 1993. Percentage of persons working one week or more during a four-week period prior to the survey (October/ November 1993)

Main area of work:	Occupied Territories		Israel	
Main area of residence:	Gaza	West Bank camps	Gaza	West Bank camps
Weeks worked main job, last month				
1	9	11	11	14
2	15	21	24	33
3	11	21	24	33
4	65	46	41	20
Work status main job, last month				
UNRWA employed	7	8	1	
Civil Administration	12	4	0	1
Other employee	7	15	4	6
Self-employed	35	25	16	1
Unpaid family worker	4	3		
Employer	7	9		1
Other	29	36	78	92
Type of payment main job last month				
Daily wage	28	30	57	49
Weekly wage	4	10	20	15
Monthly wage	30	31	21	34
Unpaid family	5	9		
Sub-contr./piece-work	32	20	3	2
n	587	368	171	133

Table 2.47 Number of work weeks, status and type of pay, by area of work and main geographical area of residence, 1992. Percentage of persons working one week or more during a four-week period in October/November 1992

Main area of work: Main area of residence:	Occupied Territories		Israel	
	Gaza	West Bank camps	Gaza	West Bank camps
Weeks worked main job, last year				
1	3	6	3	3
2	9	15	14	14
3	14	21	20	31
4	74	58	64	52
Work status main job last year				
UNRWA employed	8	11	0	
Civil Administration	12	5	0	1
Other employee	6	16	4	10
Self-employed	39	24	10	4
Unpaid family worker	4	3		
Employer	7	6		1
Other	25	35	86	84
Type of payment main job last year				
Daily wage	27	33	60	44
Weekly wage	3	7	17	14
Monthly wage	31	37	20	37
Unpaid family	5	6	1	
Sub-contr./piece-work	34	17	3	5
n	486	274	281	191

Table 2.48, Type, place and sector of employment for persons employed in the Occupied Territories in 1993, but working in Israel in 1992. Percentage of persons working one week or more in Israel during a four-week period in October/ November 1992

	Gaza	West Bank camps
Work-place in main job last month		
Gaza, own locality	97	
Gaza, other village	2	
Gaza, other town	2	
WBC, own camp		42
WB, other village		7
WB, other town		48
Arab Jerusalem		3
Type of work in main job last month		
Middle professional		1
Vocational	36	47
Mercantile	2	7
Agriculture	23	
Traditional craft	5	2
Service	26	21
Unskilled	8	22
Sector of work in main job last month		
Construction	24	40
Industry	11	19
Commerce/restaurants	2	7
Public services	31	28
Farming/fishing	23	
Transport/communication	5	7
Other	5	
n	56	47

Table 2.49 Work-weeks, status and type of pay for persons employed in the Occupied Territories in 1993, but working in Israel in 1992. Percentage of persons working one week or more in Israel during a four-week period in October/ November 1992

	Gaza	West Bank camps
Weeks worked in main job last month		
1	19	17
2	26	41
3	9	27
4	46	15
Work status in main job last month		
UNRWA employed		1
Civil Administration	7	
Other employee	7	13
Self-employed	20	34
Unpaid family worker	5	
Employer	5	16
Other	55	35
Type of payment in main job last month		
Daily wage	40	27
Weekly wage	8	15
Monthly wage	22	16
Unpaid family	5	4
Sub-contr./piece-work	25	39
n	56	47

Table 2.50, Persons outside the labour force at the time of the survey (October/ November 1993) who had worked at least one week the same month in 1992, by main geographical area of residence and gender

	Gaza	West Bank camps
Male	96	92
Female	4	8

Table 2.51 Average age and years of education, by main geographical area of residence and labour-force status

	Average age	n	Average education	n
Gaza labour force	34.0	938	10.7	938
Gaza labour force who lost job from 1992 to 1993	32.2	99	8.5	99
Gaza labour force who lost job in Israel from 1992 to 1993	29.7	66	8.5	66
WBC labour force	32.9	603	9.6	602
WBC labour force who lost job from 1992 to 1993	30.1	57	8.9	54
WBC labour force who lost job in Israel from 1992 to 1993	29.0	40	8.8	36

Table 2.52 Average age and years of education of workers in the sample employed in Israel, by year and main geographical area of residence

	Average age	Average education	n
Gaza 1993	33.1	9.5	172
Gaza 1992	31.4	9.3	282
WBC 1993	34.5	8.0	137
WBC 1992	32.8	9.8	195

EMPLOYMENT BY GENDER AND AREA OF RESIDENCE

Table 2.53 Type, place and sector of employment, by gender and main geographical area of residence, 1993. Percentage of persons working one week or more during a four-week period prior to the survey (October/November 1993)

	Male		Female	
	Gaza	West Bank camps	Gaza	West Bank camps
Main area of work				
Occupied Territories	77	73	99	93
Israel	23	26	1	7
Abroad	0	0		
Type of work in main job last month				
High professional	3	2	7	1
Middle professional	8	8	40	40
Vocational	32	28	2	20
Mercantile	15	10	23	9
Agriculture	14	3	10	4
Traditional craft	3	4	8	2
Service	14	23	8	16
Unskilled	10	22	1	7
Sector of work in main job last month				
Construction	24	24		1
Industry	10	11	1	8
Commerce/restaurants	15	10	24	8
Public services	26	35	45	50
Farming/fishing	14	3	12	4
Transport/communication	4	6	1	
Other	7	10	16	29
n	760	501	65	67

Table 2.54 Work-weeks, status and type of pay by gender and main geographical area of residence, 1993. Percentage of persons working one week or more during a four-week period prior to the survey (October/November 1993)

	Male		Female	
	Gaza	West Bank camps	Gaza	West Bank camps
Work weeks in main job month				
1	10	12	3	9
2	17	24	8	11
3	14	24	3	19
4	60	39	85	60
Work status main job last month				
UNRWA employed	5	6	17	13
Civil Administration	9	3	19	8
Other employee	6	13	7	28
Self-employed	31	18	28	8
Unpaid family worker	3	3	15	4
Employer	5	7	2	6
Other	40	51	12	33
Type of payment main job last month				
Daily wage	34	35	10	19
Weekly wage	8	12		7
Monthly wage	28	32	43	56
Unpaid family	4	6	19	8
Sub-contr./piece-work	26	15	28	10
n	760	501	65	67

Table 2.55 Type, place and sector of employment, by refugee status, males 1993. Percentage of males working one week or more during a four-week period prior to the survey (October/ November 1993)

	\multicolumn{6}{c}{Refugee status}
	Non-refuge	Gaza Refugee outside camps	Refugee in camps	Refugee in West Bank camps	Non-registere refugee	Non-refugee in camps
Main area of work						
Occupied Territories	71	82	81	74	56	74
Israel	29	18	18	26	44	26
Abroad	0	0	0	0	0	0
Type of work in main job last month						
High professional	3	5	1	2	7	5
Middle professional	3	9	14	8	0	4
Vocational	31	33	35	29	20	21
Mercantile	14	17	13	10	24	0
Agriculture	26	5	7	3	0	0
Traditional craft	1	4	5	4	0	0
Service	9	21	16	23	32	26
Unskilled	13	6	10	22	17	44
Sector of work in main job last month						
Construction	29	17	22	25	24	27
Industry	7	10	13	12	12	10
Commerce/restaurants	15	20	13	11	0	0
Public services	15	36	33	34	39	50
Farming/fishing	26	5	8	3	0	0
Transport/communication	2	6	4	6	0	5
Other	5	5	8	10	24	9
n	300	166	279	484	14	17

Table 2.56 Number of work weeks, status and type of pay, by refugee status, males 1993. Percentage of males working one week or more during a four-week period prior to the survey (October/November 1993)

	Non-refuge	Gaza Refuge outside camps	Refugee in camps	Refugee in West Bank camps	Non-registere refugee	Non-refugee in camps
Weeks worked in main job last month						
1	8	7	12	12	13	11
2	15	18	20	25	11	15
3	14	15	12	24	39	22
4	63	60	57	39	37	52
Work status main job last month						
UNRWA employed	1	7	9	6	7	4
Civil Administration	8	12	9	3		
Other employee	5	6	8	13	6	9
Self-employed	33	32	28	19	5	11
Unpaid family worker	7	1	1	3		
Employer	4	9	3	7	24	
Other	42	33	42	49	58	76
Type of payment main job last month						
Daily wage	37	27	35	36	54	9
Weekly wage	7	10	8	11	7	15
Monthly wage	23	30	33	31	33	45
Unpaid family	8	3	1	7		
Sub-contr./piece-wo	26	30	23	15	5	31
n	300	166	279	484	14	17

INDIVIDUAL ENGAGEMENT IN INCOME-GENERATING HOUSEHOLD ACTIVITIES

Table 2.57 Persons responsible for household production, by gender and main geographical area. Percentage of all adults in respective groups

	Male Gaza	Male West Bank camps	Female Gaza	Female West Bank camps
Vegetables	1	1	1	1
Fruits	4	3	4	4
Herbs	2	3	2	3
Poultry	4	4	12	5
Animals	1	1	2	1
Fish	0			
Food proc.	7	8	47	41
Crafts	2	5	7	17
Services	1	4	0	1
Mobile trade	2	4	1	1
Street trade	0	0	0	0
Household production excluding food processing	13	20	20	25
n	1744	903	1796	962

Table 2.58 Persons responsible for household production, by gender and refugee status. Percentage of all adults in respective groups

	Gaza Non-refuge	Gaza Refugee outside camps	Gaza Refugee in camps	Refugee in West Bank camps	Non-registere refugee	Non-refugee in camps
Male						
Active in food processing	6	6	10	8	3	7
Active in other household production	14	12	12	20	12	24
n	641	374	702	874	30	24
Female						
Active in food processing	49	45	45	41	40	54
Active in other household production	23	17	19	25	13	37
n	627	383	764	937	28	19

Table 2.59 Persons responsible for household production, by gender and age. Percentage of all persons in respective groups

	15-19	20-29	30-39	40-49	50-59	60+
Gaza male						
Active in food processing	5	11	6	8	7	4
Active in other household production	5	9	15	20	31	18
n	388	522	351	171	116	195
West Bank camps male						
Active in food processing	3	8	9	15	15	7
Active in other household production	9	19	28	21	32	20
n	168	338	149	90	61	96
Gaza female						
Active in food processing	13	40	68	71	65	43
Active in other household production	3	16	32	31	32	19
n	334	536	320	206	177	222
West Bank camps female						
Active in food processing	14	32	59	74	65	45
Active in other household production	11	23	35	36	34	26
n	208	309	172	82	94	97

Table 2.60 Persons responsible for household production, by gender and labour-force status. Percentage of all adults in respective groups

	Male		Female	
	Not in LF	In LF	Not in LF	In LF
Gaza				
Active in food processing	7	7	46	49
Active other household production	8	18	19	31
n	918	826	1685	110
The West Bank refugee camps				
Active in food processing	7	9	41	35
Active other household production	14	24	25	21
n	391	512	871	91

177

Table 2.61 Persons responsible for household production, by gender and employment situation. Percentage of all adults in respective groups

	Male			Female		
	Employed want no more work	Not in LF, OK	Under-utilized	Employed want no more work	Not in LF, OK	Under-utilized
Gaza						
Active in food processing	6	5	10	51	47	34
Active in other household production	20	9	12	38	19	15
n	421	595	729	71	1641	84
The West Bank refugee camps						
Active in food processing	9	5	10	33	45	24
Active in other household production	24	16	21	17	26	25
n	190	266	447	48	763	151

Table 2.62 Household production among men who lost employment in Israel from 1992 to 1993, by main geographical area. Percentage of men in respective groups

	Gaza	West Bank camps
All males		
Active in food processing	7	8
n	1744	903
Lost employment in Israel from 1992 to 1993		
Active in food processing	11	8
n	146	94
All males		
Active in other household production	13	20
n	1744	903
Lost employment in Israel from 1992 to 1993		
Active in other household production	9	20
n	146	94

FUTURE LABOUR FORCE SCENARIOS

See World Bank: "An Investment for Peace" no.2, Chapter 5 as well as Annex module "a) and c)".

Table 2.63, Gaza labour-force participation including active in household production, by gender and age (cont x 4). Percentage of all adults in Gaza

	Male					
	15-19	20-24	25-29	30-34	35-39	40-44
In labour force	15	52	65	68	68	75
Active in household production excluding food processing	5	6	12	14	15	23
In expanded labour force	18	54	67	70	71	78
n	388	273	249	188	163	101

	Male					Female
	45-49	50-54	55-59	60-65	65+	15-19
In labour force	67	62	40	31	18	3
Active in household production excluding food processing	17	27	36	18	19	3
In expanded labour force	69	74	58	39	30	6
n	71	59	57	52	144	330

	Female					
	20-24	25-29	30-34	35-39	40-44	45-49
In labour force	8	5	5	9	10	7
Active in household production excluding food processing	12	20	29	35	27	36
In expanded labour force	18	24	33	38	34	41
n	301	235	168	152	112	95

	Female			
	50-54	55-59	60-65	65+
In labour force	6	8	8	3
Active in household production excluding food processing	31	34	24	15
In expanded labour force	35	38	28	17
n	102	75	103	119

SCENARIOS FOR THE LABOUR FORCE IN GAZA 1992-2002

	LF Part.	1992	1993	1994	1995	1996	1997	1998	1999	2000	2001	2002
Male population		192	200	208	217	226	236	246	256	267	278	290
Female population		200	208	217	226	236	246	256	267	278	290	302
Labour force Males FALUP 93	47	90	94	98	102	106	111	116	120	125	131	136
Labour force Females FALUP 93	6	12	13	13	14	14	15	15	16	17	17	18
Total labour force FALUP 93	26.5	102	107	111	116	121	126	131	136	142	148	154
Labour force Males FALUP 93 Expanded	52	100	104	108	113	118	123	128	133	139	45	151
Labour force Females FALUP 93 Expanded	24	48	50	52	54	57	59	61	64	67	70	72
Labour force Male FALCOT 92	72	138	144	150	156	163	170	177	184	192	200	209
Labour force Female FALCOT 92	7	14	15	15	16	17	17	18	19	19	20	21
Labour force Male FALCOT 92	72	138	144	150	156	163	170	177	184	192	200	209
Labour force Females FALUP 93 Expanded	24	48	50	52	54	57	59	61	64	67	70	72

DETERMINANTS OF LABOUR FORCE PARTICIPATION

To study the determinants of labour force participation of men in Gaza and in the camps on the West Bank logistic regression was used.

The Gaza analysis was carried out by means of PC CARP (Statistical Laboratory 1989) in order to take account of the effects of the sample design of the survey.

The following variables were used:

AGE	Age of person
AGEREG	Age of person squared
YEAREDU	Years of education
RELHREG4	1 if Son in the household, 0 otherwise
MARHHH	1 if married household head, 0 otherwise. This variable combines the married status and headship
ADULTMAL	Number of adult men in the household
ADULTFEM	Number of adult women in the household

The model predicted correct labour force status in 73 of the cases. The coefficients were as follows:

Variable	Beta	S.E. of Beta	e^{beta}	Design effect
AGE	0.1440	0.0262	1.15	1.138
AGEREG	-0.0021	0.0006	0.99	1.259
YEAREDU	-0.0311	0.0037	0.96	1.559
RELHREG4	0.5744	0.2759	1.78	1.682
MARHH	0.9757	0.2884	2.65	1.621
ADULTMAL	-0.1645	0.0483	0.85	1.082
ADULTFEM	0.1477	0.0605	1.16	1.587
Constant	-2.0416			

The overall design effect was 1.443

The analysis of the labour force participation of men in the West Bank Camps was carried out using the procedure Logistic Regression in SPSS for Windows, as the sample design is different from the Gaza one, and cannot easily be adapted to the format required by PC CARP. Therefore standard errors are probably somewhat underestimated.

The variables were those used in the Gaza analysis, except that the variable MARSON, (1 if the person was a married son, 0 otherwise) took the place of RELHREG4 (being a son in the household). Also, the number of adult men and women in the household were not found to have an effect in the West Bank Camps.

The model predicted correct labour force participation in 75% of the cases.

The coefficients were:

Variable	Beta	S.E. of Beta	e^{beta}
AGE	0.1697	0.0400	1.19
AGEREG	-0.0025	0.0004	0.99
YEAREDU	-0.0362	0.0052	0.96
MARSSON	1.1612	0.3314	3.19
MARHH	0.9083	0.2707	3.66
Constant	-1.9037	0.6837	

APPENDIX 4 TABLES TO CHAPTER 3

HOUSEHOLD INCOME-GENERATING ACTIVITIES AS ADAPTATION STRATEGY

Table 3.1 Household production changes, by main geographical area. Percentage of all households in respective groups

	Gaza	West Bank camps
Fruits		
More	14	14
Same	76	59
Less	10	27
n	162	82
Herbs		
More	21	16
Same	74	42
Less	5	42
n	85	60
Poultry		
More	20	36
Same	62	40
Less	18	24
n	295	90
Food processing		
More	21	29
Same	56	34
Less	23	38
n	913	454
Crafts		
More	10	14
Same	70	32
Less	20	54
n	147	201

Table 3.2 Household production changes, by refugee status. Percentage of all households in respective groups

	Non-refugees	Gaza Refugees outside camps	Refugees in camps	Refugees in West Bank camps
Fruits				
More	12	21	11	14
Same	77	71	79	58
Less	10	8	10	28
n	76	39	47	79
Herbs				
More	25		13	17
Same	69	96	83	40
Less	6	4	4	44
n	41	18	22	58
Poultry				
More	25	9	20	37
Same	56	72	65	38
Less	19	19	15	25
n	131	55	106	87
Food Processing				
More	23	15	24	28
Same	54	67	53	34
Less	23	19	23	38
n	335	203	361	444
Crafts				
More	7	4	12	14
Same	70	73	69	32
Less	23	22	18	54
n	41	25	79	196

Table 3.3 Household production, by labour force participation. Percentage of all households in respective groups

	Gaza		West Bank Camps	
	\multicolumn{4}{c}{LF member in household?}			
	No	Yes	No	Yes
Active in food processing	92	97	82	93
Active excluding food processing	43	57	55	70
n	293	655	106	388

Table 3.4 Household production, by full-time employment in household. Percentage of all households in respective groups

	Gaza		West Bank Camps	
	Full-time worker in household?			
	No	Yes	No	Yes
Active in food processing	95	97	87	95
Active excluding food processing	49	60	64	70
n	601	348	263	231

Table 3.5 Household production, by unemployment in household. Percentage of all households in respective groups

	Gaza		West Bank Camps	
	Unemployed worker in household?			
	No	Yes	No	Yes
Active in food processing	95	98	90	100
Active excluding food processing	51	70	66	85
n	856	93	454	40

Table 3.6 Household production, by discouraged workers in household. Percentage of all households in respective groups

	Gaza		West Bank Camps	
	Discouraged worker in household?			
	No	Yes	No	Yes
Active in food processing	95	96	92	88
Active excluding food processing	54	50	68	64
n	681	268	337	158

Table 3.7 Household production, by under-utilized workers in household. Percentage of all households in respective groups

	Gaza		West Bank Camps	
	Under-utilized worker in household?			
	No	Yes	No	Yes
Active in food processing	94	97	87	92
Active excluding food processing	49	55	60	70
n	405	544	129	365

Table 3.8 Household production, by person losing employment in Israel in household. Percentage of all households in respective groups

	Gaza		West Bank Camps	
	\multicolumn{4}{c}{Household member worked in Israel 92 not 93?}
	No	Yes	No	Yes
Active in food processing	95	100	90	94
Active excluding food processing	52	58	68	63
n	813	135	410	84

Table 3.9 Labour force categories of household members, by household size. Percentage of all households in respective groups

	Gaza			West Bank Camps		
	\multicolumn{6}{c}{Adult persons in household}
	1 - 2	3 - 4	5 or more	1 - 2	3 - 4	5 or more
Under-utilized worker	48	54	74	67	75	83
Discouraged worker	19	22	48	22	29	48
Person working in Israel in 1992, but not in 1993	12	15	16	16	15	20
Unemployed worker	6	13	12	4	6	16
n	389	291	269	214	127	153

Table 3.10 Household production, by main geographical area. Percentage of all households in respective groups

	Gaza	West Bank camps
Plant production	20	19
Animal production	33	20
Crafts production	15	40
Services and trade	9	19
Active in food processing	96	91
Active excluding food processing	53	67
n	955	498

Table 3.11 Household production, by refugee status. Percentage of all households in respective groups

	Non-refugees	Gaza Refugees outside camps	Refugees in camps	Refugees in West Bank camps
Active in agriculture production	25	20	14	19
Active in livestock production	39	31	29	20
Active in crafts	12	12	21	40
Active in services and trade	10	6	9	19
Active in food processing	97	94	96	92
Active excluding food processing	58	51	49	67
n	347	216	378	484

Table 3.12 Household production, by sub-area. Percentage of all households in respective groups

	Gaza North	Gaza Central	Gaza South	WBC North	WBC South/Central
Active in agriculture production	19	15	24	12	25
Active in livestock production	28	39	39	25	15
Active in crafts	13	19	17	38	43
Active in services and trade	8	8	10	33	5
Active in food processing	95	96	96	98	84
Active excluding food processing	48	54	61	71	62
n	502	151	302	244	254

Table 3.13 Gaza Household production, by household size. Percentage of all households in respective groups

	Total number of persons in household		
	1 - 5	6 - 10	11 or more
Gaza			
Active in plant production	21	17	23
Active in livestock production	24	34	45
Active in crafts	9	15	26
Active in services and trade	5	9	14
Active in food processing	94	96	98
Active excluding food processing	44	54	66
n	297	462	195
West Bank refugee camps			
Active in agriculture production	19	18	20
Active in livestock production	14	21	33
Active in crafts	35	43	48
Active in services and trade	16	19	24
Active in food processing	82	96	98
Active excluding food processing	60	69	78
n	186	249	62

Table 3.14 Household production plans, by main geographical area. Percentage of all households in respective groups

	Gaza	West Bank camps
Plant production	3	5
Livestock production	5	16
Food processing	0	1
Craft production	2	12
Services and trade	3	16
Any kind	12	36
n	955	498

Table 3.15 Household production plans, by sub-area. Percentage of all households in respective groups

	Gaza North	Gaza Central	Gaza South	WBC North	WBC South/ Central
Plant production	3	2	4	4	6
Livestock production	3	7	7	20	12
Food processing	0	1	1	1	2
Crafts production	3	1	2	18	6
Services and trade	2	3	4	25	8
Any kind	10	11	15	45	28
n	502	151	302	244	254

Table 3.16 Household production plans, by refugee status. Percentage of all households in respective groups

	Non-refugees	Gaza Refugees outside camps	Refugees in camps	Refugees in West Bank camps
Plant production	5	3	3	5
Livestock production	4	7	5	16
Food processing		1	0	1
Crafts production	1	3	3	11
Services and trade	1	1	5	16
Any kind	8	12	14	36
n	347	216	378	484

Table 3.17 Household production use, by main geographical area. Percentage of all households in respective groups

	Gaza	West Bank camps
Give away home production	8	15
Sell home production	4	3
Total not exclusively for own consumption	11	18
n	955	498

Table 3.18 Household production use, by refugee status. Percentage of all households in respective groups

	Non-refugees	Gaza Refugees outside camps	Gaza Refugees in camps	Refugees in West Bank camps
Give away home production	9	4	8	15
Sell home production	6	1	4	3
Total not exclusively for own consumption	15	5	11	18
n	347	216	378	484

HOUSEHOLD INCOME TYPES AND EMPLOYMENT

Distribution of the index for household possession of consumer durables, by region and socio-economic group

Table 3.19 1993 index for household possession of consumer durables, by refugee status. Percentage of all households in respective groups

	Non-refugees	Gaza Refugees outside camps	Gaza Refugees in camps	Refugees in West Bank camps
Lower third	28	39	47	46
Middle third	32	35	36	34
Upper third	40	26	16	20
n	347	216	378	484

Table 3.20 1993 index for household possession of consumer durables, by household size. Percentage of all households in respective groups

	1 - 5	6 - 10	11 or more
Gaza			
Lower third	48	37	26
Middle third	32	33	39
Upper third	21	30	35
n	297	462	195
West Bank refugee camps			
Lower third	59	38	42
Middle third	27	39	32
Upper third	14	23	25
n	186	249	62

Table 3.21 1993 index for household possession of consumer durables, by gender of head of household. Percentage of all households in respective groups

	Male	Female
Gaza		
Lower third	35	64
Middle third	35	24
Upper third	29	12
n	848	97
West Bank refugee camps		
Lower third	46	55
Middle third	34	31
Upper third	20	14
n	445	48

PREVALENCE AND IMPORTANCE OF HOUSEHOLD INCOME TYPES

Table 3.22 Household income types, by sub-area. Percentage of all households in respective groups

	Gaza North	Gaza Central	Gaza South	West Bank camps North	West Bank camps South/Central
Labour income					
Wages	67	49	52	69	81
Main importance	61	43	47	63	76
Agricultural income	9	7	11	3	2
Main importance	4	5	8	1	1
From self employed home production	9	5	13	9	5
Main importance	3	2	5	2	3
From trade estab.	6	5	10	17	7
Main importance	5	4	8	10	4
From industry and service estab.	3	2	3	5	2
Main importance	2	2	2	3	1
Non-labour income					
Remittances	12	12	11	8	9
Main importance	5	5	5	3	3
Pensions	2	2	2	1	2
Main importance	1	1	2	0	2
Sale of properties	14	13	9	17	5
Main importance	1	4	5	7	0
Rent revenues	3	1	2	2	2
Main importance	1		1	0	0
UNRWA support	46	75	65	96	73
Main importance	8	20	17	23	5
Social benefits	10	12	11	2	7
Main importance	3	5	1	1	0
Zaqat money	7	3	7	14	3
Main importance	0			1	0
Other income	23	30	13	18	18
Main importance	7	13	7	8	7
n	502	149	298	244	254

Table 3.23 Household income types, by refugee status. Percentage of all households in respective groups

	Non-refugees	Gaza Refugees outside camps	Refugee in camps	Refugees in West Bank camps
Labour income				
Wages	61	62	56	75
Main importance	57	55	50	69
Agricultural income	21	4	2	2
Main importance	11	3	1	1
From self employed home production	12	6	9	7
Main importance	2	4	5	3
From trade estab.	8	8	5	12
Main importance	7	7	3	7
From industry and service estab.	2	4	2	3
Main importance	2	3	2	2
Non-labour income				
Remittances	11	10	14	8
Main importance	5	3	7	3
Pensions	1	1	3	2
Main importance	0	1	1	1
Sale of properties	14	13	9	11
Main importance	3	4	2	3
Rent revenues	6	1	1	2
Main importance	1	0		0
UNRWA support	4	85	89	87
Main importance	1	19	20	14
Social benefits	7	14	13	4
Main importance	3	1	3	0
Zaqat money	6	7	7	8
Main importance	0		0	1
Other income	20	16	24	17
Main importance	9	7	8	7
n	346	213	375	484

Table 3.24 Household income types, by household size. Percentage of all households in respective groups

	Gaza			West Bank camps		
	\multicolumn{6}{c}{Persons in household}
	1 - 5	6 - 10	11 or more	1 - 5	6 - 10	11 or more
Labour income						
Wages	44	64	71	64	79	91
Main importance	40	58	63	59	74	83
Agricultural income	5	8	19	3	2	3
Main importance	3	4	10	1	1	
From self employed home production	6	11	12	6	8	6
Main importance	3	4	4	2	3	3
From trade estab.	6	7	9	7	15	12
Main importance	5	6	6	4	10	3
From industry and service estab.	2	3	4	4	2	5
Main importance	1	2	3	4	1	3
Non-labour income						
Remittances	18	10	6	11	6	9
Main importance	10	4	1	5	2	1
Pensions	2	2	3	1	2	3
Main importance	1	1	0	1	1	
Sale of properties	7	13	18	13	10	12
Main importance	2	4	1	2	4	5
Rent revenues	3	3	2	1	2	4
Main importance	1	1	0		0	1
UNRWA support	61	57	51	90	81	79
Main importance	18	11	8	20	9	14
Social benefits	20	7	6	3	7	1
Main importance	5	2	1		1	
Zaqat money	8	7	3	11	6	8
Main importance	0	0		1	1	
Other income	28	19	14	21	17	11
Main importance	14	6	4	11	7	1
n	296	458	195	186	249	62

CHANGES IN INCOME SINCE 1992

Table 3.25 Changes in labour income from 1992 to 1993, by main geographical area. Percentage of households receiving the respective income types

	Gaza	West Bank camps
Wages		
More	18	15
Same	62	59
Less	20	26
n	566	374
Agricultural income		
More	13	8
Same	63	64
Less	25	28
n	88	11
Income from home production/self employment		
More	10	18
Same	79	54
Less	11	28
n	92	33
Income from trade establishment		
More	22	25
Same	63	49
Less	15	26
n	69	59
Income from industrial establishment		
More	12	41
Same	58	41
Less	29	17
n	24	16

Table 3.26 Changes in non-labour income from 1992 to 1993, by main geographical area. Percentage of households receiving the respective income types

	Gaza	West Bank camps
Remittances		
More	6	11
Same	81	64
Less	13	25
n	113	40
Pensions		
More	5	8
Less	8	64
n	19	8
Income from sales		
More	38	31
Same	44	36
Less	18	33
n	116	56
Rent revenues		
More	4	17
Same	93	74
Less	3	9
n	24	10
Support from UNRWA		
More	7	6
Same	90	71
Less	3	24
n	543	420
Social benefits		
More	11	9
Same	86	84
Less	3	8
n	101	22
Zaqat money		
More	3	7
Same	88	54
Less	9	39
n	61	41
Other income		
More	6	12
Same	83	76
Less	11	12
n	198	89

Table 3.27 Changes in wages from 1992 to 1993, by sub-area. Percentage of households receiving the respective income types

	Gaza			West Bank camps	
	North	Central	Sout	North	South/Central
More	21	13	14	27	5
Same	60	65	63	30	83
Less	19	22	24	43	12
n	336	74	157	169	205

Table 3.28 Changes in wages from 1992 to 1993, by household size. Percentage of households receiving the respective income types

	Gaza			West Bank camps		
	\multicolumn{6}{c}{Total number of persons in household}
	1 - 5	6 - 10	11 or more	1 - 5	6 - 10	11 or more
More	15	16	26	19	12	18
Same	67	62	55	52	62	64
Less	18	22	19	30	26	18
n	129	297	139	119	198	57

INCOME TYPES AND THE INDEX FOR HOUSEHOLD POSSESSION OF CONSUMER DURABLES

Table 3.29 Household income types, by index for household possession of consumer durables. Percentage of all households in respective groups

	Gaza			West Bank camps		
	\multicolumn{6}{l}{Household consumer durables by thirds}
	Lower	Middle	Upper	Lower	Middl	Upper
Labour income						
Wages	45	68	68	69	79	83
Main importance	41	62	61	64	72	77
Agricultural income	5	9	16	1	2	4
Main importance	3	5	8	1		1
From self employed home production	8	9	13	5	7	10
Main importance	4	5	2	2	3	3
From trade estab.	3	5	16	8	14	16
Main importance	2	4	13	6	7	10
From industry and service estab.	1	2	5	1	4	6
Main importance	1	2	4	1	3	3
Non-labour income						
Remittances	11	12	13	9	7	8
Main importance	6	6	3	5	2	1
Pensions	1	2	3	2	2	1
Main importance	1	0	2	0	2	1
Sale of properties	10	14	13	14	10	7
Main importance	4	2	3	4	3	3
Rent revenues	1	3	5	1	3	5
Main importance	1		1		1	1
UNRWA support	69	57	40	85	83	84
Main importance	22	10	4	18	13	8
Social benefits	20	6	4	5	5	3
Main importance	5	2	1	0	1	
Zaqat money	11	6	0	11	9	1
Main importance	0	0		1	1	
Other income	25	19	17	19	14	21
Main importance	13	5	6	10	5	7
n	361	323	265	232	168	98

THE "FAMILY EMPLOYMENT NETWORK" HYPOTHESIS

Table 3.30 Household income types of main importance, by main geographical area and unemployed worker in household. Percentage of all households in respective groups

	Gaza		West Bank camps	
	\multicolumn{4}{c}{Unemployed worker in household?}
	No	Yes	No	Yes
Labour income	71	63	82	96
Non-labour income from private sources	17	17	16	20
Non-labour income from public sources	16	21	17	4
Total	104	101	115	120
n	856	93	454	40

Table 3.31 Household income types, by main geographical area and unemployed worker in household. Percentage of all households in respective groups

	Gaza		West Bank camps	
	Unemployed worker in household?			
	No	Yes	No	Yes
Wages	59	56	74	79
Main importance	54	50	69	73
Agricultural income	9	8	2	
Main importance	5	6	1	
From self employed home production	10	7	7	2
Main importance	4	1	3	2
Income from trade estab.	8	2	12	13
Main importance	6	2	7	9
From industry and service estab.	2	4	3	4
Main importance	2	4	2	
Remittances	11	18	7	19
Main importance	5	6	3	9
Pensions	2	1	1	5
Main importance	1	1	1	3
Sale of properties	12	12	11	12
Main importance	3	2	4	
Rent revenues	2	6	2	5
Main importance	0	2	0	
UNRWA support	56	60	84	98
Main importance	13	16	15	3
Recieve social benefits	10	15	4	7
Main importance	3	5	1	
Receive Zaqat money	6	6	8	13
Main importance	0		1	1
Other income	21	19	19	10
Main importance	8	6	8	8
n	856	93	454	40

Table 3.32 Household income types of main importance, by main geographical area and "discouraged worker" in household. Percentage of all households in respective groups

	Gaza		West Bank camps	
	\multicolumn{4}{c}{Discouraged worker in household?}
	No	Yes	No	Yes
Labour income	75	59	80	83
Non-labour income from private sources	15	26	14	16
Non-labour income from public sources	15	16	20	6
Total	105	101	114	105
n	681	268	337	158

Table 3.33 Household income types, by main geographical area and discouraged worker in household. Percentage of all households in respective groups

	Gaza		West Bank camps	
	\multicolumn{4}{l}{Discouraged worker in household?}
	No	Yes	No	Yes
Wages	59	59	72	81
Main importance	55	50	67	74
Agricultural income	10	8	2	2
Main importance	6	4	1	
From self employed home production	10	8	8	5
Main importance	4	3	2	3
Income from trade estab.	9	3	13	10
Main importance	8	1	8	5
From industry and service estab.	3	2	4	2
Main importance	2	1	2	1
Remittances	13	10	10	5
Main importance	6	5	4	1
Pensions	2	2	1	2
Main importance	1	1	1	0
Sale of properties	10	18	11	12
Main importance	1	6	3	3
Rent revenues	3	2	2	2
Main importance	1	1	0	
UNRWA support	54	64	87	81
Main importance	12	15	18	5
Recieve social benefits	12	8	4	5
Main importance	3	1	1	
Receive Zaqat money	3	1	1	13
Main importance	7	4	11	3
Other income	18	27	18	18
Main importance	6	13	6	12
n	681	268	337	158

DEPENDENCY ON PUBLIC SUPPORT, EMPLOYMENT AND HOUSEHOLD WEALTH

Table 3.34 Household income types of main importance, by main geographical area and worker who lost employment in Israel in household. Percentage of all households in respective groups

	Gaza		West Bank camps	
	\multicolumn{4}{c}{Household member worked in Israel 92 not 93?}
	No	Yes	No	Yes
Labour income	68	80	81	86
Non-labour income from private sources	18	13	15	18
Non-labour income from public sources	17	9	17	11
Total	103	102	113	115
n	813	135	410	84

Table 3.35 Household income types, by main geographical area and worker who lost employment in Israel in household. Percentage of all households in respective groups

	Gaza		West Bank camps	
	\multicolumn{4}{c}{Household member worked in Israel 92 not 93?}
	No	Yes	No	Yes
Wages	56	76	75	74
Main importance	51	67	69	71
Agricultural income	8	15	2	3
Main importance	5	8	1	1
From self employed home production	9	12	6	9
Main importance	3	4	2	4
Income from trade estab.	8	1	13	8
Main importance	7	0	8	3
From industry and service estab.	3	1	2	11
Main importance	2	1	1	7
Remittances	13	4	8	8
Main importance	6	0	3	3
Pensions	2	1	2	1
Main importance	1	0	1	0
Sale of properties	10	23	9	20
Main importance	3	5	3	6
Rent revenues	2	3	2	1
Main importance	0	1	0	1
UNRWA support	57	57	85	85
Main importance	14	8	15	11
Recieve social benefits	12	4	5	4
Main importance	3	1	1	
Receive Zaqat money	7	3	9	6
Main importance	0		1	3
Other income	21	17	19	12
Main importance	8	7	8	8
n	813	135	410	84

Table 3.36 Household income types of main importance, by main geographical area and full-time worker in household. Percentage of all households in respective groups

	Gaza		West Bank camps	
	\multicolumn{4}{c}{Full-time worker in household?}
	No	Yes	No	Yes
Labour income	53	100	69	97
Non-labour income from private sources	27	4	24	4
Non-labour income from public sources	24	1	20	10
Total	104	105	113	111
n	601	348	263	231

Table 3.37 Household income types, by main geographical area and full-time worker in household. Percentage of all households in respective groups

	Gaza		West Bank camps	
	Full-time worker in household?			
	No	Yes	No	Yes
Wages	46	81	63	88
Main importance	40	76	57	83
Agricultural income	8	12	1	3
Main importance	5	5	1	1
From self employed home production	8	13	6	8
Main importance	4	3	3	2
Income from trade estab.	3	14	9	16
Main importance	3	11	7	8
From industry and service estab.	1	6	2	5
Main importance	1	4	1	3
Remittances	15	7	11	5
Main importance	8	1	5	0
Pensions	2	2	2	1
Main importance	1	1	2	0
Sale of properties	13	11	14	9
Main importance	4	2	4	2
Rent revenues	3	2	1	3
Main importance	1		0	0
UNRWA support	61	49	85	85
Main importance	20	1	18	10
Recieve social benefits	16	0	5	4
Main importance	4		1	0
Receive Zaqat money	9	1	12	5
Main importance	0		1	0
Other income	28	8	26	9
Main importance	13	0	13	2
n	601	348	263	231

Table 3.38 Household income types of main importance, by main geographical area and unemployed worker in household. Percentage of all households in respective groups

	Gaza		West Bank camps	
	\multicolumn{4}{l}{LF member in household?}
	No	Yes	No	Yes
Labour income	24	91	33	94
Non-labour income from private sources	43	7	44	9
Non-labour income from public sources	34	7	30	10
Total	101	105	107	113
n	293	655	106	388

Table 3.39 Household income types, by main geographical area and labour force participant in household. Percentage of all households in respective groups

	Gaza		West Bank camps	
	LF member in household?			
	No	Yes	No	Yes
Wages	24	75	35	86
Main importance	19	69	28	80
Agricultural income	5	11		3
Main importance	3	6		1
From self employed home production	3	13	4	8
Main importance	1	5	3	2
Income from trade estab.	1	10	4	14
Main importance	1	8	2	8
From industry and service estab.	0	4		4
Main importance		3		3
Remittances	20	9	11	7
Main importance	13	2	8	2
Pensions	2	2	3	1
Main importance	1	1	3	1
Sale of properties	12	12	9	12
Main importance	5	2	6	3
Rent revenues	3	2	1	2
Main importance	1	0	1	0
UNRWA support	65	53	89	84
Main importance	28	6	27	10
Recieve social benefits	23	5	5	4
Main importance	6	1	2	0
Receive Zaqat money	14	3	17	6
Main importance	0	0	1	0
Other income	43	11	43	11
Main importance	23	2	26	3
n	293	655	106	388

Table 3.40 Household income types of main importance, by main geographical area and gender of household head. Percentage of all households in respective groups. Percentage of all households in respective groups

	Gaza		West Bank camps	
	Gender of head of household			
Male	Female	Male	Female	Yes
Labour income	75	29	86	42
Non-labour income from private sources	16	28	14	31
Non-labour income from public sources	12	47	13	40
Total	103	104	113	113
n	842	97	445	48

Table 3.41 Household income types, by main geographical area and gender of household head

	Gaza		West Bank camps	
	\multicolumn{4}{c}{Gender of head of household}
	Male	Female	Male	Female
Wages	63	27	78	49
Main importance	57	25	73	35
Agricultural income	10	2	2	2
Main importance	6		1	1
From self employed home production	10	2	6	10
Main importance	4	1	2	3
Income from trade estab.	8	2	13	4
Main importance	6	2	8	4
From industry and service estab.	3	1	3	2
Main importance	2	1	2	3
Remittances	11	23	7	17
Main importance	4	13	3	8
Pensions	2	2	2	1
Main importance	1	2	1	0
Sale of properties	13	2	12	2
Main importance	3		4	2
Rent revenues	2	3	2	2
Main importance	0	2	0	2
UNRWA support	55	70	85	87
Main importance	10	35	12	37
Recieve social benefits	7	41	4	5
Main importance	2	11	0	1
Receive Zaqat money	5	23	6	34
Main importance	0	1	1	2
Other income	20	27	15	40
Main importance	8	11	6	21
n	842	97	445	48

THE ROLE OF NET LIQUID WEALTH AS HOUSEHOLD COPING STRATEGY

Table 3.42 Net household liquid wealth, by main geographical area. Percentage of all households in respective groups

	Gaza	West Bank camps
Purpose of selling savings		
Daily consumption	15	10
Other consumption	2	4
Housing/house building	4	9
Other investments	3	2
Other purposes	1	4
Not sold savings	7	4
No savings	67	68
Purpose of selling gold		
Daily consumption	20	15
Other consumption	4	3
Housing/house building	7	9
Other investments	4	3
Other purposes	4	3
Not sold gold	51	44
No gold	11	23
Have debt for:		
Any purpose	42	58
Consumption	17	29
Marriage	7	9
Housing	10	22
Invest excl. housing	7	11
Sources of debt		
Family	6	9
Relatives	10	7
Friends	16	22
Family and relatives	1	1
Friends and Family and/or relatives	7	8
Other than above	1	10
No loans	58	42
Debt change since border closure		
Greater	28	44
Same	7	10
Smaller	3	3
Not applicable	4	1
No loans	58	42
Difficulty repaying loans		
Yes	30	45
No	12	13
No loans	58	42
Reason for credits		
Cannot pay	19	32
Long-time practice	6	7
No regular salary	23	13
Other	5	2
No credits	46	46
n	955	497

Table 3.43 Net household liquid wealth, by sub-region. Percentage of all households in respective groups. Percentage of all households in respective groups

	Gaza North	Gaza Central	Gaza South	WBC North	WBC South/ Central
Purpose of selling savings					
Daily consumption	17	12	14	15	5
Other consumption	3	1	2	5	2
Housing/house building	5		5	14	3
Other investments	3	1	6	3	1
Other purposes	1	1	2	5	2
Not sold savings	8	8	5	3	5
No savings	64	78	66	54	81
Purpose of selling gold					
Daily consumption	21	24	18	12	17
Other consumption	3	2	7	3	3
Housing/house building	7	4	7	7	10
Other investments	3	2	5	4	2
Other purposes	5	2	3	3	3
Not sold gold	51	47	51	37	52
No gold	9	19	9	34	13
Have debt for:					
Any purpose	42	39	44	62	54
Consumption	17	17	18	34	24
Marriage	7	5	8	8	9
Housing	12	8	9	22	23
Invest excl. housing	5	8	9	15	6
Sources of debt					
Family	6	7	6	9	10
Relatives	10	10	11	7	8
Friends	14	17	18	27	18
Family and relatives	2		0	1	1
Friends and Family and/or relatives	9	4	7	7	8
Other than above	1	1	2	12	8
No loans	58	61	56	38	47
Debt change since border closure					
Greater	31	21	29	51	38
Same	7	9	6	7	12
Smaller	3	0	4	3	2
Not applicable	2	9	5	2	1
No loans	58	61	56	38	46
Difficulty repaying loans					
Yes	30	25	33	53	38
No	12	15	11	10	15
No loans	58	61	56	38	46
Reason for credits					
Cannot pay	17	24	21	33	31
Long-time practice	5	7	9	5	8
No regular salary	25	20	22	15	11
Other	6	4	5	2	2
No credits	48	45	44	45	47
n	502	151	302	244	253

Table 3.44 Net household liquid wealth, by refugee status Percentage of all households in respective groups

	Non-refugee	Gaza Refugees outside camps	Refugees in camps	Refugees in West Bank camps
Purpose of selling savings				
Daily consumption	15	17	14	10
Other consumption	1	3	2	3
Housing/house building	2	4	5	9
Other investments	4	5	2	2
Other purposes	2		2	4
Not sold savings	10	6	5	4
No savings	65	65	70	67
Purpose of selling gold				
Daily consumption	22	17	21	15
Other consumption	4	5	4	3
Housing/house building	4	8	8	9
Other investments	4	3	3	3
Other purposes	4	6	3	3
Not sold gold	54	49	48	44
No gold	8	13	13	24
Have debt for:				
Any purpose	42	42	42	58
Consumption	16	17	18	29
Marriage	7	7	7	9
Housing	9	11	10	23
Invest excl. housing	9	4	6	11
Sources of debt				
Family	7	4	7	10
Relatives	12	10	9	7
Friends	14	15	18	23
Family and relatives	2	2	0	1
Friends and family and/or relatives	6	10	7	8
Other than above	2	2	1	10
No loans	58	58	58	42
Debt change since border closure				
Greater	28	28	28	44
Same	9	4	7	10
Smaller	3	4	2	3
Not applicable	2	5	5	1
No loans	58	58	58	42
Difficulty repaying loans				
Yes	29	30	31	45
No	13	12	11	13
No loans	58	58	58	42
Reason for credits				
Cannot pay	19	15	22	32
Long-time practice	8	7	4	7
No regular salary	26	22	20	13
Other	4	5	6	2
No credits	43	50	48	46
n	347	216	378	483

Table 3.45 Net household liquid wealth, by household wealth index. Percentage of all households in respective groups

	Gaza			West Bank camps		
	\multicolumn{6}{c}{Household consumer durables by thirds}
	Lower	Middle	Upper	Lower	Middle	Upper
Purpose of selling savings						
Daily consumption	12	16	18	8	13	9
Other consumption	1	3	3	4	3	3
Housing/house building	2	4	6	6	13	7
Other investments	0	4	6	1	2	4
Other purposes	1	1	3	4	1	7
Not sold savings	2	6	14	5	2	5
No savings	81	66	49	71	65	64
Purpose of selling gold						
Daily consumption	22	23	15	15	13	18
Other consumption	4	6	3	2	3	4
Housing/house building	5	8	7	8	8	11
Other investments	2	3	6	3	2	3
Other purposes	2	3	8	3	2	5
Not sold gold	50	48	53	40	49	48
No gold	15	9	7	29	23	11
Have debt for:						
Any purpose	41	44	42	57	58	61
Consumption	21	18	10	34	27	21
Marriage	6	9	5	9	7	11
Housing	8	12	11	19	26	25
Invest excl. housing	5	7	9	8	15	9
Sources of debt						
Family	4	7	9	7	6	20
Relatives	10	11	9	9	5	7
Friends	18	15	14	22	27	16
Family and relatives	2	2	0	1	2	1
Friends and Family and/or relatives	7	8	8	7	10	5
Other than above	0	2	2	9	9	14
No loans	59	56	58	44	42	39
Debt change since border closure						
Greater	29	32	24	45	40	49
Same	6	7	8	10	11	6
Smaller	2	1	7	1	3	6
Not applicable	4	4	3	1	3	1
No loans	59	56	58	43	42	39
Difficulty repaying loans						
Yes	31	33	25	45	46	44
No	10	11	17	11	12	17
No loans	59	56	58	43	42	39
Reason for credits						
Cannot pay	31	14	10	42	28	16
Long-time practice	5	6	8	7	8	5
No regular salary	19	27	24	14	11	12
Other	1	5	10	1	3	3
No credits	44	48	48	36	50	63
n	365	323	267	231	168	98

Table 3.46 Net household liquid wealth, by main geographical area and discouraged worker in household. Percentage of all households in respective groups

	Gaza		West Bank camps	
	\multicolumn{4}{c}{Discouraged worker in household?}
	No	Yes	No	Yes
Purpose of selling savings				
Daily consumption	14	16	10	11
Other consumption	1	4	4	3
Housing/house building	4	4	10	7
Other investments	4	2	2	4
Other purposes	2	0	4	4
Not sold savings	8	5	5	2
No savings	67	68	67	70
Purpose of selling gold				
Daily consumption	18	26	14	16
Other consumption	3	6	3	4
Housing/house building	7	6	8	9
Other investments	4	3	2	4
Other purposes	4	4	3	4
Not sold gold	53	45	45	42
No gold	11	11	25	20
Have debt for:				
Any purpose	41	47	53	69
Consumption	15	22	26	35
Marriage	5	11	7	13
Housing	11	8	22	23
Invest excl. housing	7	6	13	6
Sources of debt				
Family	6	6	8	12
Relatives	10	11	6	11
Friends	14	20	21	25
Family and relatives	1	2	1	1
Friends and Family and/or relatives	8	6	8	6
Other than above	1	2	9	13
No loans	59	53	47	31
Debt change since border closure				
Greater	25	37	39	56
Same	7	7	10	9
Smaller	4	1	3	2
Not applicable	5	1	1	2
No loans	59	53	47	31
Difficulty repaying loans				
Yes	28	37	44	48
No	13	10	9	21
No loans	59	53	47	31
Reason for credits				
Cannot pay	15	29	30	37
Long-time practice	6	6	6	10
No regular salary	22	26	12	14
Other	6	3	2	3
No credits	50	36	50	37
n	681	268	337	157

Table 3.47 Net household liquid wealth, by main geographical area and unemployed worker in household. Percentage of all households in respective groups

	Gaza		West Bank camps	
	Unemployed worker in household?			
	No	Yes	No	Yes
Purpose of selling savings				
Daily consumption	14	23	10	14
Other consumption	2	1	4	3
Housing/house building	4	4	9	12
Other investments	3	9	2	2
Other purposes	1	3	4	4
Not sold savings	7	5	4	2
No savings	69	56	67	72
Purpose of selling gold				
Daily consumption	20	26	15	11
Other consumption	4	7	3	5
Housing/house building	7	5	8	4
Other investments	4	4	3	4
Other purposes	4	3	3	5
Not sold gold	52	41	43	62
No gold	10	15	25	12
Have debt for:				
Any purpose	41	54	58	63
Consumption	16	30	29	32
Marriage	7	8	9	7
Housing	10	10	22	25
Invest excl. housing	7	5	10	15
Sources of debt				
Family	6	8	10	5
Relatives	9	18	8	7
Friends	16	17	23	18
Family and relatives	1	4	1	1
Friends and Family and/or relatives	7	7	7	15
Other than above	1		9	18
No loans	59	46	42	37
Debt change since border closure				
Greater	28	34	44	50
Same	7	9	10	6
Smaller	3	2	2	6
Not applicable	3	9	2	2
No loans	59	46	42	37
Difficulty repaying loans				
Yes	29	44	45	54
No	12	10	13	9
No loans	59	46	42	37
Reason for credits				
Cannot pay	19	21	33	29
Long-time practice	6	4	7	8
No regular salary	23	26	12	16
Other	5	10	2	2
No credits	47	39	46	43
n	856	93	453	40

Table 3.48 Net household liquid wealth, by main geographical area and full-time worker in household. Percentage of all households in respective groups

	Gaza		West Bank camps	
	\multicolumn{4}{c}{Full-time worker in household?}
	No	Yes	No	Yes
Purpose of selling savings				
Daily consumption	15	14	10	11
Other consumption	2	3	4	3
Housing/house building	3	5	6	12
Other investments	1	7	3	2
Other purposes	1	2	4	3
Not sold savings	5	10	4	4
No savings	73	58	69	66
Purpose of selling gold				
Daily consumption	24	15	17	12
Other consumption	4	4	2	4
Housing/house building	6	8	10	6
Other investments	3	5	3	2
Other purposes	4	4	4	3
Not sold gold	47	57	38	52
No gold	13	6	27	20
Have debt for:				
Any purpose	43	42	56	61
Consumption	21	11	35	22
Marriage	5	9	8	10
Housing	8	14	17	29
Invest excl. housing	6	7	8	14
Sources of debt				
Family	6	7	9	10
Relatives	11	9	7	8
Friends	16	16	24	20
Family and relatives	2	1	1	1
Friends and Family and/or relatives	7	8	6	10
Other than above	1	2	9	11
No loans	57	58	44	39
Debt change since border closure				
Greater	30	26	41	48
Same	6	8	11	8
Smaller	2	4	3	3
Not applicable	4	3	2	1
No loans	57	58	44	39
Difficulty repaying loans				
Yes	32	27	43	48
No	11	15	13	12
No loans	57	58	44	39
Reason for credits				
Cannot pay	24	11	35	29
Long-time practice	5	8	7	7
No regular salary	26	19	16	9
Other	3	9	1	3
No credits	42	53	41	51
n	601	348	262	231

Table 3.49 Net household liquid wealth, by main geographical area and household size. Percentage of all households in respective groups

	Gaza			West Bank camps		
	\multicolumn{6}{c}{Total number of persons in household}
	1 - 5	6 - 10	11 or more	1 - 5	6 - 10	11 or more
Purpose of selling savings						
Daily consumption	15	15	17	11	9	10
Other consumption	1	2	4	4	4	1
Housing/house building	3	5	4	8	9	11
Other investments	2	2	8	2	2	3
Other purposes		2	2	7	2	7
Not sold savings	7	6	10	3	6	3
No savings	73	68	55	65	69	72
Purpose of selling gold						
Daily consumption	10	23	30	14	16	13
Other consumption	4	3	7	1	4	6
Housing/house building	7	7	4	10	8	9
Other investments	4	3	4	1	3	5
Other purposes	4	4	4	5	2	1
Not sold gold	58	49	44	43	46	42
No gold	14	10	7	26	22	23
Have debt for:						
Any purpose	34	43	52	52	58	75
Consumption	15	16	23	25	30	36
Marriage	6	5	13	10	5	19
Housing	5	14	7	19	23	31
Invest excl. housing	5	6	11	10	11	10
Sources of debt						
Family	4	7	7	12	9	4
Relatives	6	12	12	3	10	10
Friends	16	14	21	20	22	32
Family and relatives	1	2	2	0	1	1
Friends and Family and/or relatives	7	7	7	7	6	16
Other than above		1	3	11	8	14
No loans	66	57	48	48	42	25
Debt change since border closure						
Greater	21	30	36	38	45	59
Same	5	7	9	8	10	12
Smaller	2	3	5	4	2	4
Not applicable	6	3	2	2	2	1
No loans	66	57	48	48	42	25
Difficulty repaying loans						
Yes	26	30	36	38	46	63
No	8	13	17	14	12	12
No loans	66	57	48	48	42	25
Reason for credits						
Cannot pay	16	20	22	27	34	40
Long-time practice	7	6	6	5	8	6
No regular salary	17	25	28	11	14	13
Other	3	4	10	1	1	8
No credits	58	44	34	55	43	33
n	297	462	195	186	248	62

Table 3.50 Net household liquid wealth, by main geographical area and labour force member in household. Percentage of all households in respective groups

	Gaza		West Bank camps	
	LF member in household?			
	No	Yes	No	Yes
Purpose of selling savings				
Daily consumption	16	15	12	9
Other consumption	1	3	4	3
Housing/house building	2	5	5	10
Other investments	1	4	3	2
Other purposes	1	2	3	4
Not sold savings	2	9	1	5
No savings	77	63	73	67
Purpose of selling gold				
Daily consumption	24	19	17	14
Other consumption	2	5	2	3
Housing/house building	5	7	5	9
Other investments	1	5	5	2
Other purposes	3	4	4	3
Not sold gold	49	51	35	47
No gold	15	9	32	21
Have debt for:				
Any purpose	34	46	54	60
Consumption	17	17	39	26
Marriage	3	8	5	10
Housing	4	13	11	26
Invest excl. housing	7	7	9	11
Sources of debt				
Family	4	7	2	11
Relatives	8	11	8	8
Friends	14	17	27	21
Family and relatives	2	1		1
Friends and Family and/or relatives	5	8	6	8
Other than above	1	1	9	10
No loans	66	54	47	40
Debt change since border closure				
Greater	25	30	44	45
Same	5	8	6	11
Smaller	1	4	2	3
Not applicable	4	4	2	1
No loans	66	54	47	40
Difficulty repaying loans				
Yes	28	31	44	46
No	7	15	10	14
No loans	66	54	47	40
Reason for credits				
Cannot pay	29	15	48	28
Long-time practice	5	7	6	7
No regular salary	20	24	10	13
Other	1	7	1	2
No credits	45	47	35	49
n	293	655	105	388

Table 3.51 Net household liquid wealth, by main geographical area and lost employment in Israel In household. Percentage of all households in respective groups

	Gaza		West Bank camps	
	\multicolumn{4}{c}{Household member worked in Israel 92 not 93?}
	No	Yes	No	Yes
Purpose of selling savings				
Daily consumption	14	17	8	18
Other consumption	2	5	4	3
Housing/house building	4	6	8	12
Other investments	3	6	2	4
Other purposes	1	1	4	2
Not sold savings	7	10	4	3
No savings	70	54	70	58
Purpose of selling gold				
Daily consumption	19	28	15	13
Other consumption	4	8	3	3
Housing/house building	6	9	6	16
Other investments	4	3	2	5
Other purposes	4	5	4	1
Not sold gold	52	42	45	43
No gold	12	5	25	19
Have debt for:				
Any purpose	40	58	56	67
Consumption	14	33	27	42
Marriage	7	8	9	8
Housing	10	13	21	27
Invest excl. housing	7	3	10	14
Sources of debt				
Family	5	12	9	9
Relatives	10	12	7	11
Friends	15	24	21	28
Family and relatives	1	1	1	1
Friends and Family and/or relatives	7	10	7	11
Other than above	1	0	11	7
No loans	60	42	44	33
Debt change since border closure				
Greater	25	48	42	56
Same	7	6	10	7
Smaller	3	2	2	4
Not applicable	4	2	2	1
No loans	60	42	44	33
Difficulty repaying loans				
Yes	27	47	43	58
No	12	11	13	9
No loans	60	42	44	33
Reason for credits				
Cannot pay	19	21	31	37
Long-time practice	6	7	6	14
No regular salary	21	34	13	12
Other	5	8	3	2
No credits	49	30	48	38
n	813	135	409	84

Table 3.52 Net household liquid wealth, by main geographical area and households gender. Percentage of all households in respective groups

	Gaza		West Bank camps	
	Male	Female	Male	Female
Purpose of selling savings				
Daily consumption	16	7	10	7
Other consumption	2	3	4	3
Housing/house building	4	1	9	7
Other investments	4	1	2	4
Other purposes	1		4	2
Not sold savings	7	4	4	3
No savings	66	84	66	86
Purpose of selling gold				
Daily consumption	21	11	16	10
Other consumption	5		3	2
Housing/house building	7	3	8	6
Other investments	4	3	3	2
Other purposes	4	1	4	1
Not sold gold	50	53	46	29
No gold	9	29	20	51
Have debt for:				
Any purpose	44	26	59	47
Consumption	18	7	30	24
Marriage	6	10	9	7
Housing	11	4	23	15
Invest excl. housing	7	2	11	11
Sources of debt				
Family	6	5	10	2
Relatives	11	3	8	3
Friends	16	13	23	19
Family and relatives	1		1	1
Friends and Family and/or relatives	8	5	8	8
Other than above	1	1	9	15
No loans	56	74	41	53
Debt change since border closure				
Greater	30	16	47	24
Same	7	6	9	16
Smaller	3	1	2	6
Not applicable	4	4	1	2
No loans	56	74	41	53
Difficulty repaying loans				
Yes	31	21	47	34
No	13	5	13	13
No loans	56	74	41	53
Reason for credits				
Cannot pay	19	22	32	39
Long-time practice	7	3	8	14
No regular salary	25	10	13	8
Other	6	1	2	2
No credits	44	65	45	53
n	848	97	444	48

Table 3.53 Employment on household level, by refugee status. Percentage of all households in respective groups

	Non-refugee	Gaza Refugees outside camps	Refugees in camps	Refugees in West Bank camps
LF member in household				
No	27	32	35	22
Yes	73	68	65	78
Full-time worker in household				
No	61	62	68	53
Yes	39	38	32	47
Unemployed worker in household				
No	91	90	89	92
Yes	9	10	11	8
Discouraged worker in household				
No	78	70	67	68
Yes	22	30	33	32
Household member worked in Israel 92 not 93				
No	86	88	84	82
Yes	14	12	16	18
Total number of persons in household				
1 - 5	28	38	30	38
6 - 10	48	44	51	50
11 or more	23	18	19	13
Gender of household head				
Male	93	88	88	90
Female	7	12	12	10
n	342	215	373	478

REFERENCES

Central Bureau of Statistics, Israel. (1987) *Projections of Population in Judea, Samaria and Gaza Area up to 2002*. Jerusalem: Central Bureau of Statistics.

(1992) *Judea, Samaria and Gaza Area Statistics*. 21. Jerusalem: Central Bureau of Statistics.

(1993) *Statistical Abstract of Israel 1993*. Jerusalem: Central Bureau of Statistics.

Grootaert, Christian. (1986) *The Role of Employment and Earnings in Analyzing Levels of Living*. LSMS Working paper no 27. Washington: World Bank.

Hansen, Morris H., William N. Hurwitz and William G. Madow. (1953) *Sample Survey Methods and Theory*. New York: John Wiley.

Heiberg, Marianne and Geir Øvensen. (1993) *Palestinian Society in Gaza, West Bank and Arab Jerusalem. A Survey of Living Conditions.*. Oslo: FAFO report 151.

ILO. (1990) *Surveys of Economically Active Population, Employment, Unemployment and Underemployment*. Geneva: ILO.

(1992) *Report of the Director-General* Appendices (Vol 2) Report on the situation of workers in the occupied Arab territories. Geneva: ILO.

Lang, Erica and Itimad Mohanna. (no date) *A Study of Women and Work in 'Shatti' Refugee Camp of the Gaza Strip*. Jerusalem: Arab Thought Forum.

Statistical Laboratory. (1989) *PC CARP*. Ames: Statistical Laboratory, Iowa State University.

U.S. Bureau of the Census. (1993) *CENVAR, Variance Calculation System (IMPS 3.1)*. Washington: U.S. Bureau of the Census, International Statistical Programs Center.

World Bank. (1993) *An Investment in Peace*. Washington: World Bank.

World Bank. (1993) *Developing the Occupied Territories*. Washington: World Bank.